The Final Few Years of British Steam

Part Two

Summer 1966 – Summer 1968

An enthusiast's recollection of exploits and adventures while following the decline of steam on British Railways.

Les Wheeler

Dedicated to all the railwaymen working at the last three standard gauge British Railways steam depots, Carnforth, Lostock Hall and Rose Grove and to the members of the Master Neverers Association who gave a little dignity to a number of steam engines that continued their labours until 4th August 1968.

Cover Illustrations.

Front cover: Quite unexpectedly, Preston station is graced with the presence of Stanier 'Black 5' No. 45212 on Sunday 4th August 1968, the final day of regular BR standard gauge steam working. The engine would not only be the last to carry out a steam station pilot duty (known locally as the Preston shunt), but would also go into the history books as the last steam locomotive to carry out a normal duty for BR.

Back cover: Following overhaul to main line standard, 'Black 5' No. 45212 is seen on its inaugural test run passing through Preston station platform 2 (old platform 4) on 3rd March 2017. Almost 49 years since it was last out and about on the main line, Ian Riley has ensured a degree of authenticity with regards to the positioning of the top lamp bracket, which can be seen fixed to the right on the engine's smokebox, just as it had been in 1968 (see front cover picture). P. Fitton.

Copyright© Les Wheeler 2017

All rights reserved.

No part of this publication may be reproduced, stored in a retrieval system or transmitted, in any form or by any means, electronic, mechanical, photocopying, recording or otherwise, without prior written permission from the publisher.

First published in November 2017.

Published by Grange Publications and Les Wheeler
Hawthorn Terrace
Shilbottle
NE66 2XA
Telephone 01665 575 287

ISBN 978-0-9955548-1-8

Printed in Great Britain by The Amadeus Press Ltd.

Proceeds from the sale of this book will go towards the upkeep of the last steam engine to carry out a normal duty for British Railways on 4th August 1968, Stanier 'Black 5' No. 45212.

Of the making of "railway books" there is no end. But is this surprising? Could any other business organisation be named which covers so vast a diversity of interests as does the railway?

Of all that the railway has of interest to show, it is the steam locomotive that attracts by far the largest share of public attention. There is something essentially human about it.

Cecil J. Allen. Railway Planning & Making 1928.

Introduction to The Final Few Years of British Steam Part Two.

Records of my travels and exploits in search of steam continue from the beginning of July 1966. Throughout the previous month plans and preparations had been made for returning to Scotland, hopefully to see one or two of the handful of Gresley's 'A4's still managing to find work on express passenger duties. Steam was in its death throws north of the border and would be dispensed with by the following spring. As with many other trips throughout this sad period, it would be a question of attempting to keep one step ahead of steam's Grim Reaper.

Following the fortunes of BR steam during the final two years of its employment would often mean trips and visits prompted simply by hearing or reading about imminent changes concerning this form of motive power. Forthcoming closures of steam depots, withdrawal of the final member(s) of a particular class of engine or the termination of steams regular use on certain services, would all provide the motivation to respond as best I could to record such a fast changing scene. Some forays would also be made to areas or sheds where such locomotives had relatively recently capitulated to diesel power; on reflection, these visits had most likely been made out of a feeling of disbelief and the need to see first-hand that steam had indeed been dispensed with. Of course, with any luck, there might also possibly be one final opportunity to photograph a few engines still stored on shed or in sidings while awaiting disposal.

Subsequent to what would prove to be a not entirely incident-free escapade to Scotland, other expeditions would follow to places still relatively distant from home, including the southwest and the northeast, but not for long. Steams distribution was shrinking swiftly by the month and by March 1968 it would be confined to the northwest of England. Visits to Yorkshire and Lancashire, although not a stone's throw from the West Midlands, would be made more frequently as this form of traction found itself restricted to working within the boundaries of these two counties. Once the shackles were really on, steam would only be found in Lancashire.

Steam specials would continue to attract many enthusiasts to participate in what was often a last opportunity to travel behind a certain locomotive, often the last of its class, or over a particular line that would soon be no more. From July to December 1966 a total in excess of 40 of these would take place, during 1967 the total would reach approximately 70 and during the final eight months of standard gauge steam working in 1968 there would be 33, culminating, of course, in the 'Fifteen Guinea Special' on 11th August. Engines called upon to carry out such duties were often, but not always, spruced up, and presented the many eager photographers with subjects that were far more photogenic than the vast majority of the locos remaining at the time.

However, on the subject of well-groomed locomotives, something peculiar had started to happen - for no apparent reason, there began to appear a few other clean engines, which would have no part to play in any of the planned railtours. If you found yourself in the right place at the right time (which I fortunately did once or twice) a picture of a well-presented steam loco would be an unexpected bonus, even if it had only been cleaned on one side! Why this was happening and who was responsible will become clear later.

Things would be done and dusted as far as standard gauge steam on BR was concerned by the beginning of August 1968. On Sunday 4th August the normal, everyday rostering of such motive power would come to an end, but because of my observations on this day, an extra chapter in the form of a postscript would be needed to complete to my satisfaction a true and accurate account of steams final few hours, and those of one locomotive in particular, Stanier 'Black 5' No. 45212.

1966 July - December (Goodbye to Gresley's 'Streaks')

Plans for our Scotland trip were finalised during the first week of July. Our Freedom of Scotland Silver Tickets would be valid from 23rd of the month, but our journey would begin a week earlier. Progressively making our way north, we would visit a number of sheds before reaching Carlisle where we would spend a couple of days prior to beginning our much awaited travels around the Scottish region of BR.

On 1st July we wrote a letter to the Chief Works Manager seeking permission for us to visit Cowlairs and St Rollox Works, and his reply was received on 6th, granting us access to both on Thursday 28th. A payment of 1/- (5p) each would be charged in the form of a donation to the work's charity fund, and although I knew that I would find it difficult not to, I duly noted that photographs could not be taken at either premises.

Excursions to Saltley continued prior to setting off for Scotland and visits to the depot were made on 1st, 3rd and 10th July, with corresponding steam and class totals being 49/4, 48/7 and 37/6. Similar statistics for Tyseley, visited on 7th and 11th, were 31/7 and 31/6 respectively. Visitors of note to Saltley on 3rd were all North Eastern Region locos: Hull Dairycoates 'WD' No. 90704 and York based locos, 'B1 No. 61199 and 'K1' No. 62065. However, the depot's most interesting guest was recorded on 10th and, ironically, it was a Scottish Region engine – Dundee-based 'V2' No. 60919!

It transpired that the 2-6-2 should have worked an LCGB 'last steam' special on the Southern Region on 3rd July, but was failed at Nine Elms, supposedly with a broken spring. While fitters attended the loco, Stanier 'Black 5' No. 45493 substituted for the 2-6-0. Following successful repairs, it later ran light down the Bournemouth line to head the return trip. Fate, however, decreed that, after developing a hot box, the 'V2' would get no further than Eastleigh and the venture had to be abandoned. No. 60919 returned to Basingstoke for repairs and started its journey back to Scotland the next day, reportedly in charge of a freight train bound for the Birmingham area. Nearly a week later she had obviously still a long way to go before reaching home.

On 7th July 1966, Banbury-based 'Black 5' No. 44872 is ready to move forwards to be coaled in Tyseley MPD. Previously an Aston engine for many years, the 4-6-0 would be transferred to Croes Newydd later in October and, finally, to Lostock Hall in May 1967, from where it would be withdrawn four months later.

Making its way back to Dundee from the Southern Region, 'V2' No. 60919 is seen in the yard of Saltley MPD on 10th July 1966. A number of other reasons for the loco not heading the LCGB steam special (see above) have been proposed over the years, including the driver or fireman refusing to work the loco.

As the sun penetrates the gloomy shed building on 11th July 1966, 0-6-0PT No. 3619, having worked a trip freight, is found resting in Tyseley roundhouse. Allotted to several local sheds over the previous few years, the ex-GWR loco would officially be transferred from Stourbridge to Tyseley during the following few days. However, life as a 2A engine would be brief, and the pannier tank would be withdrawn by the end of August.

Saturday 16th July: the beginning of our second Scottish sojourn.

It was a cool, wet day and the motive power that would take us on the first stages of the day's journey was inauspicious to say the least. Dennis and I met up on the local dmu train to Snow Hill and then transferred to another dmu that would take us to Wolverhampton L. L. Here we made the short trek to the High Level station and boarded yet another dmu to Shrewsbury, arriving there at about 10.00am. By this point we had seen a total of 16 steam, two of which, 'Black 5' No 44780 and sister engine No.45132 were noted on passenger turns. We had a couple of hours before we had to catch our next train to Wrexham so we made our way to the shed, a walk of about twenty minutes.

Historically, because of its dual identity, Shrewsbury's allocation of motive power had always been a mixed bag. It was once home to both ex-GWR and LNWR engines, but by the time of this visit only one engine, 0-6-0PT No. 8718, was from such a background. This former GWR pannier tank was one of 28 steam noted on shed. The majority of the engines were of LMS origin and altogether 7 different locomotive classes were noted.

While waiting on Shrewsbury Station for our next train, several steam workings were recorded, including 'Black 5' No. 44681 with a relief passenger train to Crewe, standard 4-6-0 No. 75020 on parcels duty and light engine 'Britannia' No. 70021 Morning Star. Yet another diesel multiple unit took us on to Wrexham, our next destination, and from where, after a short walk, we gained access to the old GWR shed of Croes Newydd.

Even though the depot had been under the control of the LMR since September 1963, it still held on to a few ex-GWR engines. At this point in time it had an allocation of around thirty steam, including eight 0-6-0PT's. We noted a total of 26 steam representing 8 different varieties. While taking a photograph of standard 4-6-0 No. 75071, two of the youngest 'spotters' I'd ever seen wandering around a steam depot appeared by the side of the engine, and not an adult in sight! What the HSE would have to say about such an incident occurring today doesn't require much imagination.

We resigned ourselves to travelling from Wrexham to Chester by the same means as our previous four journeys. At last, however, we discovered were in for something far more interesting and enjoyable. The motive power this time was steam, and at the head of our train was 'Britannia' Pacific No. 70021 Morning Star seen earlier at Shrewsbury Station. The short journey, a fraction over 12 miles, with an allowance of 20 minutes, didn't ask too many questions of the engine, but it was a bonus to be hauled by steam again.

In quick succession, before we started off on the long walk to the shed, Chester station produced three steam workings, including another 'Britannia' Pacific, No. 70005 John Milton, on passenger duty. With an excursion heading in the direction of Crewe, 'Black 5' No. 45039, an Edge Hill engine, presented us with a photo opportunity while we were on Station View Bridge. After crossing the railway once more we followed the cinder path into the ex-LNWR depot.

The shed had an allocation of 28 steam of 4 different classes, so we were pleased to find that these figures were well surpassed on the day, with 35 steam on shed representing 8 varieties. In the yard we met up with No. 70021 Morning Star having her thirst quenched, accompanied by Hawksworth light 0-6-0 pannier tank No. 1628. As with other designs built in the fifties, these engines were being withdrawn almost as soon as they had been put into service. Together with No. 1638, which would be preserved, she was one of the last two remaining in use and would survive to be the final member of the class to be withdrawn. Stanier designed engines accounted for twenty-three of the steam present.

As luck would have it, while crossing back over the main line along Hoole Lane, we noted and photographed standard '9F' No. 92118, a Tyseley engine, at the head of a mixed freight train leaving Chester and heading east towards Crewe. The weather was still very dull and dreary as we continued on our way to the station, yet we were already looking forward to visiting the next shed on our itinerary, Birkenhead. Once serving the LNWR/GWR Joint Railway, this depot had dispensed with the last of its GWR locos some seven years earlier, but still had a healthy allotment of over seventy steam.

With no fewer than 56 standard '9F's comprising the major part of its allocation of steam motive power, Birkenhead could call upon nearly a third of the total of 189 still in service at this time. Other classes in its steam pool were Fairburn and Stanier 2-6-4T's, a handful of 'Jinties' and a similar number of 'Crabs'. During our visit we noted a total of 51 steam of 7 different types. As to be expected, with a total of 31 logged, '9F's were most evident. Overhauled at Crewe about four weeks earlier, one of these, No. 92048, was still very clean and was duly noted to be in ex-works condition. The day still hadn't managed to brighten up, but a few pictures were taken before we continued on, first to Birkenhead Central Station, then Liverpool James Street and from there to Ormskirk where we planned to spend the next two nights under canvas.

Left. 'Black 5' No. 45231, allocated to Chester MPD, sits inside Shrewsbury shed on 16th July 1966. The 4-6-0 would continue to be provided with employment until the end of steam on BR.

Below. On the same day Machynlleth-based standard 4MT No. 75002 is seen resting in the yard of Shrewsbury shed. During the second week of December it would become a Croes Newydd engine and would remain so until withdrawal in September 1967.

Also on 6D was pannier tank No 8718 taking a rest from shunting duties. The transfer of this engine, together with six others of the 5700 class during w/e 6th July, constituted the last re-allocation of ex-GWR engines.

Standard 2MT's No's. 78039 and 78058 were found simmering gently in Shrewsbury shed yard while awaiting their next turn of duty. The former engine would continue working for another three months, while the latter would remain in service until December 1966. All sixty-five of the class would be withdrawn by May 1967.

Built at Swindon in November 1953, standard 4MT No. 75020 stands in Shrewsbury station with a parcels train. Allocated to 6D, this loco would move briefly to Aintree and then to Carnforth where it would remain until the end of steam in August 1968.

All 16th July 1966

1966 July – December (Goodbye to Gresley's 'Streaks')

Stanier 'Black 5' No. 45130 and former GWR tank No. 3709 in the yard of Croes Newydd MPD on 16th July 1966. Withdrawal of the 4-6-0 would come in November 1967 while allocated to Birkenhead MPD.

We came across two very young enthusiasts as we continued around Croes Newydd shed, neither of whom could have been more than eight years old! Reminding me of my early trainspotting days, the boys in question are seen standing next to standard 4MT No. 75071. One of a batch of fifteen built at Swindon (lot No. 409), and fitted with double chimney in March 1961, this was the only one that was shedded further north than Bath after entering service. After three years allocated to 6C, it would be transferred to Stoke w/e 10th June and withdrawn two months later in August 1967. Disposal would take place in February 1968 at Birds Commercial Motors, Long Marston.

Following a top up of coal in the firebox, a light breeze takes the resulting smoke away from 0-6-0PT No. 3709 as it snatches a rest from duties in Croes Newydd shed yard. After 30 years of carrying out mainly tedious, menial jobs, withdrawal would come two months after this photograph was taken.

Stanier motive power on Chester shed: 'Black 5's No's. 45001 and 45064, together with '8F's No's. 48754 and, just visible, 48055. The 4-6-0's were built in 1934/35 at Crewe and Vulcan Foundry works respectively. Withdrawal would take place in the same month, March, in 1967 for 45064 and in 1968 for 45001. 16th July 1966.

1966 July – December (Goodbye to Gresley's 'Streaks')

Designed for light branch line work and shunting, Hawksworth's 1600 class 0-6-0 PT's were lightweight engines weighing a little over 41 tons. Here No. 1628, allocated to Croes Newydd, is seen taking a breather in the yard of Chester shed on 16th July 1966. This engine would be the last in the class to remain in service and would be withdrawn about a month after this photograph was taken.

Stanier 2-6-4T No. 42086 is caught basking in the sunshine at the end of Birkenhead Woodside station on 16th July. Formerly a Southern Region engine during the 1950's, the tank then had stints working out of Neasden and Cricklewood, before moving to Birkenhead earlier this month. Removal from capital stock would take place in April 1967.

Hughes/Fowler 2-6-0's, also known as 'Crabs', always seemed to suggest to me that whatever the weight of train you put behind them, they would have little difficulty in moving it. Here, even while at rest in the yard of Birkenhead MPD, No. 42727 can't help but display a powerful and imposing presence.

Sunday 17th July

Having had an early breakfast, we started off from Ormskirk on a whirlwind tour of seven sheds in the Liverpool and Manchester area. Being a Sunday had its advantages - we would undoubtedly see more steam on shed - however, buses and trains were less frequent, of course, and travelling between each depot would take that little bit longer. In spite of this, we managed to get round all seven, including the diesel and electric depot at Allerton, but not without a major problem by the end of the day.

The six steam depots on our itinerary were: Aintree, Bank Hall, Speke Junction, Trafford Park, Patricroft and, last of all, Agecroft. Aintree, a freight depot of the former Lancashire and Yorkshire Railway, housed 19 steam of 6 different types. The best time to visit this shed was undoubtedly Grand National Day, especially in earlier times when most of the specials were still steam-hauled. Next was Bank Hall, another former L&Y shed, with less than three months to go before closure. Including 4-6-0 No. 45627 Sierra Leone representing the 'Jubilee' class, we found 5 different varieties present. Most prevalent amongst the 21 steam logged were Stanier's 'Black 5' 4-6-0's with 9 of these engines noted.

The third shed on our programme, Speke Junction, had an allocation of 55 steam. Including two visitors, Stanier 2-6-4T No. 42574 of Trafford Park and Wakefield based 'WD' No. 90639 this visit produced 43 steam representing 6 different classes of locomotive. Also present was the last steam engine to be repaired at Gorton Works (in April 1963) '8F' No. 48520. From Allerton we caught the train into Manchester Central and then from Oxford Road on to Warwick Road station, which left us with a relatively short walk to Trafford Park the former Cheshire Lines Railway shed. Once assigned some of the last members of the famous 'Director' class as well as 'Jubilees' and 'Britannia's', its allocation was now predominantly Stanier 'Black 5's and Fairburn 2-6-4T's. During our visit we noted a total of 32 steam representing 5 varieties.

Patricroft, the penultimate depot visit for the day, was formerly of the LNWR. Its steam allocation had increased to 78 by 1959 and included a small stud of 'Jubilee' class 4-6-0's. Unfortunately, these had long gone and its allotted steam power had by now been reduced to about 60, with two thirds being standard varieties. Indeed, nearly half of the 48 steam logged belonged to the standard 5MT 4-6-0 class. Three other types were also noted - Stanier 'Black 5' and '8F', and standard 3MT 2-6-2T.

Speke Junction shed on 17th July 1966. Built in 1886, the depot would continue to service steam engines until its closure in May 1968.

During a brief visit to Manchester Central station on Sunday, 17th July 1966, Stanier 2-6-4T No. 42644 was found on pilot duty. Allocated to Trafford Park shed, the engine would continue in employment until March 1967.

It was late afternoon when we left Patricroft and made the short walk to catch the bus that would take us to the last shed. We had hoped that we might fit in Newton Heath, too, but at this point we realised that it wouldn't be possible. Time was moving on and we didn't arrive at Agecroft until late evening. With its allocation of steam having fallen from around 55 in the 1950's to 26 by April 1965, it had experienced a steady increase again and its allotment was now back up to around the 40 mark. We didn't envisage seeing a great number engines or indeed much variety, but on noting the last engine we were pleasantly surprised to find the total had reached a creditable 36 with 4 different classes represented. Interestingly, two of the three remaining Johnson 0-6-0 tanks were on shed, No's 47201 and 47202, the latter of which was fitted with condensing apparatus and would be the last of the sixty-strong class to remain in service.

Built at the Vulcan Foundry in 1901, Johnson 0-6-0T No. 47202 casts a clear shadow while standing in the yard of Agecroft MPD on 17th July 1966. One of sixty in its class, it was fitted with condensing apparatus (as were most of this type), which facilitated working through the tunnels of the Metropolitan Line in the London area. Two weeks after this photograph was taken the engine would be transferred to Newton Heath, from where it would be withdrawn in December.

It had been a really enjoyable day. We had seen 198 steam on shed and I had copped just over half of them. We had taken longer than planned, however, and when we left Agecroft we knew that it was going to be a close call as to whether we would make it back to Liverpool in time to catch the last train out to Ormskirk. While we could run to help save time, we couldn't do anything about the frequency or indeed the timekeeping of either the buses or trains that we needed to use.

Our legs failed to carry us quickly enough from the bus to Manchester Central and we arrived breathless two or three minutes after the 9.45pm had departed for Liverpool. This left one more train we could catch, the 10.30pm, which was due to arrive in Lime Street at 11.33pm. Stopping at nearly every station en-route, the thirty-four mile journey seemed to take forever, and even with a generous schedule we knew by the time we reached Allerton that we would be about 8 minutes late into Lime Street. From here we needed to get across to Exchange, about half a mile away, to catch the last train out to Ormskirk at 11.44pm. Needless to say, we ran all the way only to find that the train had already left… and so began our introduction to the joys of hitch hiking!

We now had to find our way out of the city centre and locate the road that would take us to Ormskirk. If I remember correctly, the first person we asked for directions replied rather aptly that the road we needed was the Scotland Road! Thankfully we didn't have to wait long for our first lift, which got us as far as Aintree. As the night wore on, however, there were fewer and fewer vehicles on the road. Our second lift didn't materialise until quite a while later, but as luck would have it we were dropped off only a few minutes walk from the campsite. It had taken us over three hours to complete the last stage of our journey, which couldn't have been more than about 12 miles. Not quite the way we planned to get back, we eventually crawled into our tent a little after 3.00am.

Monday, 18th July.

We broke camp in bright sunshine, which had no doubt been illuminating the tent almost as soon as we had got to bed. It wasn't the earliest of starts, but we were soon on the train heading firstly for Burscough Junction and then, after a short walk to Burscough Bridge, to the seaside town of Southport for our first shed visit of the day. We didn't realise that the depot had closed on 6th June, and with only a handful of steam as part of its allocation before this date, we weren't surprised to find only three diesel shunters and Stanier 2-6-0 No. 42968 present.

Before leaving Southport an hour or so was spent on Chapel Street station during which time 'Mogul' No. 42968 appeared and took on water. This engine would be the only member of the forty-strong class to be preserved and which I would regularly see long after steam had finished on BR. From Southport we travelled east to Wigan and visited Springs Branch. The shed was completely rebuilt in the early fifties and would continue to service steam until its closure in early December next year. Of all the depots visited during this trip this one produced the greatest variety of steam power. We noted a total of 45 representing 11 different classes. Included in the those present was 'B1' No. 61306, which would be preserved and later be given the name Mayflower, previously bestowed on classmate No. 61379. A full list of locomotives on shed is given in appendix 16.

Once back at Wigan North Western station we caught the first available train to Preston, headed by Brush Type '4' No. D1620. After spending a few minutes here, and noting Kingmoor-based 'Black 5' No. 45217, in charge of a passenger train, we caught the bus to Lostock Hall. This shed would of course continue to have an active steam allocation until 4th August 1968 - the last day of normal steam working on BR. As with the previous depot, we found quite a mix of steam power present with 10 different classes amongst the 43 residents. Varieties noted were as follows: Fairburn 2-6-4T (3), Fowler 0-6-0T (2), Stanier 2-6-4T (4), Ivatt 2-6-0 (4), Stanier 'Black 5' (9), Stanier '8F' (13) 'Britannia' (2), standard 5MT (1), standard 2MT (4) and 'WD' (1). Following the taking of a few photographs we headed back to Preston Station.

Several steam were noted on the way to Carnforth, our next destination, including 'Britannia' Pacific No. 70025 Western Star. As previously mentioned, since 1950 the depot here had a continuous allocation of about 40 steam, but there had been an increase over the past year and it now had 50 to call upon. We noted 47 such locos representing 9 different classes, including 'Jubilee' No. 45675 Hardy, a Leeds Holbeck engine, 'WD's No's 90633 and 90707 both Wakefield locos and 'Britannia' No. 70052 Firth of Tay allocated to Kingmoor.

From the shed we walked into the town to buy some food for our evening meal, which we would have after setting up camp at Bolton-le-Sands. The campsite couldn't have been better situated - well, not if you were interested in steam or liked being next to a main railway line - you could watch the trains come and go without leaving your tent! Which is exactly what we did until dusk, by which time we had seen five steam-hauled freights headed by 'Black 5's No's 45221 and 44773, standard 5MT No. 73100 and 'Britannia's' No's 70017 Arrow and 70042 Lord Roberts. Before heading into the Lake District tomorrow, we would 'spot' on the local station for a while, and then move on to Carnforth in the hope of seeing some steam-hauled summer specials and relief passenger trains.

Above. Stanier Mogul No. 42968 takes on water on a hot and sunny 18th July 1966 while standing in Southport station.
Below. Hull (Dairycoates)-based 'B1' 4-6-0 No. 61306 at rest in Springs Branch (Wigan) MPD. This engine would also be preserved after withdrawal from normal service in October 1967.

Top. Front ends in the evening sunshine at Lostock Hall MPD. From nearest the camera: 'Black 5' No. 45368, Ivatt 2-6-0 No. 43118, Stanier 8F's No's 48263 (L) and 48470 and 'WD' No. 90351.
Above. Ivatt 2MT No. 46400 at rest in the yard of Carnforth shed with the depot's coaling stage in the background. This Lostock Hall allocated engine would see another 10 months service before ceasing work in May 1967.
Both 18th July 1966.

Tuesday 19th July

The day began bright and sunny with a wide expanse of clear blue sky. We left the tent in situ and spent an hour or so on Bolton-le-Sands station noting several steam workings before catching the local service into Carnforth. While the sunshine persisted and the day gradually got warmer and warmer, we thoroughly enjoyed watching frequent steam movements through and around the station. We noted nine passenger trains with steam in charge: four hauled by 'Britannia' Pacifics No's 70009 and 70036 outward and return, four by 'Black 5's' No's 45420, 45445, 44905 and 45278 and one by 'Jubilee' No. 45675 Hardy. Altogether we logged 25 steam and 11 diesel movements, nine of which were Brush Type '4's. Needless to say, I made good use of my camera during the day with a few pictures to be reasonably pleased with.

As much as we would have liked to continue our observations at the platform end for the rest of the day, we needed to make preparations for the next stage of our journey. Once back at the campsite, we had something to eat (most likely a Vesta curry!), packed our gear and returned to Carnforth. Leaving the main line here, our train would take the route of the old Furness Railway to Barrow, from where we faced a good walk to reach the depot. After seeing so many passenger turns in the hands of steam earlier in the day, I suppose we were hoping the trend would continue. However, confirming what we really expected, English Electric Type '4' No. D231 Sylvania came in to the station and sat ready to take us further on our way.

Barrow had an allocation of about a dozen steam, so we weren't expecting it to be bursting with activity. Indeed, the number present mirrored its allotment, with just 12 such engines noted representing 5 different varieties. Three of the last remaining Midland 0-6-0's No's 44311, 44394 and 44500 were present and looked as if they had recently been withdrawn. Also on shed were three 'Jinties' No's 47373, 47667 and 47675. The services of No. 47373 would be dispensed with last of all, when the shed closed five months later on 12th December.

From Barrow we continued by dmu to Seascale where we would camp overnight on the beach. It was a warm summers evening with a sea breeze noticeable by its absence when we selected the spot to pitch our tent. We had the beach to ourselves as we drank the last of our pop and watched the sun slowly sink into the sea. As the light began to fade our final thoughts were no doubt about tomorrow and the prospect of reaching Carlisle another great railway centre. Before arriving there, however, we would break our journey to see what steam locos were on Workington shed.

We slept soundly for about two or three hours until we were abruptly awakened by the sound of voices. Very close by we heard a number of lads and girls in high spirits laughing and giggling. This went on for a few minutes and then, suddenly, it seemed as though they were all around us, and we wondered if they were about to pull the tent down. Two of them, if not more, collided with the guy ropes and swore loudly as the tent partly collapsed. I looked out to see a group of twelve or so naked teenagers making their way down to the sea for a midnight swim. I think this was part and parcel of what became known as the swinging sixties, although, no doubt, similar bouts of exuberance had happened many times before this decade had begun!

'Jubilee' 4-6-0 No. 45675 Hardy enters Carnforth station with a northbound parcels train. One of a handful of this class to survive into 1967, it would remain in service for a further 12 months.

'Britannia' Pacific No. 70009 Alfred the Great draws into Carnforth station with a relief passenger train for the Lake District. Based at Norwich when new in May 1951, like many other of its classmates it would end its days shedded at Carlisle Kingmoor.

Ready to continue its journey northwards from Carnforth station with its mixed freight train, 'Britannia' pacific No. 70018 Flying Dutchman is met by 'Black 5' No. 45278 with a relief express passenger train.

All above 19th July 1966.

Top. Carnforth station on what was turning out to be a very warm 19th July: 'Britannia' pacific No. 70009 Alfred the Great arrives with a southbound relief passenger train, presumably a balanced working to that featured opposite. This time, however, the locos headlamp code shows it to be at the head of an express rather than an ordinary one.

Above: On the same day, Fairburn 2-6-4T No. 42252 rests in the yard of Barrow MPD its home shed. Further allocations to Tebay, Low Moor and Normanton would take place before the engine would cease work and face its final journey, to the scrapyard, in October 1967.

Wednesday 20th July

The morning was overcast and dull, completely at odds with the fine weather of the day before. After breakfast we broke camp, packed our rucksacks and made the short walk to the station. While sitting and waiting for our train, Fairburn 2-6-4T No. 42236, allocated to Barrow MPD, appeared with a northbound parcels train. Having taken a photo of the engine, the driver invited us on to the footplate, from where further pictures were taken looking towards the front of the loco. Shortly after stepping down on to the platform a very clean Lostock Hall Ivatt 2-6-0, No. 46499, came through the station with an inspection saloon carrying a number of railway officials.

The twenty-mile journey to Workington was uneventful with no engines seen en-route. The depot, which was only a few minutes walk from the station, produced 12 steam of 5 different types. Most evident was the Ivatt 4MT 2-6-0 class with seven members noted. Also resting on shed was No. 42236 seen earlier at Seascale. This former LNWR shed would close on 1st January 1968 but, many years later, the building would be bought by The Great Central Railway based at Loughborough with the intention of carefully demolishing it and then putting it back together to house steam once more.

Carlisle Citadel was reached early in the afternoon and from the station we set off for Upperby, the nearer of the two depots still servicing steam. Last year I failed to get round the shed after bumping in to a dog and his policeman; seeking to dispel any thoughts about it happening again I kept telling myself I couldn't possibly come across them again and, even if I did, they wouldn't remember me… would they?

Nervous and apprehensive we walked down the cinder track towards the depot. Neither of us were convinced we would manage to get round the depot without a problem, but with the effort we were making to keep our eyes peeled I think we would have spotted a mouse a hundred yards away let alone a dog or anyone remotely looking like they we wearing a blue uniform. As it turned out we needn't have been so concerned. We logged all the engines on shed without anyone, seemingly, being interested in our presence. Only 15 steam were present representing 5 different classes. Three 'Britannia' Pacifics were noted - No's 70022 Tornado, 70024 Vulcan and 70032 Tennyson.

Kingmoor was reached after a short bus ride from the city centre and once again, just like last year, we knew exactly where we were heading sometime before we arrived. With so many engines ready for their next turn of duty, the resulting pall of smoke rising way above the depot couldn't help but advertise its position. Its allocation of around 120 steam twelve months earlier hadn't changed a great deal and presently stood at 115, including two 'Black 5's, No's. 45082 and 45097, withdrawn the preceding week. This was a remarkable number considering the continued onslaught on steam stocks since our previous visit. Regrettably, the depot's last active 'Patriots' had gone, and so, too, had the few remaining 'Clans' and 'Scots', although No. 72006 Clan Mackenzie and No. 46115 Scots Guardsman, withdrawn the previous May and January respectively, were still to be found in store. The 'Scot' of course would be preserved, but the 'Clan' would not be so fortunate. All told we noted 67 steam on shed - thirty-four of which were Stanier 'Black 5's - representing 9 different classes.

From Kingmoor we walked back to the main road we had cycled along the previous summer, caught the bus out to Blackford and headed for the campsite adjacent to the A7, which would be our base for the next two days. The Waverley Route was only half a mile away and on the evening we noted two Birmingham R.C. & W. Type '2' diesels No's D5311 and D5318.

Noted as 'still in store' during our visit to Carlisle Kingmoor on 20th July 1966, was 'Royal Scot' No. 46115 Scots Guardsman. Built in October 1927, it had completed a little over 2,000,000 miles by January 1961. Good fortune would mean a new life in preservation beckoned.

While on the way back to Citadel station from Kingmoor shed, we spotted '9F' No. 92009 crossing the river Eden with a northbound mixed freight. First allocated to Wellingborough, the standard 2-10-0 entered traffic on 12th March 1954. On paper at least, the '9F' was allocated to Saltley no fewer than four times during its working life. The locos final transfer (of twelve) would take it from Kingmoor to Carnforth in January 1968, from where it would continue in service for another three months. 92009 would be one of the last of the class to be withdrawn.

Thursday 21st and Friday 22nd July

Both days were spent relaxing. The weather had become very hot and sticky and my postcards to mum and dad written over the two days mentioned how the sky had remained a constant blue, the temperature had relentlessly hovered around 80f, and that I was rather sore from sunburn! Citadel Station, visited on both days, provided plenty of steam workings, a fair number of which were passenger turns entrusted to, in the main, 'Black 5's and 'Britannia' Pacifics.

On Friday morning we delayed breaking camp and caught the bus into Carlisle early in the afternoon. Once on Citadel station, the countdown to midnight (when our Freedom of Scotland tickets became valid) began and, even though there was no lack of steam activity, time seemed to stand still. Impatience was getting the better of us because we were so looking forward to moving on into Scotland but, thankfully, after what felt like an eternity (I was convinced the station clock needed rewinding!) Saturday was under way. The waiting wasn't quite over at this point however - it would be another hour or so before our expedition around Scotland would begin.

Built at Crewe in October 1948 and allocated to Bletchley for many years, Upperby-based Ivatt 2-6-2T No. 41222 stands in Carlisle Citadel station on 21st July 1966 with a parcels train. It would be withdrawn on the shed's closure in December.

Saturday 23rd July

We had decided to catch the 11.45pm ex-Newcastle, arriving at Citadel at 1.10am. This service had through carriages to Stranraer where it was scheduled to arrive at 4.55am. We knew that it stood a fair chance of being steam-hauled, and so it turned out when into the station came 'Black 5' No. 45126, a Kingmoor engine, only a few minutes late. From what I remember we left pretty well on time and, even though the train was very busy, we managed to find a couple of empty seats. We now needed to keep alert so we would be ready to get off the train at Dumfries and visit our first Scottish shed of the week.

At 2.15am the train entered a deserted Dumfries station and by 2.25am we were inside the depot. We hadn't realised that this former Glasgow and South Western shed had lost its steam allocation six weeks earlier at the end of May, so I suppose we were fortunate to find a solitary Stanier 'Black 5' present, No. 45480, with large cabside numbers to help us identify it in the dark!

We hurried back to the station to ensure that we were in good time to catch the sleeper from London, which had left Euston at 8.40pm and was due at 2.59am. We were aware that steam might well be in charge of this train, too, and so it proved. As the train came into the station it appeared to be hauled by a 'Black 5'. However, No. 44790 proved to be the pilot engine and sharing the roster was 'Britannia' Pacific No. 70041 Sir John Moore. Both engines were allocated to Kingmoor and had a long, heavy load behind them. There weren't any seats available in the few ordinary carriages available, and passengers were sitting or lying in the corridors and vestibules. We eventually succeeded in finding a few square feet free of bodies so we could sit down but, because of the cramped conditions and the sunburn to contend with, it was one of the most uncomfortable journeys by train I can remember. How envious I was of all the people tucked up in bed in the sleeping cars! Needless to say, we didn't get any shuteye and with lots of windows open the only enjoyable part of the experience was the intermittent sound of the exhausts of the engines working hard at the head of the train.

The two locos finally eased their way into a cool and wet Sranraer at about 6.20am and, though feeling tired, we were looking forward to visiting the shed here. Originally serving both the Caledonian Railway and the Glasgow and South Western Railway, since 1950 its allocation had never been more than about sixteen engines, and this figure had dwindled over the past few years to only three by the time of our visit. It was close to 7.00am when we arrived at the shed and noted 2 different varieties of loco ('Black 5' and standard 2MT) amongst the 7 steam present.

Leaving Stranraer on the 7.35am service to Glasgow Central, our next destination, Ayr, was reached at 9.10am. We changed here to catch the 9.20am service to Kilmarnock as far as Newton-on-Ayr, which would leave us with a ten-minute walk to Ayr shed. Once again we were steam hauled, albeit only for a mile, this time by standard 4MT 2-6-0 No. 76102. We logged a total of 30 steam in residence representing 5 different classes, with Hughes-Fowler 'Crabs' (11) and Stanier 'Black 5's' (12) dominating. This former G&SW depot would continue to service steam for a further two months before closing at the beginning of October. We had given ourselves an hour to complete the visit and get back to the station in time to catch the 10.38am to Kilmarnock. We managed this quite comfortably, but we were starting to feel the effects of our irregular and inadequate sleep pattern. Later the same day this lack of sleep would catch up with us, and we would find ourselves in a very tricky situation.

Getting to Hurlford, the next G&SW shed on our schedule, required us to catch the bus to Barleith Halt (by this time closed), from Kilmarnock, from where it was a short walk to the shed. A total of 12 steam were logged representing 7 different varieties. Standard designs were in the majority with eight such engines noted, including three 3MT 2-6-0's, No's 77017, 77018 and 77019, which the shed received when new in 1954. There was very little in the way of activity, and it appeared few jobs remained for these engines. Like Ayr, this depot would finish with steam well before the end of the year and would close on 3rd October.

En-route to Glasgow Central from Kilmarnock we noted a southbound passenger train at Barrhead with Stanier 'Black 5' No. 45442 piloting 'Jubilee' No. 45697 Achilles. From Central we caught the train to Cartsdyke, hopeful that after the short walk to Greenock (Ladyburn) we might find a couple of steam on shed. We recorded just 5 locomotives in residence - all, unfortunately, diesel shunters. So, tired and disappointed, it was back to Central Station, where to welcome us was the pleasing sight of our second 'Jubilee' of the day No. 45593 Kolhapur at the head of a southbound express.

In the hope of getting a glimpse of an 'A4' we decided to head for Buchanan Street station. After noting a number of diesels, mainly North British Type '2's, we had our first glimpse of not a 'streak' but the widely travelled class 'A2' No. 60532 Blue Peter. She coasted into the station with the 3.45pm ex-Aberdeen, as I recall spot on time. Once I had photographed the engine, we were soon off again to try and complete our shed bash for the day by fitting in both Hamilton and Motherwell depots.

Hamilton had been closed to steam for about three-and-a-half years and was found to be housing dmu's and a few diesel shunters. Motherwell, however, although with a much reduced steam allocation from the ninety or so it had at the beginning of the 1960's, was expected to produce a reasonable number steam of several varieties. It did just that with 20 steam noted of 6 different classes, including 'A2' No. 60528 Tudor Minstrel, which had been recently withdrawn, leaving only two members of the once forty-strong class still active. Also present was standard 5MT No. 73154 the last steam engine built at Derby works.

We had been up and about for almost forty hours as we made the journey once more back to Glasgow Central station and couldn't wait to reach Beattock where we would camp for the night. Our train, the 9.50pm sleeper to London, would take about 90mins to get to Beattock, so we relaxed in our seats and tried hard not to nod off. Well, we arrived at the bottom of the well-known incline presumably on time, but completely oblivious to where we were and to anything that might have been going on around us. Not surprisingly, while resting in the comfortable compartment we had succumbed to fatigue and following a brief spell of drowsiness, had fallen fast asleep. Indeed, so deep were our slumbers that we were completely unaware of reaching and spending 15 minutes in Carlisle station before our train continued its journey south!

Left. With a little over three months left of its working life, 'Crab' 2-6-0 No. 42919 stands simmering in Ayr, its home depot, on 23rd July 1966.

Below. As it slowly makes its way into Glasgow Buchanan Street station with the 3.45pm ex-Aberdeen, 'A2' 4-6-2 No. 60532 Blue Peter is watched by an admirer. The last of the class to be withdrawn later in December, the engine would be fortunate enough to be preserved. 23rd July 1966.

Having reached the buffer stops of Buchanan Street station, Blue Peter waits for the empty stock to be removed so it can return to St Rollox shed for servicing. The Glasgow Evening Citizen van in the background had just dropped off the latest edition of the newspaper and the driver of the 'A2' had managed to secure a copy to read while waiting to take his engine back to shed. Owned by Beaverbrook Newspapers Ltd., the paper would cease publication in 1974.
23rd July 1966.

Seen standing beside mounds of rubble in Motherwell shed on 23rd July 1966, 'A2' No. 60528 Tudor Minstrel looks clean and ready for work, even though she had been reported as being withdrawn the previous month. It was now left to classmates 60530 Sayajirao and Blue Peter to continue flying the flag for the 'A2's.

Sunday 24th July

For some reason I stirred at about 2.15am as we were passing through - no it couldn't be - Warrington! I immediately woke Dennis and we both very quickly realised that we were now travelling without valid tickets and Crewe was our next stop - what, we wondered, would we do if we were asked for them? Now wide awake and dreading that the guard might materialise at any time, we decided to pretend we were still asleep in the hope it would deter him from asking for proof of travel. Fortunately for us he didn't appear and with great relief we got off the train at about 3.15am. What we didn't realise, however, was that things were going to get a lot more problematic as the day progressed.

Sitting on a luggage trolley, we gathered our thoughts while noting the movements of a variety of diesels and electric locos until it was light. We had looked at the timetable and decided to delay our return initially to Carlisle and then Glasgow until we had 'bunked' the sheds - well it was Sunday and there would be a good number of extra locos taking a rest! North Stabling Point was visited at 4.45am, the Diesel Depot at 5.00am and lastly the sole remaining steam depot, Crewe South, at about 5.15am, where we found a healthy total of 77 steam representing 8 different classes.

Being on a tight budget we didn't have sufficient funds to pay for the journey back to Carlisle, so we agreed to take the chance of pleading our case if we were asked for our tickets, and hope that the guard had a sympathetic ear! With Brush Type '4' No D1854 in charge of our train, we left Crewe at 7.50am. Calling at all stations on the way, it would take the best part of two hours to reach Preston. The journey seemed endless, and after every stop we expected to be asked for our tickets. As we stepped down on to the platform at Preston, we couldn't believe how fortunate we had been. There had not been a sign of the guard since leaving Crewe and we had managed about a third of our journey back to Carlisle without any additional expense. But would we be as lucky during the next stage of our trip?

During the hour or so we had to wait for the 9.50am ex-Liverpool Exchange to arrive, two steam locos were noted: Fairburn 2-6-4T No. 42105 and 'Black 5' No. 44848 with a passenger train. Headed by 'Black 5' No. 44737, our train to take us to Carlisle and on to Glasgow arrived on time. Unfortunately, Brush Type '4' No. D1939 replaced the Stanier 4-6-0 and it was behind the diesel loco that we departed for the north - well, not exactly north to begin with, more southeast. We soon realised what was happening - we were heading for Bamber Bridge, would then turn east for Blackburn, and then north to Hellifield and on to the Settle to Carlisle line. Not the best of routes in view of the circumstances!

The laying of long-welded track between Crewe and Glasgow was taking place and these engineering works were no doubt the reason for our diversion. With an extra thirty-six miles to cover to get to Carlisle using the Settle route, uppermost in our thoughts was the increased possibility of having to produce valid tickets. Tiredness was a constant companion and after we left Hellifield we slept fitfully in a compartment we had all to ourselves. We reached the outskirts of Carlisle and then Citidel Station itself with, thankfully, no sign of anyone being remotely interested in checking our tickets. Happily, we had reached the point where our Freedom of Scotland passes were accepted once again.

It was late afternoon by the time we arrived in Glasgow, and the first of its depots we should have visited a lot earlier in the day, St Rollox. Amongst the many diesels, we noted 5 steam of 4 different varieties, including, gently simmering inside the shed, No.60034 Lord Faringdon, one of only three 'A4's still working. Also present and in steam was 'Britannia' Pacific No. 70034 Thomas Hardy. From here we set off for Polmadie, which we expected to produce a large number of diesels but also a good smattering of steam, too.

With the evening sun casting some brightness on the shed's variety of motive power, we gradually made our way round this former Caledonian Railway depot. Last July when we visited Polmadie we logged 28 steam of 7 different varieties. This visit produced 39 steam representing a similar number of different classes. Standard 2-6-4T's were the most prolific with fourteen present and, on this occasion, there were also four 'Britannia' class locos - No's. 70002 Geoffrey Chaucer, 70006 Robert Burns, 70010 Owen Glendower and 70011 Hotspur. The depot would continue to cater for steam up until the 1st May the following year when steam traction would cease being used in Scotland.

Like Polmadie, the next shed we visited, Corkerhill, employed a small allocation of steam right up until its elimination from Scottish metals. We logged a total of 30 steam amongst which were 8 different varieties. During the fifties and early sixties a small stud of 'Jubilees' had been allotted to the depot, so it was a pleasing to find No. 45675 Hardy, a Leeds Holbeck engine, which we had previously noted at Carnforth in charge of a relief passenger train, resting here between duties. Standard locos were much in evidence with twenty-one recorded.

Having only a few months left before closing to steam in November, Eastfield, the last shed on our itinerary, had no more than a handful of such engines as part of its allocation. Nevertheless, we noted 8 classes amongst the 15 steam present, including 'A4' No. 60024 Kingfisher undergoing repair work after failing in the Glasgow area earlier in the month. The possibility of being hauled by one of these engines during the next few days was already beginning to look extremely doubtful.

Absolutely exhausted, we reached Buchanan Street at about 9.30pm in good time to catch the 9.50pm train to Edinburgh Waverley where we planned to spend the night in one of the waiting rooms. It was about 11.30pm when we settled down to try and get some sleep. As we stretched out on the seats the door opened and two other enthusiasts joined us. They were both from Leicester and were travelling around Scotland in search of steam too. No sooner as we had introduced ourselves and started chatting another two lads appeared carrying very heavy rucksacks. Once their contents had been revealed it was easy to see why they were obviously both so laden. They had decided to return home with a few mementos in the form of shed plates, oil cans etc. It transpired that they were from Rugby and had reached the end of their holiday and were heading south the following day. To lighten their load they offered us two sizeable spanners and so I had one and the lads from Leicester the other. I have to admit, needless to say, that by the end of the week I too had 'collected' one or two similar oval shaped souvenirs.

Originally fitted with a corridor tender, 'A4' Pacific No. 60034 Lord Faringdon awaits its next turn of duty inside St. Rollox MPD. There wouldn't be many more jobs for this engine, and it would be withdrawn before the following month was out. 24th July 1966.

Seen stored in the yard of Polmadie shed on 24th July, standard 2-6-4T No. 80058 had been withdrawn about a week by the time this picture was taken. Built at Derby in January 1955, it remained allocated to 66A for all of its relatively short life.

Condemned at the same time as No. 80058, Fairburn tank No. 42176, a Greenock (Ladyburn) engine for a number of years, had only the prospect of being towed from Polmadie to McLellan's scrapyard, Langloan.

Derby built standard 5MT No. 73063, withdrawn the previous month, would soon be facing the cutter's torch at Motherwell Machinery and Scrap Co., Wishaw; it had been a Polmadie engine since new in September 1954. The two 2-6-4 tanks, No's 80086 (L) and 80116, would continue in service until steam finished in Scotland in May 1967. 24th July 1966.

'Black 5' No 44997 stands in the yard of Perth MPD its home shed on 25th July 1966. The 4-6-0 may well have been the last steam loco in service in Scotland. Although official withdrawal would take place on 6th May 1967, employment continued after this date - see caption accompanying colour picture on page 132.

Monday 25th July

Following an uncomfortable and restless night, I woke at six am and decided it was pointless to try and get back to sleep. I took the opportunity to write a postcard to mum and dad and brought them up to date with our exploits and telling them where we were off to next: Perth, Dundee, Thornton, St. Margarets and Haymarket sheds. After posting the card we had coffee and biscuits for breakfast and started to log the various locos arriving and departing. Several steam were noted, including 'Black 5's No's. 44952, 45053, 45084, 45162, 44791, Fairburn 2-6-4T's No's. 42273 and 42691 and standard 2-6-4T No. 80006.

After saying farewell to the other lads we caught the 9.33am to Perth, behind BR Type '2's No's. D5125 and D5129. We had learned from our experience over the weekend and, although we both catnapped during the journey, we were determined not to fall soundly asleep and wake up in Inverness the train's ultimate destination! Arrival at Perth was a couple of minutes early and by 11.15am we were making our way round the depot. With only about a half of the number of steam present compared with my visit a year earlier, it didn't take long to note down the 18 on shed. The variety of steam power had taken a tumble, too, with only 4 different classes represented.

Two locos worthy of note were 'Britannia' No. 70008 Black Prince and withdrawn 'A4' No. 60026 Miles Beevor minus its tender. Interestingly, the tender that had been attached to the 'streak' was the one originally attached to 'Mallard' when she reached 126mph during a breaking test in July 1938. Of course, much of the former 'A4' would end up on sister engine No. 60007 Sir Nigel Gresley during its restoration. With regards to the tender, a fellow enthusiast, Peter Groom, after addressing an RTCS meeting informed me about the saga surrounding its fate. It would appear to have been purchased from the scrapyard by a company in Sheffield, which used it for industrial purposes. Many years later it was offered to the 'A4' preservation Society, but by this time only parts like the wheels and axles could be salvaged and the rest had to be disposed of. Perth would continue with a small allocation of steam until closure the following May when the few remaining were removed for breaking up.

By midday we were back on Perth Station and looking forward to catching the 12.10pm to Dundee, from where we would make the short walk to Tay Bridge steam depot once of the North British Railway. Its steam allocation had been reduced to 26, but the depot still had the last two working 'A2's' and a handful of 'V2's'. Noted on this visit were 6 different classes amongst the 17 steam present. No sign of the ubiquitous Blue Peter, but the other 'A2' No. 60530 Sayajirao was on shed, accompanied by two 'V2's' No's. 60813 and 60819. One of the last seven sheds in Scotland to retain a steam allocation, it would close the following year on 1st May.

By mid afternoon, after a short journey by train to Thornton Junction, we were making our way round Thornton shed. This was a former NBR depot, too, and during the fifties could assemble fifteen or sixteen different varieties of steam motive power, amongst a total allocation hovering around the one hundred plus mark. Like so many other MPD's up and down the country, its allocation reflected the relentless replacement of steam; representing four different classes, it now had thirty-nine such engines to call upon. We noted 39 steam present (eighteen seemingly stored) during our visit, with 5 classes represented as follows: 'B1' (8), 'J36' (2), 'J37' (6), 'J38' (12) and 'WD' (11). During the time spent at the depot I reeled off a 36-exposure film and copped nine steam.

Resting in the sunshine: Thompson 'B1' No 61262 stands simmering outside its home shed, Dundee, on 25th July 1966. After reallocation to Dunfermline later in September, the engine would complete its time in service there in April 1967.

Gresley class 'J38' No. 65931 rests in the yard of Thornton Junction MPD on 26th July 1966. A total of thirty-five were built in 1926 and the design had a longer boiler, shorter smokebox and smaller driving wheels than the 'J39's. A number of its classmates had had 'J39' boilers fitted over the years, but the above engine has the original design. Two months after this photograph was taken the 0-6-0 would be withdrawn.

Above. 'J38' No. 65920 sits below the coaling stage of Thornton Jnct. MPD on 25th July 1966. Transferred from St Margarets, its home shed for many years, to Dalry Road in October 1964, the 0-6-0 became a 62A engine the following March. Withdrawal would come in a little over three months time.

Right. Looking extremely grimy and work weary, 'J36' No. 65345 is seen in Thornton MPD on 25th July 1966. Except for the whole of 1966, when allocated to Bathgate, the 0-6-0, from 1948 onwards, had always been a Thornton loco. As tired and jaded as she looked, she would be the last of her class to be withdrawn in May 1967.

With Type '2' diesel No. D5315 at its head, we caught the 4.47pm back to Waverley and then the bus to St Margarets, yet another former North British shed. At the beginning of the fifties this depot had a considerable allocation of steam totalling 221 engines of 26 varieties. Indeed, it boasted the largest provision of steam power of all the Scottish sheds. Even by the start of the sixties it had 22 varieties amongst its still healthy allocation of 175 steam. Its decline over the last six years was mirrored in its allotment of steam power at the time of our visit - down to just 23, with only two ex-LNER engines (both 'V2's) still operating from the shed and a solitary class 'J36' No. 65234 acting as a stationary boiler. With 7 different classes represented, we recorded a total of 18 steam, with no visitors worthy of special mention.

Haymarket diesel depot was visited at the end of the day and from there we caught the train to Glasgow, arriving at Queen Street at about 9.50 pm. Although unlikely to be an 'A4', tonight, with any luck, we would travel behind steam, and during the journey get some much needed sleep. The 11.00pm from Buchanan Street was scheduled to take nearly four and a half hours to Aberdeen and when we arrived at the station 'A2' No. 60532 Blue Peter (named after the horse that won the 2000 Guineas and Derby in 1939) was already at the head of the train. There wasn't a great number of people using the service, and we found an empty compartment in the first carriage behind the engine from which we could take in the sounds of the loco as it made its way north. Making full use of the extra space we slipped off our shoes and lay out across the seats. As the train made its way out of the station and through the suburbs we listened to the 'A2's' crisp exhaust and, before reaching the open countryside, had fallen fast asleep.

Tuesday 26th July

The guard woke us up from our slumbers as he made his way through the carriages announcing we had arrived at Aberdeen and that the train terminated here. It was 3.20 in the morning and we didn't really want to leave our comfortable compartment. Reluctantly we did so, and sat for a while in the waiting room before setting off for Ferryhill. This shed had never had a large compliment of steam and was always capable of housing all of its engines under cover. It had quite an interesting early history, which I didn't discover until many years later. The Caledonian shared their site with the NBR after it had acquired the right to house its engines in the depot. What followed, especially once the new twelve-road shed had been completed in 1908, was incessant wrangling concerning the charges levied by the Caledonian for stabling, lighting up, sand, water, turning etc., resulting in a mountain of correspondence between the two companies!

At 4.00am, as the sun was rising, we were making note of the locos on shed. Blue Peter was being serviced and was gleaming in the early morning sunshine; and while we were admiring her, the driver invited us on to the footplate! Also being prepared for its next turn of duty was Stanier 'Black 5' No. 44703 which, a little over a month later on 3rd September, would haul the last steam rostered Aberdeen to Glasgow express (1.30 pm). A total of 6 steam were noted, including three 'A4's' No's 60004 William Whitelaw (minus tender and awaiting scrapping), 60009 Union of South Africa (minus tender) and, undergoing repair 60019 Bittern in a very clean and presentable condition. The sixth loco present was 'B1' No. 61262.

4.00am on the morning of 26th July 1966: Ferryhill based 'Black 5' No. 44703 has been prepared ready for work. The Horwich built 4-6-0 cost £14,450 when new and entered traffic in August 1948. In December, approximately three months after hauling the last steam rostered Aberdeen-Glasgow express, the loco would be deemed surplus to requirements and be withdrawn. Below. The early morning sunlight is reflected off the 4-6-0's relatively clean motion.

The final picture of 'Black 5' No. 44703 captures the loco leaving Aberdeen with the 6.20am passenger service to Perth. With a well-prepared bed of coal in place, the fireman has time to spend a few moments looking out from the cab. 26th July 1966.

Taken from almost the same spot in July 2006, the view below shows how the track layout and signalling have significantly changed over the years.

The sunny start to the morning continued as we sauntered back to the station. The next steam passenger turn was the 6.20am to Perth, which earlier in the year had been diagrammed for an 'A4', but was now most likely to be a 'Black 5'. So, it came as no surprise when No. 44703 reversed slowly up to the line of carriages sitting in the bay platform and waited for the signal to start its ninety-mile journey south. We, on the other hand, would be heading north and into very wet weather to visit Kittybrewster and Inverness MPD's and Inverurie Works. Although this would be more of a diesel day, we planned to stop off at Dunfermline on our way back and visit its steam depot.

Type '2's meet at Inverurie. North British No. D6155 is Piloting No. D5329, while No. D6152 is nearest the camera. The number of NB diesel electrics recorded during our visit to Inverurie works reflected how problematic they were. Ten of the fourteen main line diesels present belonged to this class, and within 30 months of steam finishing on BR all 58 members would be consigned to the history books. 26th July 1966.

Once a St Margaret's engine, 'J36' No. 65288 was transferred to Dunfermline in December 1963. Pictured in the yard of the latter depot on 26th July 1966, she would eventually face withdrawal in May 1967, and then the cutter's torch at Arnott Young's in the November.

Following successful visits to the above sheds and works we reached Dunfermline and arrived at the depot in bright sunshine. A total of 17 steam were noted, eight of which were 'WD's. Other classes represented were 'J36' (1), 'J37' (1), 'J38' (3), 'B1' (3), and standard 4MT 2-6-0 (1).

By the time we reached Edinburgh we had covered approximately 265 miles and, although we hadn't seen a great number of steam, we had had a pleasant and enjoyable day. Tonight we would be under canvas at Little France campsite, about a three-mile bus ride south of the city centre, which we had used as a base last year.

Wednesday 27th July

We were now into our fifth day travelling around Scotland. Steam wasn't as much in evidence as the previous year, but we were still having a great time. Today we would leave our gear in the tent and travel light. After breakfast, on another clear and sunny morning, we caught the bus into the city centre and briefly looked in at Waverley before heading off to St. Margarets shed.

There hadn't been much change in the collection of stable mates since our visit two days earlier. Amongst the six 'new faces' was 'V2', No. 60919, which I had last seen at Saltley shed on 10th July. She had obviously succeeded in making her way home following the aborted special run she should have made on Southern metals a week earlier. Altogether we logged a total of 19 steam with 7 classes represented as before. With no rucksacks to carry, we enjoyed the walk back to Waverley and were soon aboard the 10.33am dmu service to Dunfermline Lower Station.

'V2' No. 60813 is seen in Dundee MPD. Once a St Margaret's based engine she was transferred to Dundee in April, where she would remain until withdrawal later in November. The 2-6-2 was the only member of the class to be fitted with small ('shovel-rim or trough type') smoke deflectors on top of the smokebox alongside its stovepipe chimney. 27th July 1966

'J37' 0-6-0 No. 64620 stands close to Dundee Tay Bridge MPD at the head of a pick up freight on 27th July 1966. Introduced in 1914, these engines would continue to give good service for over fifty years. The engine would be the last of its class to remain in service, and would be withdrawn when Scottish steam capitulated in May 1967.

Comparing my log with that for the previous night's visit to Dunfermline, it soon became evident that only two engines, 'WD's No's 90041 and 90489, had been found employment. The remaining locos on shed had been noted the day before and there had been no new arrivals overnight. Once again there were 6 different varieties of loco represented. The apparent lack of work for these engines made me wonder exactly how many were still being used in Scotland on a regular basis; a good number it seemed were idling their final days away in store awaiting official withdrawal. Unfortunately, I didn't identify those engines I'd found in steam, which would have helped to produce a better assessment of their use, but the picture wasn't encouraging.

The next steam depot on the day's schedule was Dundee Tay Bridge. On this occasion it produced 16 steam, one engine fewer than when we visited two days earlier. The 'A2's were noticeable by their absence, which left 5 classes represented as follows: 'Black 5' (2) Ivatt 2-6-0 (1), 'V2' (1), 'B1' (6) and 'J37' (6). Comparing the engines present on both visits revealed, like the situation at Dunfermline, that only a handful of the engines noted were actually being found anything to do. After taking a few photographs, we crossed over the main line to access the former Caledonian shed, Dundee West. For a number of years in the fifties this depot had stored or repaired steam locos from Tay Bridge, but in 1958 had been refurbished as a diesel depot.

During the two-hour journey back to Edinburgh (behind E.E. Type '4' No. D265), we talked about what we were going to do during our last two days in Scotland. Tomorrow, after breaking camp, we decided we would travel across to Glasgow and with any luck visit Cowlairs Works, followed by Eastfield, St. Rollox, Polmadie and Bathgate MPD's. On the evening we planned to catch the 11.00pm from Buchanan Street to Aberdeen and even though the chances were slim, we hoped the motive power would be an 'A4'. The only active member of the class we had noted over the last few days, No. 60034 Lord Faringdon, had not been seen since the previous Sunday, so perhaps we might have the next best thing, an 'A2'. We weren't looking forward to Friday and the fact that we would have to head south to Carlisle before our ticket expired. However, we agreed that, after bunking Ferryhill depot for the last time, we would visit our final Scottish shed at Carstairs, before heading to Edinburgh, possibly behind steam, and then finally back across to Glasgow.

Thursday 28th July

Rising early, we had breakfast and packed the tent and our belongings and caught the bus to Waverley Station. We then travelled by dmu to Glasgow Queen Street and on by bus for our 10.30am visit to Cowlairs Works. Here we noted 12 steam (No's 57566, 44722, 44992, 45357, 60041, 60836, 61029, 61140, 61278, 62059, 73096 and 90020) representing 7 different classes. 'A3' No. 60041 Salmon Trout, we were told, was being dismantled for spares for Flying Scotsman. Former Caledonian '3F' 0-6-0 No. 57566, withdrawn in August 1963 and bought for £900 through the Scottish Locomotive Trust Fund, was in grey primer. Two 'foreign' locos being overhauled were standard 4-6-0 No. 73096, a Patricroft engine, and 'K1' 2-6-2 No. 62059, allocated to Blyth.

We caught up with 'A4' No. 60034 Lord Faringdon in Eastfield and it appeared that she was awaiting repair. In addition to this loco we recorded a further 14 steam on shed - No's 42690, 42734, 42917, 44699, 45273, 61008, 61342, 65912, 73146, 80007, 80051, 80054, 90117 and 90468 - representing 8 different varieties. Looking in my logbook, the pattern of little employment for steam power was evident once again, with only two locos having left the depot and a similar number arriving since our previous visit four days earlier.

The second 'A4' of the day was noted in St. Rollox. Having been repaired by fitters in Eastfield depot, No. 60024 Kingfisher was in steam and sat inside the shed building. Other locos noted were No's 44998, 73149, 73150, 73151 and 73153. If not employed on an earlier express, we both hoped that Kingfisher would head the 11.00 pm to Aberdeen and provide us with a real treat before the end of our trip. Following the short journey to St Rollox Works we noted 15 diesels present, eight of which belonged to the Birmingham RCW Type 2 class. Next on our programme was Polmadie, the last of the Glasgow sheds we would visit. A total of 5 varieties were present amongst the 23 steam locos logged, and for every steam engine noted there were three diesels. Its use of steam would steadily decrease until the following May, the time of its closure, when only twelve would be left allocated to the depot.

From Polmadie we boarded the trolleybus back to the city centre, walked across to Queen Street and caught the 3.30pm to Falkirk High Station. After a short bus journey from here we arrived at Bathgate, home of the named 'J36' No. 65243 Maude. I wanted to photograph her last year, but didn't bother, as she was deep inside the shed building. This time I was hoping that she would be less camera shy and that I'd find her out in the open but, once again, she was hidden inside the depot. Determined to capture her on film, I took several pictures inside the dim building, with the best result proving to be the one of her name painted on the middle wheel splasher! We didn't realise that she had been withdrawn a few days before our holiday had begun and that she would be bought and preserved by the SRPS. Other engines present were No's 46462, 61307, 65267, 65319, 78046 and 78047. The shed would close to steam about two weeks after our visit and several of its remaining engines would be transferred to Edinburgh St. Margarets.

While walking through the centre of Glasgow from Queen Street to Buchanan Street Station to catch the 11.00pm to Aberdeen, we jokingly speculated that we would probably find ourselves behind a 'Black 5' rather than a 'streak'. Well, it wasn't either. It was No. 60532 Blue Peter, the 'A2' we had travelled behind a few nights before. On reaching the front of the train, we stood for a while next to the engine and in the failing light took two or three hand held photographs of her without a flash. Barely printable, the pictures take me back to the two runs we were fortunate to experience behind this powerful and well-proportioned engine. It reminds me, too, that the 'ugly blot' would not have to be endured for much longer. In three months time the remaining 'A4's' would have gracefully succumbed to the diesel invasion and their duties curtailed. From 7th November (the same day that my local shed, Tyseley, would close to steam), Buchanan Street would cease to operate and its services would be transferred to Queen Street.

We boarded the first carriage behind the loco and once again found an empty compartment where we duly made ourselves comfortable. The sounds and atmosphere of being hauled by an express passenger engine in Scotland were not going to last much longer, so the journey ahead was to prove a special one. While we wanted to get some much needed sleep, we also wanted to savour our last run behind an 'A2'. Consequently, at least to begin with, sleep came intermittently, but we both remember the start of the journey and leaving the outskirts of Glasgow and, of course, listening to the powerful beat of the exhaust of Blue Peter as she gathered speed and headed into the night.

Late in the evening of 28th July 1966, 'A2' Pacific No. 60532 Blue Peter stands in Buchanan Street station with the 11.00pm service to Aberdeen. Working steam specials and tours far and wide during the last few months of its career, Blue Peter would finally be put into store later in December.

Friday 29th July

Our last day in Scotland was already underway when we awoke as Blue Peter entered Perth station on time at 12.40am. After about twenty minutes the driver was given the 'right away' and we opened our window fully so that we could listen to the engine moving its train northward once more. We can't remember reaching Forfar so we must have been dead to the world again, which we remained until reaching Aberdeen. Informing people that the train would not be going any further, once again it was the voice of the guard that woke us up. Leaving the cosiness of our compartment we spent the next hour and a half in a far less comfortable waiting room, and then, tired but undaunted, we started off for the shed.

A footnote in my logbook informs me that I started noting the locos at 5.10am. On this our last visit to the depot we recorded the following steam: 'Black 5's No's 44703, 44794 and 44879; 'A4's No's 60004 William Whitelaw, 60009 Union of South Africa and 60019 Bittern; 'A2' No. 60532 Blue Peter and 'WD' No. 90628. 'Black 5' no. 44794 was being prepared for duty so we guessed that she would be taking charge of the 6.20am to Perth. If we were proved right, we would change our plan of travelling on the Bon Accord and spend another two hours behind steam. We were right, and arrived at Perth behind the Stanier 4-6-0 about two minutes early at 8.30 am.

While waiting for the 9.40am to Euston that would take us as far as Carstairs, we noted 'A4' No 60024 Kingfisher (light engine) and English Electric Type '4' No. DP2, which was under going trials on the west coast main line. Travelling via Stirling, Coatbridge and Motherwell we arrived at our destination on time at 11.34am. It had been a restful couple of hours with few engine numbers taken on the way. We were now looking forward to visiting the shed and then, if we were lucky, a final ride behind steam into the capital.

The shed was duly 'bashed' and amongst the 14 steam logged the following classes were represented: Fairburn 2-6-4T (1), 'Black 5' (7), 'B1' (1), 'Britannia' (1), standard 5MT (2) and standard 4MT 2-6-0 (2). The 'Britannia' present, No. 70040 Clive of India, was a Kingmoor-based engine. The shed seemed quiet with little activity; indeed, it appeared once more that work was in short supply and several of the steam locos had been placed in store. Little did we realise how things were about change. The afternoon and evening would provide an unforgettable contrast with the most lively and energetic finish to the week as we could have wished for.

Once back on the station we watched the arrival of Stanier 4-6-0 No. 44791 with the 12.15pm ex-Edinburgh. We had a few minutes to wait after this before our train, the 1.14pm to Waverley, got under way. We knew that there would be a good chance that this service would be steam-hauled, most likely by a 'Black 5'. However, much to our delight and disbelief there wasn't one but two of these engines ready to head this relatively short train - only three or four carriages from what we can remember.

We were soon joined by several other steam enthusiasts armed with tape recorders and stopwatches keen to save the sounds and log the performance of the two engines during their relatively short journey to Edinburgh. Together with these other devotees we hurried to the end of the platform to talk to the crews. Driver Mc Intosh was on the regulator of pilot engine No. 45319 and sister engine No. 45492 under the control of Driver Creighton. They seemed taken aback, yet pleased, at the level of interest being shown both in their engines and their role in what for them, I suppose, was a 'run of the mill' turn of duty.

I wondered if this would encourage them to put on a bit of a show and play to the audience that they knew would be travelling behind them. I didn't have to wait long to find out. Immediately after being given the 'right away', the two locos with both regulators shoved fully open made a thunderous departure - the run it appeared was going to be nothing less than spectacular.

The 'Black 5's fairly rocketed out of the station and the lads with the stopwatches couldn't believe the early pace the drivers were setting. Those recording the resultant deafening roar of the locos were equally bemused. With a light load of three or four carriages off the 9.00am ex-Liverpool to Glasgow train, and two engines together capable of producing about 2,500 horsepower it soon became apparent that, even with the inconvenience of a stop at Haymarket, Edinburgh would be reached well ahead of schedule. Dennis and I decided to try to determine our speed, too, and although our timings in no way could be described as being precise, we agreed that our top speed had hovered around 90 mph and could have been a little higher. We pulled into Waverley at 1.40pm a journey time of 26mins at an average speed in the region of 64mph for the 28-mile journey.

A flying start: 'Black 5's No's. 45319 (pilot) and 45492 power their way out of Carstairs with the 1.14pm bound for Waverley on 29th July 1966.
It wouldn't be long before both enginemen would move on to working with diesel traction but, fortunately for us, Drivers McIntosh (No. 45319) and Creighton provided us with an experience that we would never forget.

We jumped down on to the platform just prior to the train coming to a stop and made straight for the two engines which, with safety valves fully lifted, were both unreservedly declaring how much steam they had to spare. We spoke briefly to the two drivers, thanking them for an exhilarating and enjoyable run into Edinburgh, and then asked them to sign (or should that be autograph!) their names next to their engine's numbers recorded in our logbooks. Although we parted with a farewell of 'long live steam', I wondered afterwards whether the crews couldn't help but look forward to switching from the relatively crude and dirty working conditions of the steam footplate to the comparable luxury and delights of a diesel cab.

Almost there: the end of an exciting journey is only seconds away as the 'Black 5's approach Edinburgh Waverley. Both allocated to Carstairs, No. 45319 would remain a 66E engine until withdrawal in May 1967, while No. 45492 would move on to Motherwell (66B) before ceasing work later in December.

29th July 1966.

Extraction from my notes for Friday 29th July 1966: the drivers' signatures next to their respective locos will forever be a reminder of one of the most exhilarating runs behind steam that I've ever experienced. It wasn't long afterwards that I felt a little guilty in not asking the two firemen for their autographs too.

Fairburn 2-6-4T No. 42273 and 'V2' No. 60919 were noted before boarding the dmu from Waverley to Glasgow Queen Street; a tedious journey with no steam noted en-route. After walking across to Central Station, we had time to reflect on the day's highs and accepted that the journey home held no prospect of further steam haulage; it would be a dull all diesel affair from now on… or would it?

We were due to catch the 9.30 pm to Euston as far as Carlisle, arriving there about 15mins before the expiry of our railrover tickets. Once on Central station, however, we discovered that there was a special excursion (1X39), which we could catch instead. This train was due to leave at 8.55pm and would take the route of The Thames-Clyde express through Kilmarnock, Dumfries and Annan to Carlisle. The journey was a circuitous one and would obviously take longer, but any thoughts of taking the later train were instantly dismissed when we saw the special was double-headed by steam! What a superb way to finish off our Scottish adventure.

Two standard engines, 4MT 2-6-4T No. 80046 (pilot) and 5MT 4-6-0 No. 73079 were in charge of what seemed to be a long train, comprising at least fourteen carriages. A steady stream of passengers took up their seats before our departure; once underway we gathered speed slowly, there was to be no repeat of the fireworks earlier in the day. In fact, a note in my logbook suggests a top speed of about 60mph during the entire journey. As we entered Kilmarnock there was a very large crowd awaiting our arrival and, even though the compliment of carriages was a generous one, every available seat appeared to have been taken when everyone had got on board.

Thirty-eight miles later, and a little under an hour into the journey, the train made an unscheduled stop at Auchinleck so the engines could take on water. With a capacity of less than half of the standard 4-6-0, it was the tank, I presume, that was more in need of having its thirst quenched, and Carlisle was still seventy-seven miles away! Citadel Station was finally reached with twenty minutes to spare before our 'railrover' tickets expired. Our 'bash' around Scotland had come to an end, but what a good end it had been with over 230 miles behind steam.

Saturday 30th July

Until now I have refrained from mentioning the World Cup. The fact that England had reached the final against West Germany meant that I had something else to look forward to, and all being well I would watch the match on television later in the day. Our return to Birmingham from Carlisle, hauled by a Brush Type '4' throughout, was uneventful. I didn't do much spotting during the journey - a lot of the time was spent relaxing and catching up with much needed sleep. Even so, I managed to note six steam en-route, including three 'Britannia' Pacifics No's. 70016 Ariel, 70028 Royal Star and 70036 Boadicea. Several days later after studying my notebook and producing the usual statistics, I realised I had logged a grand total of 1,048 different steam locos during the two week trip (for those recorded on shed see appendix 16).

Uneventful as our journey home may have been, a few miles away from Carlisle the day was proving far from incident free as far as Driver Peter Norris and Fireman Tony Gillett were concerned and, indeed, for a guard who would be more than thankful that England had managed to make the final of the World Cup.

Together with fellow Lostock Hall men, Drivers J Burke and P. Doyle, Peter was involved in three special trains returning holidaymakers to Scotland from Blackpool. Following the completion of his turn of duty as far as Carlisle, he agreed to take forward from Kingmoor sidings the 11.45am ex-Glasgow (Polmadie) to Morecambe empty stock train later in the day.

After preparing 12A 'Britannia' No. 70017 Arrow for the trip to Morecambe, the 4-6-2 was backed on to its train comprising twenty bogies. All started well, but at approximately 1.20pm on reaching the curve at Bog Junction, Peter suddenly saw a stationary train ahead - the 3.20pm Carlisle to Liverpool (Tuebrook) freight, and realised that with 500 tons behind him he was not going to be able to stop!

The Pacific ploughed into the guards van, which was lifted clear of the track, up the embankment and in the process demolished a platelayer's hut. Immediately next to the van was a bogie bolster carrying steel girders many of which were badly bent as a result of the engine continuing forwards and colliding with this the last truck comprising the freight train. Fortunately, the guard was not inside his van. Trying to listen to the news about the Cup Final, and finding the reception was not very good, he decided to take advantage of his train being held up and climbed up the embankment to get a better signal just before the crash.

Above. A small crowd has gathered along the wall at the top of the embankment to watch the start of the proceedings to clear the track of debris and re-rail the 'Britannia'.

Left. A few hours later and the breakdown crane is ready to engage in some heavy lifting. The freight train has continued on its way and, once the first carriage and No. 70017 Arrow are back on the track, another engine will take up the empty stock working. Sustaining substantial front-end damage, the 'Britannia' was officially withdrawn on 1st October and taken via Shrewsbury to Cashmore's, Newport for disposal. Both courtesy of the Evening News & Star, Carlisle.

August

After the adventure of Scotland and England's triumph over West Germany, the days that followed seemed both uninspiring and uneventful. I suppose it was the anti-climax to such a thrilling two weeks away, and of course the historic cup win and all the fervour and excitement that that had brought with it. I was looking forward to developing the films I had taken, but at the same time anxious about how well the pictures would turn out. Indeed, the results suggested that the replacement Halina Paulette was only marginally better than the previous camera, with some negatives incorrectly exposed and many lacking sharpness and clarity. Even so, a few, when printed over forty years later, were worthy of being enlarged to 10" x 8" and even being framed.

Not long after returning home, I had cause to look at one or two railway magazines that had been published earlier in the summer, and in one of them an article that I hadn't noticed before produced a chuckle or two. It referred to an announcement made by BR and read as follows:

'British Railways are for the first time offering prizes in a novel initiative test for young people who use Railrover tickets which are available until the end of October. The competition is open to holders of these tickets under 25years of age, who are invited to write to BR Headquarters after their holidays describing where they went and what they did'

Railway World, June 1966, News of the Month, p.230.

The first prize of £50 for my age category was certainly a tempting one, but somehow I didn't think that my exploits would be viewed in quite the way they were required to be, even though I believed I had fulfilled the criteria of using the ticket 'in the most interesting and constructive way.'

I was soon into the usual routine of recording steam locally again, and cycling to familiar places like Bromford Bridge, Bordesley and the Button Factory, as well as regularly bunking Birmingham's two remaining steam sheds. Three days after returning from Scotland, I made the first of ten visits to Saltley during August. Totals for steam present and number of classes represented on 2nd, 11th, 16th, 18th, 20th, 21st, 22nd, 23rd, 24th and 31st were correspondingly as follows: 30/5, 30/5, 31/5, 35/6, 38/5, 41/5, 38/6, 34/5, 35/4 and 42/6. Visiting 'B1' No. 61161 of Wakefield was logged on 2nd and was further noted on each visit up to and including 21st August. Two further guests also from Wakefield MPD, 'B1' No. 61024 Addax and 'WD' No. 90651, were noted on 22nd with the 'B1' still in residence the following day. During my final visit of the month, Leeds Holbeck 'Jubilee' No. 45697 Achilles, last seen during the Scottish trip at Barrhead, was found in steam in No. 3 roundhouse. Other visitors on 31st included two Patricroft standard 5MT 4-6-0's No's 73045 and 73158 and York-based '9F' No. 92231.

Tyseley was visited on 3rd, 20th and 21st August with steam and class totals recorded of 28/8, 23/8 and 29/8 respectively. On 21st four engines (No's 44730, 45015, 45324 and 73158) were in the queue outside the diesel depot awaiting attention on the wheel turning lathe (WTL), while No's 3607, 3619, 4646, 44715, 44780, 45280, 45287, 45349, 46457, 48061, 92001, 92118 and 92203 were noted in steam. Transferred from Colwick to Heaton Mersey on 20th of the month, 'Black 5' No. 45324 was probably en-route to its new home shed in the northwest.

During the second week of the month Keith Satterly, one of the lads we had met on Waverley Station, contacted me and invited me to stay with him for a few days in Syston near Leicester. From Keith's we could travel around the North and East Midlands - areas that were unfamiliar to me. We visited a number of sheds between 27th and 30th August, including Leicester, Derby, Toton, Tinsley, Canklow, Staveley, New England, March and also Loughborough and Derby Works. Steam wouldn't feature strongly as many of the depots had already closed to this form of motive power, but I was hoping to photograph a number of engines I hadn't seen before, even though most of them by this time would have either been withdrawn or placed in store.

The trip got under way with a visit to at Derby Works Open Day on 27th August. Steam guests were 'Britannia' Pacific No. 70028 Royal Star, standard '9F' No. 92118 and Stanier '8F' No. 48350. The MPD was home to 16 steam representing 4 different classes. Stanier '8F's were most evident totalling thirteen. The other three varieties were standard '9F' (No. 92159), 'Black 5' (No. 45003) and 'B1' (No. 61238 Leslie Runciman).

Toton was visited on the same day and, although it had been closed to steam from the end of December 1965, there were two Stanier '8F's in steam. Both of the engines were photographed - No. 48361 as she was leaving the depot and No. 48127 standing in the shed yard. One further Stanier 2-8-0 was present, No. 48101, which had been a Saltley engine since the beginning of the year and now withdrawn. Altogether, with stored standard 2MT 2-6-0's No's 78013, 78020, 78028, 78044, 78055, 78061 and 78064, we recorded a total of 10 steam. There was obviously no urgency to remove the condemned engines as a number of reports confirmed they were all still awaiting disposal two months later.

Several sheds were visited the following day, including Canklow, which had been closed to steam since 11th October 1965. Like Toton, it went on providing facilities for visiting steam engines up until a week or two after we had been round the depot. It had two Service locos designated to it, both 'B1's and numbered 30 and 32 - formerly BR No. 61050 and No. 61315 respectively. The latter engine was on shed and was used regularly for steam heating purposes in Sheffield Nunnery Carriage Sidings. We also found several ex-Midland railway tank engines in store in the yard all of which had been last employed in Staveley Iron Works. A total of 11 steam were recorded representing 4 different varieties.

Allocated to Birkenhead for nine years, Kitson saddle tank No. 47005 had also been a Preston engine for a couple of months. Seen here in Canklow on 28th August 1967, the 0-4-0 had been withdrawn from its final home shed, Langwith, the previous December.

Looking as work weary as No. 47005, Deeley 0-4-0T No. 41533 was to be found further along the row of what appeared to be redundant engines in the yard of Canklow MPD. Previously a Staveley (Barrow Hill) engine, it would be transferred to Langwith from where it would be officially withdrawn at the end of the year.

Built in 1880, Johnson 'half-cab' 0-6-0T No. 41708 shared the same fate as the other two engines above - at least as far as its final allocation and withdrawal date were concerned. Good fortune then stepped in and the engine was preserved (see opposite). It briefly held the record of being the oldest running loco on BR. Canklow MPD, 28th August 1967.

Thirty-one years after being noted in Canklow MPD, the 1F, having been beautifully restored, finds employment on the Swanage railway. It is seen at Harmans Cross station awaiting the arrival of standard 2-6-4T No. 80104 on 29th May 1998. The view of the cab shows the driver on the less than spacious footplate - the half-cab would be perfectly suited to working on a warm summer's day, but the need for more cover in less clement weather (often secured with a make-do sheet of tarpaulin) can clearly be appreciated.

On 29th August we bunked New England and March sheds. Both had been diesel depots for sometime, so it was a surprise to find three steam engines in the latter shed. The first noted was 'B16' No. 61572, withdrawn on 20th September 1961, and the second, 'J15' No. 65462, which had ceased working on 16th September 1962. The Midland & Great Northern Joint Railway Society had purchased both these locos. The last of the trio was 'B1' No. 26 a Service engine formerly BR No. 61138. Including those noted on the way home, a total of 51 steam had been logged during the trip with 13 different classes represented.

September / October

A tour of the northeast had been advertised in the August edition of Railway World and had stirred our interest. Organised by the Walsall Locomotive Society for a fare of 80/-, it would take place over the first weekend in October and comprise visits to twenty-two sheds. Dennis and I were now ever more eager to see steam further afield and somehow managed to find the funds to pay for the trip before all the places had been taken.

My 'O' level results had reflected the effort I had put into them. Disappointed, but not surprised, I was back at school and in the 6th Form at the beginning of September with the prospect of re-sits later in the term. Dennis had been more successful with his studies and had applied and been accepted for an engineering course at Derby Locomotive Works, which he started on 19th of the month.

Forays to Saltley and Tyseley sheds proceeded unabated throughout September. Saltley was visited nine times on 2nd, 6th, 9th, 10th, 13th, 18th, 21st, 22nd, and 25th with the number and variety of steam holding up fairly well as follows: 42/5, 43/5, 46/6, 45/5, 42/6, 39/5, 35/5, 35/5 and 36/6 respectively. Noted on 6th was visiting 'B1' No. 61173 a Wakefield engine and Oxley 'Black 5' No. 44812 being cleaned while under repair. On 9th and subsequent visits throughout the month, I noted the presence of withdrawn Stanier 2-6-4T No. 42436, last allocated to Lostock Hall. Tyseley, visited on 9th, 10th, 12th, 18th, 19th and 25th, consistently produced a greater variety of motive power but with fewer engines present compared with Saltley. Totals for steam locos logged and classes represented being: 15/7, 20/6, 20/8, 27/7, 22/8 and 31/7 respectively. On 10th, the shed was host to no less than eight ex-GWR 0-6-0PT's and, noted on 18th 19th and 25th, was 'Manor' class 4-6-0 No. 7808 Cookham Manor, which had been bought out of BR service by a Great Western Society member the previous year.

Still looking presentable after being cleaned for the Altrincham Railway Excursion Society's 'Holyhead & Brymbo' railtour on 21st August, 0-6-0PT No. 9630 stands over the ashpit in Tyseley shed yard on 10th September 1966. Together with sister engine No. 9610, they would haul the SLS (Midlands Area) 'Farewell to the GWR Pannier Tanks' special the next day. Unfortunately, 9630 would blow its left hand cylinder while climbing Hatton Bank and would be hauled back to Tyseley shed by a Brush Type '4'.

With its nameplates and cabside number plates safely stored away, No. 7029 Clun Castle is seen inside Tyseley diesel depot on Monday 19th September 1966. The following weekend they would be replaced ready for the engine to work the outward and return legs of a Talyllyn Railway Preservation Society special between Banbury and Shrewsbury.

At 9.30pm on the evening of Friday 30th September, Dennis and I met outside the Hall of Memory in the city centre ready to join the coach tour to the northeast originating from Walsall. Looking forward to the shed bash that lay ahead, we joined the group already aboard and left Birmingham shortly before 10.00pm. This was a new way to travel to see steam for both of us, and because of the excitement of it all we didn't get much sleep before reaching our first shed, Consett, at 5.25 in the morning… only to find it empty!

The next two depots we visited, North and South Blyth, kick-started the day and made up for its disappointing beginning. Both sheds were shrouded in a sea fret, which didn't enhance the photographic opportunities. Amongst the swirling mist I noted 21 steam on the former shed with 5 different classes represented, and 8 steam on the latter comprising 2 varieties. Earlier in the year, on 11th June, Brush Type '2' No. D5632 had undergone tests at Blyth, but there was no sign of this loco and the only diesels in residence were two 0-6-0 diesel shunters, No's D2330 and D3324 both on North shed.

The day progressed at a frenetic pace and we squeezed in a further seven steam depots. Totals for steam present and varieties represented at each of these were as follows: Tyne Dock 9/2, Sunderland 10/3, West Hartlepool 12/4, Thornaby 1/1, York 25/8, Goole 11/3 and Hull (Dairycoates) 40/8. Overnight accommodation was provided in Hull and on the evening Dennis and I spent an hour or so on Paragon Station, but recorded only dmu's and an English Electric Type '3' No. D6784.

Early on the morning of 1st October 1966, the two lads next to the turntable have duly noted Worsdell 'J27' No. 65833, and their attention turns to the other locos inside Sunderland MPD. The 0-6-0 would be removed from capital stock in May 1967.

Two other residents of 52G, 'J27's No's 65873 (left) and 65817, would soon be in the viewfinder of the enthusiast seen taking a photo of engines on the opposite side of the shed. No. 65873 had just been withdrawn but its accompanying classmate would survive in service until the following May.

We were back on the road bright and early the next morning and resumed our journey south visiting a further eleven steam sheds. Totals as previously noted were as follows: Normanton 18/6, Wakefield 71/7, Stourton 25/5, Leeds Neville Hill 2/2, Leeds Holbeck 28/6, Farnley 11/5, Bradford Manningham 13/3, Low Moor 14/4, Huddersfield 7/5, Mirfield 20/6 and Royston 25/4. Neville Hill had closed to steam some three months earlier but I've included it here because it was housing two preserved ex-LNER engines - class 'K4' 2-6-0 No. 3442 The Great Marquess and class 'N7' 0-6-2T No. 69621.

Over the weekend we had covered a total of 630 miles and visited 21 steam depots. Including a few engines seen working while travelling between or going round the sheds, we had noted a total of 378 steam representing 21 different classes. Most prolific were 'WD's (100), Stanier '8F's (52), Ivatt 4MT 2-6-0's (37), Thompson 'B1's (31) and Stanier 'Black 5's (31). Ex-LNER classes noted in addition to the 'B1's were 'K1', 'K4', 'Q6', 'J27' and 'V2'. Wakefield shed had by far the greatest number of steam present with 71 recorded. Nevertheless, half of the depots visited had fewer than fifteen steam on shed. It was clear that steam in the northeast was slowly succumbing to the diesel assault, just as it had done in many other areas.

Very few of my photographs turned out satisfactorily and even though the weather hadn't helped, I knew that part of the problem lay with the camera and a more expensive one was out of the question. I had developed my films as instructed, but the problems with incorrect exposure, scratching and indeed the graininess of the negatives persisted. The challenges they presented many years later when I decided to print them created further disappointment and frustration but, fortunately, the results with a few proved the effort to be worthwhile.

Left. 'K1' No. 62045 had been a West Hartlepool engine for five months by the time this picture was taken of her in the shed yard. Work would be found for the loco for a further twelve months before being condemned. Below. Also standing out in the mist and rain was sister engine No. 62004 together with WD No. 90230, which had recently been transferred to W. Hartlepool from Ardsley MPD. The 'K1' would be officially withdrawn in December while the 'WD' would soldier on until the following May; the shed would close later in the September.

Regular visits to Birmingham's two remaining steam depots resumed after our trip to the northeast. Neither shed would continue with an active steam allocation for much longer; Tyseley would officially close in four weeks time, leaving Saltley as the city's only shed continuing to use steam power and provide servicing facilities for engines working into the area from other divisions. Even though I had known about this sad news for a while, I still couldn't believe it was going to happen; Tyseley was somewhere I had visited numerous times over the past few years and had afforded me many hours of pleasure.

I made four visits to the ex-GWR shed during October on 9th, 16th, 23rd, and 30th. Engine and class totals were correspondingly as follows: 33/9, 37/9, 28/7 and 28/9. A number of the depot's locos would be removed for cutting up following its closure, but others would be more fortunate and gain a reprieve, albeit for only a short while. Standard '9F's No's 92001 and 92215 were two such engines - they had been earmarked for further employment once their transfer to Wakefield shed had taken place. No doubt in preparation for her journey north, No. 92215 was noted on the wheel turning lathe in the diesel depot on 16th. On the same day over a third of the locos logged were of GWR origin and were as follows: 0-6-0PT's No's 3619, 3625, 4635, 4696, 9610, 9630 and 9774, 2-6-2T No. 4176, 0-6-2T No. 6697, 'Castle' class 4-6-0 No. 7029 Clun Castle and 'Manor' class 4-6-0 No. 7808 Cookham Manor. Pannier tank No. 9630 was still missing a cylinder head (a result of the damage sustained while hauling a steam special with sister engine 9610 up Hatton Bank over a month earlier) and had now been officially withdrawn. As the month progressed fewer and fewer engines were found in steam. Only two were ready for duty on each of the last two visits on 23rd and 30th, while 'Black 5's, No's. 44832 and 44812 were recorded correspondingly as receiving attention on the WTL.

Saltley was visited on the same days 9th, 16th, 23rd, and 30th. Totals for locos present and classes represented were 38/5, 29/5, 26/5, and 27/5 respectively. Steam turns were diminishing here, too, and during each of these visits only a handful of engines were noted in steam and ready for work. Interestingly, on the first of my four Sunday visits I logged no fewer than fourteen standard '9F's, a total that I wouldn't see surpassed before the shed closed to steam. Two of the class, No's 92234, which had passed through Crewe works for overhaul and put back into service on 11th October, and 92029, were exceptionally clean when logged on 16th and 23rd respectively. Stanier 2-6-4T No. 42436 remained stored in the yard throughout October, and had now been on shed for almost two months.

November

On Friday 4th November I decided to walk to Tyseley shed from home via the canal. I suppose I wanted to spin out the proceedings so that the trip would last that little bit longer; it would undoubtedly be the case of 'better to travel hopefully than to arrive'. Feeling pretty despondent, I made my way towards the north yard and could see in the distance a 'Black 5' in steam as well as smoke appearing from the roof of the old passenger shed building, which helped raise my spirits a little.

With two days to go before the shed's closure to steam, I walked round the depot not really able to come to terms with or accept that the end was so close. I noted 15 steam locos as follows: No's 1638, 3619, 4176, 7029, 9610, 9630, 9774, 44663, 44859, 44915, 45052, 46442, 46457, 46509 and 92030. 'Black 5's, No's 44915 and 45052 and Ivatt 2-6-0 No. 46457, were in steam together with class 5101 No. 4176 continuing its heating duties. Stanier 4-6-0 No. 44859 and Standard '9F' No. 92030 stood in the yard of the diesel depot waiting to be moved into the shed building for wheel re-profiling work to be carried out. No. 7029 Clun Castle was found deep inside the diesel depot where, over the coming weeks, it would be given a fresh coat of paint.

Before leaving, I wandered back into the steam shed to make a note of the information on the roster board dated 4th November. The details read as follows: Snow Hill Pilot 44761; Aschurch 6697; Oldbury 46457; Halesowen 4696; Dudley 45292; out of service – 46509, 4635, 3625, 9630, 46442; Mileage exam 44663; not to be fired 45052, 9774. What I discovered some years later, however, was the possible inaccuracy of the RCTS 1969 Stock Book that listed 0-6-0PT No. 9774 as being the last representative of her 863 strong class in running stock. My records question this as sister engine No. 4696 was still at work and appeared back on shed on 6th November, the day the depot closed to steam. Out of steam on both of these days, No. 9774 hadn't moved.

As well as the '9F's already mentioned, a few more of Tyseley's engines would escape withdrawal and continue working once their transfer to other depots had been completed. For example, Ivatt 2-6-0 No. 46457, after its trip to Oldbury, would be despatched forthwith to its new home, Carlisle Upperby; 'Black 5's No's. 44663 and 45052 would eventually be re-allocated to Oxley and Shrewsbury respectively and No. 45292 after its turn of duty to Dudley would become a Stoke engine. Pannier tank No.4696 wouldn't be so lucky. Subsequent to her day out at Halesowen on shunting duties, she would join the growing ranks of other condemned engines.

With four months to go before closure to steam, Saltley's No. 3 shed looks far from ending its association with this form of motive power on 6th November 1966. From left to right: withdrawn '8F' No. 48477, '9F' No. 92152, 'Black 5' No. 44981, '9F' 92002, '8F' No. 48085 and 'Black 5' No. 44872.

Top. Soon to become a Birkenhead engine, former Crosti-boilered '9F' No. 92029 is seen looking reasonably clean when noted in Saltley No. 3 shed on 6th November 1966 (see colour photograph of loco on page 134). Also in residence this day was visiting 'B1' No. 61289, a Hull Dairycoates loco. The 4-6-0 would remain at Hull until withdrawal in June 1967; the 2-10-0 would finish work five months later in the November.

1966 July – December (Goodbye to Gresley's 'Streaks')

On reaching Small Heath Station following my visit to Saltley on Sunday 6th November (see details below) I continued cycling along Golden Hillock Road, Warwick Road and unenthusiastically on to Tyseley. Within a few hours the shed would no longer offer steam servicing or minor repair facilities. Since my visit two days earlier three engines had departed - No's. 44915, 45052 and 46457, and a similar number had arrived - pannier tanks No's. 3625 and 4696 and 'Black 5' No. 44808. Seven different classes were to be found amongst the 15 engines noted, all of which were cold. Significantly, No. 44808, after having its fire dropped, had been moved to the end of the queue outside the diesel depot ready for its turn on the WTL. This observation led me to wonder if steam locos would continue to be sent to Tyseley for wheel re-profiling; could it be that after 58 years this wasn't quite the end of seeing steam engines being repaired and serviced here?

The queue for Tyseley's wheel-turning lathe on 6th November 1966: 'Black 5's, No's 44808 and 44859 at the rear, sandwich '9F' No. 92030 in the yard of the diesel depot. Once the work has been completed they would head back to their respective depots of Oxley, Stoke and Wakefield. Interestingly, No. 44808 was withdrawn by the end of the following month.

As I cycled home I thought more and more about this possibility. I knew that a number of other officially closed steam sheds had continued for some time to have visits from engines based in areas where there was no alternative form of motive power available. But would Tyseley continue to attract steam engines that were in need of the diesel depot's wheel-turning facilities? By the time I reached home I'd decided that I would continue with my visits, very much hoping that this would be the case.

The immediate future of West Midland's steam was bleak to say the least. Except for the odd working to Banbury (usually a Saltley engine), steam traction on the local former Great Western lines would be largely confined to the Wolverhampton area. Oxley, for a while yet, would continue to provide facilities for steam engines, including the last steam-hauled passenger train in the region, the 3.10pm SX Paddington to Shrewsbury on from Wolverhampton. However, steam would still feature significantly on freight services from the district to Crewe via Wellington and Market Drayton, at least until their transfer to the Western a.c. lines.

Further trips to Tyseley were made on 13th and 20th November. During the first visit my hopes of the shed continuing to provide facilities for steam were realised when, amongst the 14 engines present, it was immediately apparent that there had been two new arrivals in the form of Stanier 'Black 5's No's. 45024, an Edge Hill engine, and 45440, allocated to Springs Branch, both needing attention to their wheels. Even more of a reward came on my next visit on 20th when the number of steam on shed had further increased to 17, and included 'Britannia' Pacific No. 70002 Geoffrey Chaucer. Nevertheless, I was still to find an engine actually in steam, and wondered if these visitors were being hauled dead to and from the depot.

Saltley during this time hadn't been overlooked and trips were made to the shed on 2nd, 4th, 6th, 13th, 20th and 27th of November. Totals for engines noted and classes represented were 23/5, 27/6, 32/6, 32/6, 27/6 and 27/5 respectively. 'B1' 4-6-0 No. 61289 a Hull Dairycoates engine (noted on my visit there six weeks earlier) was logged during my visits on 6th, 13th and 20th. 'Black 5' No. 45409, allocated to Stockport Edgeley, was recorded on shed and in steam on 27th after being noted in Tyseley waiting for her turn on the WTL, or 'on the factory' as the shed staff called it, the week before. This observation went some way to answering my question about how these visitors were getting to and from the ex-GWR depot.

December

Five trips were made to Saltley during December on 4th, 11th, 18th, 25th and 28th. Steam totals noted and number of classes represented for each of these visits was 26/6, 21/5, 23/5, 24/5 and 19/5 respectively. The totals for engines on shed look quite reasonable considering the depot had only three months or so to go before closure to steam. However, included in these statistics were 9 withdrawn engines waiting to be removed for scrap; add to this the fact that on average for each visit (excluding Christmas Day) there were only five engines in steam, then a more accurate and depressing picture emerges.

Not recorded in steam since the middle of August when it spent most of the time standing in No.3 shed, Stanier '8F' No. 48477, allocated to Tyseley, is seen in the yard of Saltley MPD on Christmas Day 1966. Its official withdrawal had taken place sometime in September.

Above. '9F' No. 92013 had been transferred from Banbury to Saltley in September only to be withdrawn the following month, presumably as a result of problems with its left cylinder. Seen in the yard of the shed on Christmas day, I would last record its presence in the depot on 22nd January 1967. Disposal would take place the following May at G. Cohen, Kettering.

Left. Stanier '8F' No. 48107 was a Midland engine for many years. By this time a Stockport Edgeley loco, the 2-8-0 is seen at rest in Saltley No. 3 shed on Christmas Day 1966. Having previously been allotted to Leicester Midland, Wellingborough, Kettering and Coalville, the '8F' would finally move to Heaton Mersey before being withdrawn in April 1968.

Tyseley was visited only once in December, on Christmas Day. Not an engine, engineman, fitter or mouse stirred as I made my way through the unnatural silence to make note of the locos present. If on duty, Mr Field, the shed master, was no doubt in the comfort of his warm office. Altogether, I recorded 15 steam on shed representing 6 different classes. Standard 4-6-0 No. 73127 had been left sitting on the WTL; it would have to wait until after the holiday period before being removed and steamed again so it could head back to Patricroft its home shed. Sister engine No. 73130 was in the queue for the lathe, together with 'Black 5's No's. 44663, 44833, 44840, 45089 and 45241. See appendix 17 for engines present on both sheds on Christmas Day.

Above. Standing outside Tyseley diesel depot, 'Black 5' No. 44663 is ready to take its turn on the lathe for wheel re-profiling. Previously a 2A engine (see picture page 238, Part One), she was transferred on the shed's closure to steam, initially to Oxley, and then at the beginning of December to Heaton Mersey. Withdrawal would come in May 1968. Left. With its bunker now empty of coal, ex-GWR pannier tank No. 4696, waits to be removed to Cashmores, Great Bridge to be cut up. Both Christmas Day 1966.

As 1966 petered out, I knew that once the New Year started to unfold there were going to be some far-reaching changes for the family. It looked certain that we would be moving home and would no longer live in or near to the city. Mum, who worked at Frank R Ford in Sparkbrook, had been given the opportunity to move to a new council house in Droitwich Spa when the factory relocated there sometime next spring. We would not be the only members of the wider family to move away; for a variety of reasons several of my aunts and uncles would begin new lives in more modern homes well away from their roots, and travel back into the city to work.

Continuing my education at Pitmaston Boys' in Hall Green would present a problem - I was not due to finish there until next summer. Droitwich was about 22 miles away, and to get to school on public transport would be possible but to do so in reasonable time would be difficult. Even more important, of course, was the question of how I would be able to continue seeing my girlfriend, Jackie! Not believing for one minute that it would happen, I suggested that having a two-wheel upgrade in the form of a motorbike would solve the problem. Mum argued from the outset that a scooter would be a safer option: I would have to wait and see if she would come round to my way of thinking.

A further 1,298 steam engines had been withdrawn, leaving a total of 1,689 in capital stock when the year came to a close. Steam's last strongholds had been greatly reduced and the few remaining Gresley 'A4' Pacifics that Dennis and I had travelled to see in Scotland had finally been taken out of service by the end of September and replaced by diesel traction. Their last booked run between Glasgow and Aberdeen was made on 3rd September, but it would appear that their final express passenger working occurred later in the month.

Owing to a shortage of motive power at Ferryhill, No 60024 Kingfisher had remained in service as standby. Having worked several freight turns to Dundee and Perth, the Pacific found itself on the 8.25am Glasgow Buchanan Street to Aberdeen eleven days later on Wednesday 14th September. This followed being called upon to replace a failed NBL Type '2' diesel on the 5.15pm Aberdeen - Glasgow the previous evening. Steam in Scotland had only the matter of a few months left before its employment would come to an end. Locally, my chances of seeing steam on a regular basis were receding quickly, too. With Saltley shed now providing very few steam locos for local freight, and its closure to this form of motive power on the horizon, it was clear that I would have to travel to more distant places to experience first hand the special atmosphere associated with a working steam depot and, indeed, to witness steam out and about and still fulfilling a useful role on BR.

Although now absent from many parts of the country, there were still one or two areas where steam had not yet capitulated to diesel and/or electric traction. In the Midlands, for example, steam was still much in evidence around Stoke-on-Trent and at the beginning of the autumn approximately 90% of freight turns were in the hands of this form of motive power. And, interestingly, reported in the November issue of Railway World was the use of 'Jubilees' No's 45581 Bihar and Orissa and 45596 Bahamas and 'V2' No. 60831, for crew training (to "pass-out" firemen as drivers) while working the Heaton-Manchester parcels turns for employees still required to handle steam locos. Further to this news was added the possibility that some North Eastern Region men, made redundant through rationalisation, might transfer to the SR where train cancellations had taken place because of staff shortages.

Something had happened of great significance during the year, however. With Marylebone as its Terminus, our youngest main line railway, The Great Central, had closed on 3rd September after only 67 years of operation. This in turn meant that through trains such as those from Poole to York had to be re-routed, with this particular service having to run north from Oxford via Worcester to Birmingham New Street, Derby, Chesterfield and Sheffield Midland. It was expected that these new arrangements would also see the end of steam working from the Southern Region through to Banbury.

Ironically, because of the ongoing electrification of one particular route on the SR, and the decision to continue to use steam until its completion (diesels had started to make their presence known, but were equipped with electric train heating - the Southern's coaching stock was still steam heated), Waterloo would take on the mantle of being the last of London's main line stations to regularly see steam-hauled express passenger trains. Oliver Bulleid's Pacifics would continue to head many of the services to Bournemouth and Weymouth as the New Year unfolded, but for exactly how long was difficult to predict. Like many other enthusiasts, my attention and desire to see these engines before they, too, disappeared would increase as time moved on.

On 31st October, Birmingham New Street had had the power turned on, and forecasts were that on 6th March next year a fully electrified service would be introduced at the start of the new timetable between Coventry, Birmingham and Wolverhampton. Interestingly, the new structure, once completed, would signal the end of open access - there had never been ticket barriers before because of the public right of way running through the middle of the station.

Some of the classes seen in normal service for the last time during the year included the 'A4's, 'A3's, 'A2's and 'A1's, the 'N' and 'U' on the Southern Region, and the 57XX pannier tanks formerly of the GWR, which only five years earlier had numbered 563. The last members of the LMS '4F' 0-6-0 class had also become extinct as had Fowler's 2-6-4 tanks. Hanging on by a thread were a few members of such classes as 'Jubilee' (8), 'J36' (3), 'J37' (4), 'J38' (3), ex-LMS Stanier 2-6-0 (1) and '3F' 0-6-0T (4), informally known as 'Jinties'. The first of the London transport coaches (driving trailer of unit No. 037) bought by BR for use on the IOW had been shipped to the island on 1st September and transported by road from Fishbourne to Ryde St Johns MPD. Three days later on 4th it was hauled from Ryde St Johns Rd station to Shanklin and back for platform clearance tests. With a few, including No's 22, 24 and 31, held in reserve for engineering and permanent way duties that would be required over the following months, the class O2 0-4-4 tanks that we had journeyed to see in the spring hauled their last passenger trains on 31st December. No's 14, 17, 22, 24, 27, 28 and 31 were all in steam on the final day.

Fewer steam engines meant less need for maintenance facilities, and once again a further swathe of sheds had either closed to steam or shut completely during the previous twelve months. Such depots included Agecroft, Ayr, Banbury, Bank Hall, Leicester, Bescot, Nuneaton, Holyhead, Carlisle Upperby, Doncaster, Darlington and Colwick to name but a few. The demand on the railways workshops was declining too. On 2nd April, the day Dennis and I had set off in search of Southern steam, after much of its machinery had been dismantled and delivered to Crewe, Darlington Works, the birthplace of probably the world's most famous engine, Flying Scotsman, officially closed.

1967 (Farewell to Oliver Bullied's Pacifics).

January / February

New Years Day: the beginning of the penultimate year of steam having a role to play in the day to day running of British Railways. Saltley, which I had visited so frequently over the last few years, had less than three months left as a working steam depot. I was up early, and after cycling the 2_ miles or so from home, was once again making notes of the engines on 2E. Five different classes were represented amongst the 21 steam present with only four ready for duty. Nine of the locos were in store following official withdrawal and one of these, Stanier '8F' No. 48351, had managed to reach her 17th consecutive year as a Saltley engine.

A further five visits were made to the former Midland Railway shed during January on 3rd, 8th, 15th 22nd and 29th. Totals for engines present and classes represented were correspondingly 16/4, 20/4, 22/5, 27/5 and 28/6. The number of engines noted in steam fluctuated between one (1st Jan.) and nine (22nd Jan.) with an average of four ready for work on any one of my five visits. Three guests in steam on 29th were Normanton-based 'WD' No. 90682, Holyhead allocated 'Black 5' No. 45405 and Kirkby-in-Ashfield '8F' No. 48128. Throughout the month '8F's dominated the steam power present and averaged 13 per visit. The shed's last two Ivatt 2-6-0's were removed for scrap on 2nd, but Stanier 2-6-4T No. 42436 seemed to have taken up permanent residence and remained stored in the yard for the rest of the month.

Stanier '8F' No. 48128 stands over the ashpit in Saltley MPD yard on 3rd January 1967. Previously allocated to such depots as Wellingborough, Kettering, Toton, Westhouses and Burton, the 2-8-0 became a Saltley engine the previous month and would move to Stoke on the closure of 2E. This would turn out to be her final move, and she would become surplus to requirements and be withdrawn sometime in May.

Officially transferred to Birkenhead during the early part of the previous November, '9F' No. 92152 was still bearing the hand painted 2E shed code when back at Saltley on 3rd January 1967. Later in November, after spending exactly a year as an 8H engine, the 2-10-0 would be withdrawn.

On the closure of Saltley to steam, '8F' No. 48351 would become a Crewe South engine early in March. When Crewe finished with this form of traction, too, the loco would be re-allocated for the final time and Trafford Park would become its last home shed. The 2-8-0 would be withdrawn in January 1968.

In order to see a greater number and diversity of steam, I decided to take myself off to Chester and Birkenhead on Saturday 7th January. Although I didn't realise it at the time, this would be the general direction I would need to travel regularly to catch the final glimpses of such engines working during the coming months.

En-route to Chester twelve steam were noted, eight of which were in charge of mixed-freight trains. The shed was home to 43 steam with 9 different varieties represented as follows: 'WD' (1), '9F' (3), '8F' (7), 'Black 5' (20), 'Jinty' (4), Stanier 2-6-4T (1), standard 2MT 2-6-0 (1), 4MT 2-6-0 (4) and 5MT (2). All four 'Jinties' had been withdrawn and seventeen engines were noted as being fired and ready for work. This was my final visit to the depot known as 6A and whose code had never changed since 1935. Before leaving Chester for the fifteen-mile journey to Birkenhead, several steam movements were logged (three 'Black 5's and two '8F's) all of which were light engine. A solitary '9F' was seen at the head of a freight train before I arrived at Woodside Station.

With the fire doors clearly still open, Hughes-Fowler 2-6-0 No. 42942 is seen in the yard of Birkenhead MPD on 7th January 1967. Built at Crewe works, the loco entered traffic in December 1932 and was the last of its class to remain active, carrying out its final duty - the 5.40am Bidston Yard to Dee Marsh pick-up goods - on 14th January. A week later on 21st January the engine was officially withdrawn from service, and would eventually head south one final time to be broken up at J. Cashmore, Great Bridge.

After making the short walk to the shed, I listed 49 steam representing 7 different classes. Including all five 'Jinties' allocated to the shed, and 'Black 5' No. 45044, which had been derailed on 21st October at Synthite Chemical Works, Mold, Flintshire, ten of the engines had been officially withdrawn. Scotland's last remaining Hughes-Fowler 2-6-0's based at Ayr and Hurlford depots had been retired the previous month leaving just two of the once forty-five strong class still working from Birkenhead. Indeed, one of the pair, No. 42942, had worked two passenger turns - the 2.45pm Birkenhead to Chester and 9.08 pm Chester to Birkenhead - as a farewell to the class on 31st December. As can be seen she was very much alive when I noted her presence, while surviving sister engine No. 42727 was cold. Thirty of the forty-nine steam present were standard '9F's.

The return journey home added a little cheerfulness to what had been a cold, dull and miserable day, but not at the outset. The first leg of the journey involved travelling on the uninspiring 1.43pm dmu service to Chester. However, my decision to catch the 2.35pm Inter-City express from here to Snow Hill proved to be wise one and I soon realised that I would be travelling at least part of the way back to Birmingham behind steam. Stanier 4-6-0 No. 45132, earlier noted on Chester MPD, would take the train for the first forty-two miles of its journey to Paddington as far as Shrewsbury. We departed on time and arrived at Shrewsbury, after stops at Wrexham, Ruabon, Chirk and Gobowen, at exactly 3.40pm as scheduled.

Transferred from Bolton early in November, Fairburn tank No. 42133 had been a Birkenhead engine for two months when pictured in her final home depot on a dull and dreary 7th January 1967. Below. In charge as far as Shrewsbury, 'Black 5' No. 45132 leaves Chester with the 2.35pm Inter-City service to Birmingham Snow Hill.

Without delay I made my way to the front of the train to take a photograph of the engine before the waiting Brush Type '4' replaced her. The day had been gloomy and overcast, and had somehow managed to deteriorate further. The engine was now shrouded in mist and murk with the lights of the station struggling to provide the slightest glimmer of brightness. Ever the optimist, with what little light remained, and a relatively fast film in the camera, I thought I might just get a passable picture. The results, however, were not as good as I had hoped for, but the pictures still remind me of an exciting run behind steam.

Following a spirited run to Shrewsbury, 'Black 5' No. 45132 is about to be replaced by a Brush Type '4' for the remainder of the journey to Birmingham. In three months time, thirty-two years after being built, the 4-6-0 would be withdrawn and taken to Cohen's, Morriston to be broken up.

During the following two months Stanier's 'Black 5's continued to produce some outstanding runs while hauling these services and, on 4th March, No. 44917 found herself in charge of the final steam-hauled run on British Railways timed at a-mile-a-minute. The allowance for a fraction over the 18 miles between Gobowen and Shrewsbury was 18 minutes and 44917's actual time was recorded as 17min. 19sec., with a maximum speed of 86mph. Further reports of some quite extraordinary performances appeared in O S Nock's article 'The Great Western Route To Birkenhead (Railway Magazine, May 1967) two of which were described as 'remarkable' and as it turned out fittingly involved No. 44917. Sometime in the few weeks before the 4th March, there's no date for either of the runs, the first log records the engine achieving an actual time of 16min. 23sec., with a top speed of 92mph. The second, however, shows a further improvement on this feat; again with a load of 6 coaches the same locomotive achieved an even more impressive run with an actual time of 16min. 15sec., with a maximum speed of 96mph. As Nock rightly pointed out these performances made one 'sit up and take notice' and were something unexpected for such engines in their 'declining years'.

I was grateful to be back inside the warm and well-lit carriage. After leaving Shrewsbury, I looked through the numbers of the engines I'd recorded during the day and, after consulting my Combined Volume, discovered I'd copped 6 steam out of a total 110 noted. Including 18 engines officially withdrawn, further observation revealed that sixty-nine locos were cold. As with the steam leg, the next forty-two miles to Snow Hill, including stops at Wellington and Wolverhampton, was also scheduled to take an hour and five minutes. As the train made its way through the fog and failing light, it became more and more difficult to see anything through the window other than reflections from within the carriage. As a result my mind began to wander and I started to think about where my next trip might take me.

Tyseley was visited three times in January, on 3rd, 22nd and 30th. Resident preserved engines continued rubbing shoulders with both stored locos and those still in service, which had been sent to the diesel depot for wheel re-profiling using its wheel turning facilities. Totals for steam present and different classes represented for the above dates were 18/7, 12/6 and 12/6 respectively. On 3rd, I watched Brush Type '4' No. D1673 remove two Ivatt 2-6-0's, No's. 46442 and 46509, from inside the shed building to join fellow classmates No's. 46421 and 46454 in the yard, ready I suspected to be moved together for the last time to the breaker's yard.

While engaged in my second visit to Tyseley on 22nd, one of the shed staff told me all four Ivatt 2-6-0's had been taken away to be cut up, confirming what I thought had been happening three weeks earlier. Two of the four remaining pannier tanks, No's. 9610 and 9630, seemed to have suffered a similar fate, as they were nowhere to be found during this or indeed any subsequent visits to the depot. Somewhat puzzlingly, No. 9774, absent on 22nd and 30th January, had reappeared by the time I made my way round the shed on 5th February! She was back inside the roundhouse with sister engine No. 4696. Perhaps the RCTS information mentioned earlier was correct after all, and No. 9774 was indeed the last of the '5700' class to remain working. A total of 13 steam representing 6 different classes were noted on this day.

Tyseley MPD, Tuesday, 3rd January 1967. The wait for the final journey continues: pannier tank No. 4696 stands next to the shed's crane, while Brush Type '4' No. D1673 is ready to move Ivatt 2MT No. 46442 (out of the picture) into the yard prior to removal for scrapping. Withdrawn the previous November, approximately a month after the 2-6-0, the 0-6-0 tank looks ready for further work rather than the scrapyard.

On 3rd January 1967, with connecting rods removed, and looking every bit like a candidate for withdrawal, standard class 5MT No. 73130 of Patricroft shed, has in fact been prepared for its wheels to be re-profiled. The 4-6-0 is seen waiting outside the diesel depot for its turn on the lathe. A copy of the repair record for this engine's visit to Tyseley caught my attention, and can be seen on page 134 together with an explanation of why it is so intriguing.

On the way to Saltley on 5th February I found it difficult to comprehend that steam would not be welcome here in four weeks time. Indeed, it would not be the only shed in the Midlands to close its doors to steam over the weekend of 4th / 5th March; Oxley, too, would cease to operate with a steam allocation from this time on. This Sunday visit witnessed Saltley catering for 17 steam representing a small variety of 4 different types. Tucked away in the third roundhouse, a notable guest was ex-GWR 0-6-0PT No. 3607. She had been a 'local' engine for many years and after her home depot, Stourbridge, closed to steam she had been transferred to Tyseley in July 1966. The last time I had seen this engine was on 31st August and she was withdrawn soon afterwards - certainly by the beginning of October. Where she had been for the last four months is a bit of a mystery. The other engines on shed comprised Stanier '8F's (14) 'Black 5' No. 44913 and standard 2-6-0 No. 76037.

Before February came to an end two further visits were made to Saltley on 11th and 18th. The total number of steam present was 18 and 16 respectively. Including pannier tank No. 3607, three varieties were to be found on the first visit, with '8F's again most prominent. Surprisingly, only one 'Black 5' was noted, No. 44876, an Oxley engine. On the 18th 0-6-0PT No. 3607 was still on shed (see picture page 73) with a footnote in my logbook suggesting that, with middle wheels removed, she appeared to be under repair! The other fifteen locos all belonged to Stanier's '8F' class with No's. 48336, 48529, 48556 and 48728 in steam.

Fresh out of Derby works, BR Type '4' 'Peak' No. D145 stands in the north yard of Saltley MPD yard on 18th February 1967. Built in December 1961 and first allocated to Derby, it would be withdrawn on 11th October 1981 and wouldn't quite complete twenty years service.

Previously allocated to Sheffield Grimesthorpe, Hellifield, Toton, Saltley, Kirkby in Ashfield and Coalville, '8F' No. 48105, now an Oxley engine, is seen in Saltley No. 2 shed on 18th February 1966. The 2-8-0 would remain active for a further three months before being withdrawn in June.

Ex-GWR pannier tank No. 3607, withdrawn last October, appears to be under repair in Saltley's No. 2 shed. Last allocated to Tyseley, its middle driving wheels have been removed and can just be seen in front of the engine. Perhaps there were problems with the loco's motion, which resulted in such action being taken so that removal to a scrapyard could take place.

Tyseley was also visited on 18th February. Including eight 'Black 5's, an '8F' and standard 5MT 4-6-0 No. 73045, a Patricroft engine, the number of steam locos on shed had increased to 15. Two of Stanier's 4-6-0's in the queue for the WTL (No's. 44675 and 44928) were Carlisle Kingmoor engines. Now complete with a fresh coat of paint, 'Castle' class 4-6-0 No. 7029 Clun Castle, looking immaculate, was noted inside the diesel depot. A total of 7 different varieties of steam power were present on this day. February was significant, of course, as it marked the end of the 'complete' overhaul of steam locos working on BR, after 'Britannia' Pacific No. 70013 Oliver Cromwell was out shopped from Crewe Works on 2nd.

Tyseley MPD, 18th February 1967. Frequently found inside the diesel depot at this time, No. 7029 Clun Castle looks ready for its part to play in the next planned special on 26th of the month, the LCGB Severn and Dee Railtour.

With a full tender of coal ready for its journey back to its home shed of Carlisle, 'Black 5' No. 44675 is seen at the rear of the wheel lathe queue outside Tyseley diesel depot on 18th February 1967. The 4-6-0 would be withdrawn after completing a further six months employment.

March / April

The weekend of 4th / 5th March would be a poignant one. To mark the end of through services on the Great Western route between Paddington and Birkenhead four steam specials were planned - two on the Saturday organised by Ian Allan Limited, and two on the Sunday entitled 'Farewell to the GWR Birmingham to Birkenhead Route' arranged by the SLS. From Monday 6th the new timetable would mean Snow Hill would cease to have any main-line services. This of course was the beginning of the end and the eventual closure of the station would come in 1972. The final 'Cambrian Coast Express' would run on Saturday 4th with standard Class 4-6-0 No. 75033 in charge of the up train from Aberystwyth to Shrewsbury and No. 75021 at the head of the down train between Shrewsbury and Aberystwyth. The last through train from Paddington would leave on the Sunday evening at 4.10pm and the final up train, a sleeping car service, would depart Birkenhead at 9.40pm.

On Friday 3rd March I decided to take the day off school and pay my last respects with a visit to Wolverhampton and, on returning back to Birmingham, a final visit to Saltley before the shed closed to steam the following Monday. Having caught the 10.04am emu to Wolverhampton High Level, I took the bus, which passed quite close to Oxley Shed, and, for what I thought would be the last time (in fact I would return again in August), made my way up the cinder path leading to the depot. Like Saltley, 2B would close to steam in a couple of days. I recorded a total of 26 steam present (see appendix 18) as follows: Stanier '8F' (9), 'Black 5' (11), standard '9F' (3), standard 4MT 2-6-0 (2) and Ivatt 2-6-0 (1). Only 5 engines were in steam: No's. 44865, 48531, 92123, 92152 and 92159.

On my way back to Low Level Station I stopped off at Dunstall Park and the nearby carriage sidings. Here I found and photographed much neglected 'Black 5' No. 44805 on steam heating duties. Further workings noted while next to the sidings involved 'Black 5' No. 45006 with an oil train and Stanier '8F' No. 48728 light engine. A quick look-in at High Level station before catching the train back to Snow Hill produced another steam working, this time a trip freight headed by '8F' No. 48177. Once back on the former GWR Low Level station, 'Black 5' No. 44812 was noted heading a mixed freight. Later the following week I heard the news that on the Sunday of the same weekend Wolverhampton's last trolleybus was taken out of service and all routes were now in the hands of diesel-powered buses. Interestingly, the few women trolleybus drivers affected were not permitted to drive PSV vehicles, and could not continue their employment with Wolverhampton Council unless they returned to the rank of conductress!

En-route to Birmingham I noted 'Black 5' No. 45062 in steam and while passing through Wednesbury Central three withdrawn engines - No's. 48274, 48428 and 76035 - most surely destined for Cashmores the breakers yard at Great Bridge. No more steam were noted during the remainder of the journey and, seemingly as a foretaste of how things were soon to be, Snow Hill seemed much quieter than normal with little happening to disturb the peace.

First allocated to Crewe North when new in February 1945, 'Black 5' No. 44865 would move nine times during its lifetime. Other depots, the 4-6-0 worked out of included Llandudno Jnct., Aston, Willesden and Tyseley. Seen here in her home shed of Oxley on 3rd March 1967, a final transfer to Crewe South would prove to be the engines last. Removal from capital stock would come later in September.

Above. Making its way on to Oxley, its home shed, on 3rd March 1967, is '8F' No. 48450. The 2-8-0 would shortly be moving to Crewe South before being reallocated for the final time to Edge Hill from where it would be withdrawn later in September.

Left. In filthy external condition and standing amongst track-strewn litter, Stanier 'Black 5' No. 44805 was found on steam heating duties in Oxley carriage sidings on the same day. Bearing the name of its previous shed, Saltley, on its buffer beam, this Oxley engine would keep ahead of the withdrawals after closure of this and its next two home sheds, Chester and Stoke, but would be condemned at the beginning of August 1967, shortly after its final move, to Crewe South.

'Black 5' No. 45006, another Oxley engine, saunters past Oxley carriage sidings with a train of oil wagons on 3rd March 1967. Also destined to move to Crewe South on the closure of its home shed, it would be taken out of service later in September.

With two guards vans in tow, '8F' No. 48177 drifts through Wolverhampton High - Level station on the afternoon of 3rd March 1967. Transferred from Colwick during w/ending 4th February, the 2-8-0 would complete a month's allocation at Oxley before being withdrawn on the shed's closure.

I walked across the city centre to New Street station and caught the local service to Saltley, which would leave me with a ten-minute walk to the shed. It was most unusual for me to get to the depot this way, which added to the sense of change I was experiencing. No more would I use the well-cycled route and follow the normal pattern of trips to a place that I had got to know so well. Looking at the wider picture, this weekend would witness the end of regular steam working in the Birmingham Division and indeed the Shrewsbury area of the Stoke division. Enthusiasts from my neck of the woods would no longer enjoy seeing steam going about its business on a daily basis locally; if they wanted to continue to see such engines in the future, they would have no option but to join those who were already having to travel, in some cases not inconsiderable distances, to witness everyday working steam.

As I had done countless times before, I stopped at the top of the ramp and waited for a few minutes to see if there were any engines about to leave or come on to the shed. With no sign of any such movements, I entered the first of the three roundhouses and found two '8F's in residence, No's. 48603 and 48690. Both engines were cold, with this part of the depot still and quiet with only the echo of my footfall to be heard. Sharing a similar silence in the second roundhouse was '8F' No. 48128 and 'Peak' No. D111. The 2-8-0 had only been a Saltley engine for about three months, was in steam and doubtless looking forward to moving on to Stoke, her next home depot. 'Black 5' No. 45038, also in steam and the sole occupant of the third roundhouse, would join her in her move to the Potteries. Three further '8F's were in the yard, No's. 48645, 48538 and 48133, making a total of 7 steam representing 2 different varieties. No's. 48538 and 48690 were two of the last three steam engines to be transferred to Saltley during week ending 4th February. The other engine, No. 48728, was not about, although after being withdrawn the following week, I would come across her inside Crewe South depot on 30th April and again, still inside the shed building, on 10th August.

One of my last pictures of steam on Saltley shed. Just prior to moving into the yard, Stanier '8F' No. 48645 is seen standing in No. 3 shed on 3rd March 1967. Transferred to the depot the previous December, the 2-8-0 would soon find itself based at Chester from where it would be withdrawn in July.

As I walked the short distance to the No 8 (the City's inner circle route) bus stop, I don't think I comprehended what this last visit had really meant. I had been fortunate to find that Tyseley, in spite of its closure to steam, had in fact continued to play host to a trickle of engines in need of its wheel turning facilities. But Saltley would not see such motive power anymore. I persuaded myself to hold on to the idea that I might witness, at least for a while, the servicing of the odd isolated steam working from somewhere like Stoke, where steam was still very much in evidence, although I didn't hold out much hope of it actually happening. I had pedalled many miles and spent many a happy hour making notes of the engines on this shed and, according to my surviving logbooks, had visited the depot a total of 177 times.

On Sunday 5th March I cycled to Tyseley on my way to see Jackie. I knew that 'Clun Castle' had been prepared for its second outing of the weekend and would begin its journey from Tyseley Station. After watching its departure along with many more enthusiasts, I wandered down to the shed via the carriage sidings where a very clean Stanier 4-6-0, No. 44680, was waiting to follow in the 'Castle's' footsteps with the second of the two specials to Birkenhead; twelve days later on 17th, the 'Black 5' would briefly be in charge of the Royal Train between Wellington and Donnington where she remained overnight on steam heating duty. This, I believe, was one of the very few times before steam finished on BR that this form of motive power was in charge of the Royal Train. Unfortunately, I had finished my film taking pictures of 7029, and was disappointed that I wasn't able to photograph this lovely clean engine too.

Tyseley produced 15 steam, eight of which were Stanier 4-6-0s. One of these, No. 44928, allocated to Carlisle Kingmoor, was noted occupying the WTL. However, by the beginning of July, after travelling so far for this special attention, her services would no longer be required and she would be withdrawn. Also present was preserved 'K4' No. 3442 The Great Marquess and, not quite of similar status, 0-6-0 light pannier tank No. 1638 almost completely repainted. The shed, even after closure, could still boast a relatively wide variety motive power with a total of 7 different classes represented. On 24th March I found the shed host to 5 steam, four of which were ex-GWR locos - No's. 1638, 4176, 4696 and 7029 - together with standard 5MT 4-6-0 No. 73132 in the yard of the diesel depot.

Being both admired and much photographed on 5th March 1967 while standing in Tyseley station, 'Castle' class No. 7029 Clun Castle is seen at the head of the SLS 'Farewell to the GWR Birmingham - Birkenhead Service' special.

Seven months later on Saturday 14th October Clun Castle was heading north again at the head of a an LCGB (North West Branch) 'Castle to Carlisle Railtour' from Preston to Carlisle via Shap and return via the S&C to Hellifield. A few days afterwards, Lostock Hall Driver, Peter Norris, received a letter from Patrick Whitehouse (shown opposite) thanking him for the enjoyable run behind the 4-6-0. His fireman, John Roach, ably assisted Peter throughout and, hopefully, he too received a similar message of gratitude. Such was the significance of the engine's performance while in the hands of Peter and John that it was referred to later by O. S. Nock in his book The GWR Stars Castles and Kings. Involved in a number of railtours up until steam finished on BR, Peter would continue to carry out his normal duties, an eventful one of which is commented upon later.

1967 (Farewell to Oliver Bulleid's Pacifics)

Spring evolved into summer and my visits to Saltley were now much less frequent. My hopes of seeing the odd steam loco from neighbouring Divisions still relying on this form of motive power had not come to fruition. I noted that the water tower and adjacent ash pit by the coaling stage appeared to have been used towards the end of March and again in early April, but whether one or two isolated steam workings had actually happened I'll never know. Contrary to reports that only one '8F', No. 48538, remained in store after the shed's closure to steam, I recorded on 17th May, for what would turn out to be the last time, the three Stanier 2-8-0's that had been withdrawn on 6th March. No. 48133 was in number three roundhouse and No's. 48538 and 48690 in the yard. I visited the depot one further time on 8th July and discovered that the Stanier '8F's had finally departed and only diesels remained.

Predictably, Tyseley now became the focus of my attention. Each time I concluded a visit I was pleased to have noted a few steam on shed. Visits on 8th, 11th, 18th, 22nd and 28th April produced the following respective totals for locos present and classes represented: 9/5, 9/5, 2/2, 8/6, and 7/6. On 11th I found 'Black 5' No. 45411 inside the shed building with a fire laid and slowly raising steam. Her 4,000-gallon tender was being filled equally slowly via a small hose attached to an adjacent standpipe. On the same day standard 5MT 4-6-0 No. 73071 was found in the diesel depot on the WTL. Two engines were in steam inside the shed on 18th, '8F' No. 48684 and 'Black 5' No. 45040. 'Britannia' Pacific No. 70049 Solway Firth, a Kingmoor engine, was in the yard of the diesel depot awaiting use of the wheel turning facilities. Interestingly, this was the last steam locomotive to be named by BR in May 1960, following by some two months the naming of '9F' No. 92220 Evening Star.

My visit to Tyseley on 28th April was something special. Not because I found '8F' No. 48684 in steam inside the steam shed once more, although that in itself was interesting, but because it was my first trip to the shed on my brand new Lambretta scooter; no longer would I have to walk, cycle or catch the bus. I could be at the depot from home in the matter of a few minutes and, more importantly, it would open up possibilities of seeing steam at more locations than would be possible if having to reach them by train. The significance of seeing the '8F' again will be explained later.

During one of my visits to Tyseley at around this time, I came across several bundles of paperwork (correspondence, shopping proposals, repair cards etc.) that had been discarded and presumably left for binning or burning. I quickly looked through some of the documents that hadn't been fully exposed to the elements and took them home with me. Once safely stored, I didn't look at them closely for many years. I have included copies of a few that I think make for interesting reading and that are directly associated with my visits to the shed, or relate to individual locomotives noted during the period in question.

One item that I believe merits a special mention at this point, and to which I alluded to in Part One when recalling a trip to London on 27th February 1965, is a circular issued by the Divisional Manager's Office, Birmingham following a tragic accident on the footplate of 'Britannia' Pacific No. 70051 Firth of Forth. The contents, while referring to the loss of life, the reasons for the blowback and the implications concerning proper maintenance, did not give any details of the driver and his actions. Many perhaps know about what happened, but I reckon his bravery and selflessness deserve to be highlighted again here.

The driver in question was Wallace Arnold Oaks a Crewe-based engineman. While travelling at about 60mph near Winsford a 'blowback' occurred filling the cab with smoke and flames. The fireman of an up train stopped to pick up the injured men and reportedly looked into the cab and saw that the handbrake had been applied, the regulator partly shut and the blower valve left open.

It would seem that Driver Oakes did not leave his engine and train until it had stopped; he had applied the brakes and reduced the blowback as best he might and was satisfied he'd done all he could to ensure the safety of the passengers. As a result he suffered 80% burns and a week later on 12th June 1965, died in Wythenshawe Hospital, Manchester at the age of 33. That wasn't quite the end of the story, however. At Euston station on 19th February 1981, following the posthumous award of the George Cross, BR named Class 86 electric locomotive No. 260 Wallace Oaks GC and, fittingly, in September 2017 his George Cross medal was purchased by the NRM for public display.

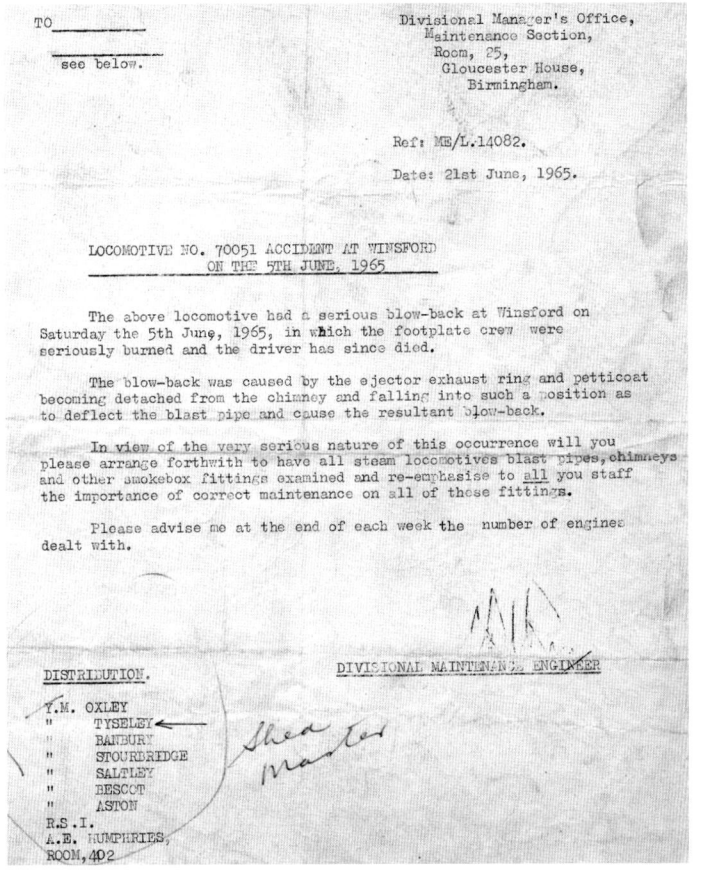

Two weeks after the tragic incident at Winsford the letter shown (left) was issued from the Divisional Maintenance Engineer, Mr E. R. Williams, to staff at the depots listed. No doubt the seriousness of the accident prompted a swift response both by the shedmasters concerned and their fitters etc. However, it would appear from the need to send out a second memorandum to Mr Field (below), that there had been a breakdown in communication, and that clarification was requested with regard to an updated list of engines having been examined.

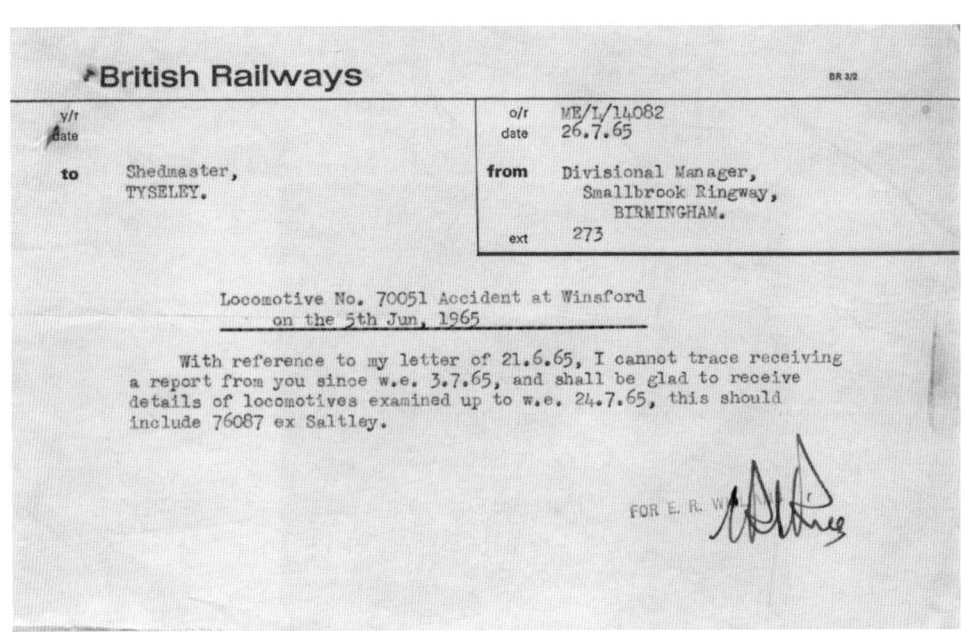

On 30th April, two days after first using my new mode of transport, I was off to Stoke, Crewe and Shrewsbury. I can't think why I didn't take my camera with me on this trip, but I have my old notebook to remind me of the engines I saw during the day. Stoke, the first of the three sheds I visited, had a total of 47 steam representing 5 different classes. One of the twenty Stanier 'Black 5's present, No. 45060, was recorded as having a badly damaged front end and appears to have been withdrawn sometime during the previous month.

From Stoke I headed initially for Newcastle-under-Lyme and then for Crewe and its last remaining steam shed. South depot had several more classes of engine present than Stoke with a total of 10 varieties amongst the 82 steam logged. Inside the shed building I found the remains of No. 71000 Duke of Gloucester, minus its valve gear and cylinders, together with preserved 'A4' No.4498 (BR No. 60007) Sir Nigel Gresley. 'Black 5' No. 44680, last seen on 5th March in the sidings at Tyseley ready to head a special, was noted as still in pristine condition. The total number of engines on shed was an impressive one, yet I listed only 12 in steam, including '8F' No. 48684, which I referred to when visiting Tyseley on 28th. Its movements will be dealt with when reviewing my trips to this depot next month.

Later in the afternoon I arrived at Shrewsbury and after calling in at the station made for the shed. It didn't take me long to list the few steam locos at rest here - only 16 representing 5 different varieties, with standard 2MT 2-6-0 (5) and 4MT 4-6-0 (3) engines making up half of the total logged. During the day I had seen 10 different engine varieties and noted 145 steam locos, just two of which were cops. Even though it was a Sunday, with less of a demand for motive power, most of the locos were cold. Except for the odd one or two, their general unkempt and grubby appearance, left me in no doubt that they were now seeing out their final few months of service. No films to develop after this trip, but I had travelled over 130 miles boosting both my riding skills and confidence as a result.

May

Visits to Tyseley on 7th, 17th and 27th May produced steam totals of 10, 12 and 9 respectively, with 7 varieties represented on each occasion. On 7th, six months after the depot had officially closed to steam, there were two engines on shed worthy of special mention. 'Britannia' Pacific No. 70049 Solway Firth, was once again in steam after attention to its wheels on the profiling machine, but of greater significance was the presence of Stanier '8F' No. 48684, also in steam. It would appear that this engine, after returning to traffic following similar profiling repairs on 28th April, had left Tyseley and returned to its home depot of Heaton Mersey. However, after noting it on Crewe South shed in steam on 30th April, it must have worked a freight into the Birmingham area, and found itself back at Tyseley for servicing before heading north again.

Looking resplendent in its new coat of paint, small pannier tank No. 1638 provides a source of cheer in the old steam shed on 27th May 1967. Built at Swindon in 1951, the engine was first allocated to Llanelli shed to work the Bury Port to Gwendraeth valley line. Privately purchased after withdrawal in August 1966, the tank would move to Buckfastleigh later in November.

Tyseley diesel depot, 27th May 1967: seen waiting for their turn on the wheel turning lathe is standard 5MT No. 73128, allocated to Patricroft and, below, Carlisle Kingmoor-based 'Black 5' No 44902. The Stanier 4-6-0 would continue in service until November 1967, while the standard would not face withdrawal until May 1968.

We moved in to our new house in Droitwich Spa during the third week in May, and I immediately discovered that from the back door leading to the garden, the track of the ex-GWR Birmingham to Worcester line was no more than 25 yards away! What a pity steam was no longer employed on this route - it would have been so easy to take photos either from my bedroom window or the bottom of the garden. Regrettably, the line was now frequented by dmu's, 'Hymeks', 'Peaks', Brush Type '4's' and English Electric Type '3' diesels, none of which inspired me to reach for my camera!

Southern steam featured more and more in my thoughts at this time. Travelling south on my scooter to record on film a few of the engines still being usefully employed was not only very tempting, but was now a real possibility. But time was short: the deadline for steams elimination was now set for early July, so I decided to contact Dennis to see if he could manage to make another expedition south. Unfortunately, being at work meant that it wasn't possible, but we agreed that somehow we would meet up before it capitulated to electric and diesel traction. I was reaching the end of my studies at school and, although certain questions would no doubt be asked about my absence, could take time off more easily.

Tuesday 30th May

A year earlier I had travelled south to see steam on the South Western Division of the Southern Region and relied on my pushbike to carry me there and back. Today I was looking forward even more even more at the prospect of doing this journey - I would still be on two wheels, but I'd have an engine beneath me to do the work rather than relying on pedal power! I would now be able to cover the same route in a fraction of the time, but there would be an added cost of course - my scooter required to be filled with petrol, which at the time was about 5/6d (27 1/2 pence) a gallon. Once again Salisbury MPD would be my first objective, and as I set off I wondered how the number of steam on shed would compare with the previous year's visit.

Well, 3 different engine varieties were noted amongst the 11 steam present, compared with 6 and 17 logged respectively the year before. Five engines werc in steam, No's. 34023 Blackmore Vale, 34108 Wincanton, standard 2-6-0's No's. 76007 and 76031, and standard 4MT 4-6-0 No. 75074. After taking a few pictures, I was back on to my Lambretta and off to Bournemouth.

'West Country' Pacific No. 34104 Bere Alston was new to traffic in April 1950. Seen here inside Salisbury shed on 30th May 1967, her nameplate has been removed, but externally the engine still appears well cared for.

On the same day Salisbury was also home to standard 4MT No. 76007. Transferred from here to Bournemouth the previous month, the 2-6-0 would continue in service until the end of steam on the Southern on 9th July.

'West Country' Pacific No. 34108 Wincanton began its revenue earning days at the same time as No. 34104. Allocated to Bournemouth when new, it had been a Salisbury engine since November 1963. It is seen being cleaned inside its home shed on 30th May 1967.

Quite what the deliberations of the two workers were before they became aware of my presence I don't know. Perhaps their discussions were about earlier times at Salisbury shed, and how things had changed on the railway over the last few years. The loco next to them is 'Battle of Britain' class No. 34052 Lord Dowding.

1967 (Farewell to Oliver Bulleid's Pacifics)

While tucking into a packed lunch, I spent a few minutes on Central station and logged 'West Country' No. 34040 Crewkerne and standard 2-6-0 No. 76026 both working passenger trains. Accessing the depot through the gate at the end of the yard adjacent to the station, I noted 12 steam present representing 5 different varieties. Five engines were in steam and ready for their next turn of duty - No's. 34004 Yeovil, 34034 Honiton, 41224, 76009 and 80146.

The driver of standard 2-6-0 No. 76026 seems very focussed as he enters Bournemouth Central with a local stopping train on 30th May 1967. His charge began revenue-earning service in October 1953 and would not quite reach 14 years employment before withdrawal later in July. On the same day, sister engine No. 76009 basks in the summer sunshine in the yard of Bournemouth MPD. In the matter of a few weeks, their services would be dispensed with and they would eventually be broken up at Cohen's, Morriston and Cashmores, Newport respectively.

Two views of 'West Country' Pacific No. 34034 Honiton while resting in Bournemouth shed on 30th May 1967. Built in July 1946 and allocated to Stewarts Lane, its final twelve months in service would be spent operating out of Nine Elms. Rebuilt in August 1960 after completing almost 637,000 miles, its final mileage would climb to 942,133. Withdrawn a little over four weeks after these pictures were taken, it would be despatched to Buttigiegs of Newport and be cut up the following April.

1967 (Farewell to Oliver Bulleid's Pacifics)

Left. Also standing out in the sunlight was Crewe built Ivatt 2-6-2T No. 41224. Over the previous few years the engine had worked out of several sheds including Bedford, Wellingborough, Barnstaple, Exmouth Jnct. and Nine Elms. Pictured in Bournemouth, her final depot, on 30th May 1967, the tank would cease working at the beginning of July. See page 124 for colour photograph and further details about the engine.

Below. On the same day, standard 4MT tank No. 80146 is seen resting between duties in the yard of Bournemouth, its home shed. Built at Brighton works, the 2-6-4 tank entered traffic in October 1956 and would continue working until the beginning of July before being withdrawn and sold for scrap to Birds Commercial Motors.

Leaving Bournemouth in gradually deteriorating weather, I made the relatively short journey to Eastleigh, arriving there in teeming rain. The shed was host to a reasonable variety of steam power and six different classes were noted among the 18 locos present. The following seven engines were in steam: No's. 30067, 34060 25 Squadron, 34095 Brentor, 75076, 75077, 80016 and 80139. I spent a brief time afterwards on the station and witnessed two steam workings headed by 'Battle of Britain' class No. 34090 Sir Eustace Missenden, Southern Railway and standard 4-6-0 No. 75068.

While the rain hammers on the shed roof, USA tank No. 30067 keeps dry while simmering inside Eastleigh MPD.

Built at Swindon in December 1955, Standard 4MT No. 75077 has been left outside Eastleigh's shed building in the pouring rain. Its short working life would soon be over; after ceasing work at the beginning of July, the loco would be taken to Kings of Norwich to be broken up.

With the heavy rain showing no signs of easing, I donned my waterproofs again and set off for Weymouth where, like the year before, I would spend the night at my great aunt's boarding house. Needless to say, on reaching the town a slight detour was made so I could make my fourth and final shed visit of the day. I didn't expect to see a significant number of engines here and indeed so it turned out. Of the four depots, Weymouth had the fewest steam on shed with a total of 8 present representing 3 different varieties. Half of the locos logged belonged to the 'Merchant Navy' class and four engines, No's. 35003 Royal Mail, 35013 Blue Funnel and standards No's. 73085 and 76009 (seen earlier in Bournemouth MPD) were noted in steam (See appendix 19 for all steam engines recorded on the four depots).

After a substantial and most welcome dinner we sat and spent the evening sharing family news, together, of course, with a brief resume of what I'd been up to during the intervening twelve months, including, but in much more detail, the trip to Scotland. Retiring to bed, I fell fast asleep while thinking about what tomorrow had in store and the fact that within a few weeks Southern steam would be no more.

Withdrawn earlier in March, 'Merchant Navy' class Pacific No. 35026 Lamport & Holt Line stands in the yard of Weymouth, its last home shed, on 30th May 1967. The 4-6-2 entered traffic in December 1948 and had completed in excess of 858,000 miles by the time it had been removed from capital stock. The locos final journey would take it to J. Cashmore, Newport where it would be cut up later in September.

Standard 5MT No. 73118 King Leodegrance (the father of Guinevere in Arthurian legend) has clearly seen better days. Resting in the yard of Weymouth shed on 30th May 1967, the 4-6-0 had initially been allocated to Nine Elms when new in December 1955. Now working out of Guildford MPD, the loco would be withdrawn at the end of Southern steam in July. Disposal would be carried out by J. Cashmore's, Newport.

Wednesday 31st May

My great aunt insisted that I had a full cooked breakfast before I left, so I didn't make it to the shed as early as I thought I might. Weymouth was renowned for having the best sunshine record in England and the day was already shaping up to support this fact. Even though yesterday's weather had deteriorated rapidly during the afternoon, as I made my way round the brightly sunlit shed, there was no doubt that summer had arrived. There had been a few changes amongst the 'guests' overnight with five newcomers since my visit the evening before. With the arrival of two 'West Country' Pacifics there were 4 different classes now represented out of a total of 10 steam on shed. I spent a short while on the station and noted four steam (No's 34024 Tamar Valley, 34040 Crewkerne, 35028 Clan Line and 76026) all involved with passenger workings. I took several colour photographs in and by the approaches to the station all of which turned out quite well (see pages 136 and 137).

All too soon it was time to leave Weymouth and start my homeward journey. However, I hadn't quite finished my shed bash - the route home would allow further visits to Bournemouth and Salisbury MPD's together with a brief stop at Wareham. Both sheds produced the same number of engines as the previous day with only a few changes in 'clientele'. At Wareham I noted rebuilt 'Battle of Britain' class No. 34060 25 Squadron on passenger duty, and while on Bournemouth Central I logged 'Merchant Navy' No. 35003 Royal Mail, standard 2-6-0's No's. 76007, 76009, all light engine, and, heading a semi-fast passenger train, standard No. 76026. A quick call in at Salisbury station before heading north produced two steam workings involving unrebuilt 'West Country' No. 34023 Blackmore Vale and standard 4-6-0 No. 73029. During the two days I had recorded a total of 60 steam representing 8 varieties, with 33 different engines in steam. And cops? Just five.

Ready to begin another day's labours, initially with an express for Waterloo, 'Merchant Navy' No. 35028 Clan Line is about to leave Weymouth MPD on 31st May 1967.

Looking very work weary and scruffy, standard 5MT No. 73085 Melisande (its name meaning strong and industrious) is seen resting in Weymouth MPD on 31st May 1967. Steadfast, too, the 4-6-0 remained in traffic until steam finished on the Southern Region.

Taking a breather between duties in Bournemouth MPD on 31st May 1967, standard 4MT 2-6-4 tank No. 80011 was one of eleven remaining in service at this time. Allocated to Tunbridge Wells when built in July 1951, it would not quite complete sixteen years employment when withdrawn on 9th July.

Top left. The front ends of 'West Country' Pacific No. 34024 Tamar Valley and standard 4MT No 76011 exemplify the differences in appearance and outline that locomotive design could produce. Top right. Another view of the front of No. 34024 while standing in the yard of Bournemouth shed on 31st May 1967. Above. Derby-built standard 5MT No. 73020 entered traffic in October 1951 and was initially allocated to Chester. Seen here standing next to Type '3' diesel No. D6514 inside Salisbury shed on the same day, the 4-6-0 was by now a Guildford engine, and would have five further weeks of employment before being condemned.

Battle of Britain class No. 34089 602 Squadron on Salisbury MPD. No doubt the cleaners at Ramsgate, the engines first home shed, would have kept the loco clean and tidy but, surprisingly, Salisbury, the 4-6-2's final home depot, still had staff who took a pride in the appearance of their engines even at this late hour. 31st May 1967.

Bullied Pacific No. 34104 Bere Alston, the last 'West Country' constructed at Eastleigh, and the last to be rebuilt there in the spring of 1961, remains out of steam inside Salisbury shed on 31st May 1967. Completing almost 700,000 since new, the engine would cease working next month and be broken up at Buttigiegs, Newport.

Seen being cleaned yesterday, Salisbury shed has another fresh looking engine to call upon: built at Brighton in April 1950, No. 34108 Wincanton had clocked up over 800,000 miles since entering traffic. Its projected life expectancy would not be realised, of course, and withdrawal from service would follow in a few day's time.

Allowing its crew time to have a chat with an onlooker (out of picture), 'West Country' No. 34023 Blackmore Vale waits to move out of Salisbury station and on to shed (see overleaf). A little over 21 years old, the Pacific remained in its original form with 'air smooth' casing until withdrawal at the end of Southern steam. Good fortune meant that the engine would not face the cutter's torch and would be preserved by the Bulleid Preservation Society. 31st May 1967

'West Country' Pacific No. 34023 Blackmore Vale is ready to be coaled and watered while on Salisbury MPD. During the first two years of its working life, the engine carried nameplates with the alternative spelling of the Vale i.e. Blackmoor, which it would use once again when preserved.

Standard 5MT No. 73029, also in the yard of Salisbury shed on 31st May 1967, was first allocated to Blackpool when new in January 1952. Following moves to St Philips Marsh (twice), Carmarthen, and Swindon, the 4-6-0 reached Weymouth in September 1958. It then remained on the Southern Region with its final move in June 1966, to Nine Elms, from where it would be withdrawn in a little over a month's time.

June

In the matter of a few weeks Southern steam would be nothing more than something to discuss and reminisce about. As soon as I was home I began thinking of when I could return south for what would be a final goodbye. I contacted Dennis, and he was keen to make the trip, too, although he knew it might prove difficult to take time off work. However, during the first couple of weeks in June we managed to come up with a programme that suited us both; we would say our farewell to the few engines still working over the first weekend in July.

On 10th June I made my only visit of the month to Tyseley. Engines noted on shed were: No's. 7029 Clun Castle, 44805, 44902, 45368, 45382, 48107, 73128, 75048 and 92045. It wouldn't be long before I was on a further steam bash ahead of its banishment from yet another part of the country. While really looking forward to the trip, my enthusiasm and eagerness to see such locomotives fulfilling an active and important role was tempered significantly by the fact that another chapter in their history was about to be concluded. Once steam had finished on the Southern Region, the only Pacifics left working would be the 'Britannia's, and how much longer they would continue to see employment in the northwest was anybody's guess. And, of course, with the withdrawal of the few remaining USA tanks, there would be no more 0-6-0 tank engines remaining on BR to help meet the demands of the more menial and tedious tasks of shunting and trip freight work.

It was with mixed feelings that I packed a few clothes on the evening of Thursday 29th June, and made sure that my films (courtesy of my uncle once again) were safely stored inside my case. The following morning I left home at 7.00am and arrived in Guildford by about 11.00am. I made straight for the shed and found it host to five engines - USA 0-6-0T No. 30072, standard 4-6-0s No's. 73092, 73118 King Leodegrance and 73155 and standard 2-6-0 No. 77014, all in steam.

USA 0-6-0 tank No. 30072 standing in the yard of Guildford MPD on 30th June 1967. Having been bought to replace the ageing 'B1', 'D1' and 'E1' class tanks to work in Southampton Docks, four of the original fourteen would be preserved, including No. 30072.

Standard 5MT No. 73092 rests inside the shed building of Guildford MPD on 30th June 1967. The 4-6-0 entered traffic in October 1955 and was despatched to Patricroft, where it was based until its first reallocation, to Shrewsbury, in August 1958. Further moves took place until the engine found itself on the Southern Region, firstly allotted to Eastleigh and, finally in October 1965, to Guildford. Just visible in the background is English Electric Electro Diesel No. E6045.

I wasn't due to meet up with Dennis until later in the afternoon at Euston, so I parked my scooter at the station and travelled up to London on the train. 'Battle of Britain' No. 34089 602 Squadron was noted at Weybridge in charge of a down mixed freight, and a further five steam locos were seen between Clapham Junction and Waterloo Station: No's 41298, 34093 Saunton, 34095 Brentor, 34102 Lapford and 82019. I had time to bunk Nine Elms before meeting Dennis, so I caught the first train out to Clapham and then the No. 77 bus to Brookfield Road at the end of which was the shed entrance.

As can be imagined, both the depot and a good number of its residents were very run down by this time. How the shed staff had managed to keep going I really don't know. Morale, especially amongst the fitters, must have been as low as it could possibly get; yet they had some how managed to keep the small number of steam locos running despite the make-do-and-mend policy they had had to follow. Perhaps a little in the extreme for me, David Shepherd's well-known painting of the depot summed up its dilapidated state, but both its pitiful appearance and indeed the awful condition of a number of the engines it housed, was certainly close to his interpretation and portrayal of this once important and thriving depot. I noted 28 steam on shed representing 8 different classes, with eight locos in steam. Two 'Merchant Navy' class engines, No's. 35008 Orient Line and 35028 Clan Line, were remarked upon as being very clean and carrying what I believe were their original nameplates.

Displaying the local light engine/empty stock head code, Swindon built standard 3MT 2-6-2T No. 82019 stands in Waterloo station resting between duties. Remaining in service for 14 years 10 months, this engine had the longest life of the 45 members of the class. Below. Unrebuilt 'West Country' No. 34102 Lapford arrives at Waterloo with a boat train from Southampton. Watched by a porter, I wondered if he envied the crew on board the engine and of course the higher pay that their jobs would provide. New to traffic in March 1950, the Pacific would cease working a week later having achieved a final mileage of 593,438.

Time for a breather: after reaching the buffer stops, No. 34102 Lapford rests in Waterloo while two passengers seem deep in conversation and in no hurry to leave the station. BR standard four-car unit (4-REP) No. 3006, an earlier arrival, stands next to the Pacific. 30th June 1967.

Back to the beginning: built at Crewe in 1951, Ivatt 2-6-2T No. 41298's first shed was Bricklayer's Arms from where it was mainly employed on empty stock workings into and out of London Victoria. Its final shed, Nine Elms, (see next picture) used it for exactly the same purpose, except of course the station in question was now Waterloo. On 30th June 1967 the loco is seen at the approaches to Waterloo on empty stock duty, just as it was engaged at the outset of its working life.

A fine study of Ivatt 2-6-2T No. 41298 resting in the yard of Nine Elms on 27th April 1967. Transferred from Bricklayers Arms to Barnstaple Junction in 1953, the loco was put to work on the branch lines in the area. A decade later she could be found working along Weymouth Quay on boat trains and local passenger turns. Withdrawal would come on 9th July when steam finished on the SR, but the tank would be fortunate enough to be purchased from BR by the Ivatt Locomotive Trust, and can now be found at Havenstreet on the Isle of Wight. Author's collection.

On 30th June 1967, 'Merchant Navy' class No. 35030 Elder Dempster Lines receives attention from a fitter inside Nine Elms shed. The loco entered traffic on 1st April 1949, and in June the following year was named after what was at the time one of the UK's largest shipping companies.

On the same day, standard 2-6-4T No. 80143 simmers in the sunshine in the yard of the depot. First allocated to Neasden when new in September 1956, it would leave Nine Elms for Bird's Commercial Motors, Risca to be broken up later in the autumn.

Whenever I was making my way round the shed, Nine Elms coaling stage always seemed to be such an imposing structure. Standing close by, and appearing somewhat dwarfed by comparison, are 'West Country' Pacific No. 34093 Saunton and Ivatt 2-6-2T No. 41298. Both engines would be withdrawn at the end of steam working on the Southern Region.

Having returned from Waterloo (see earlier photographs pages 99-100), 'West Country' No. 34102 Lapford, after being turned, has made its way to the side of the shed building to take on water. 30th June 1967.

Following No. 34102 Lapford past the coaling stage, is Ivatt 2-6-0T No. 41319. It would appear that the engine is under the control of the young fireman, while the driver keeps a watchful eye on his handling of the tank.

I was only too aware that I had made my last visit to yet another steam shed while travelling on the bus back to Clapham Junction; in the matter of a few days Nine Elms would close for good. London, once such an attraction for me and countless other trainspotters, too, would, in a week or so, no longer have any BR steam regularly working in to its main stations, or along its numerous freight routes. But I had the next two days to look forward to and enjoy; it was time to make the most of what steam were still working, and to savour the experience before it was gone forever.

Once on Clapham station I decided to take in for a while what this busy Junction had to offer. There was very little in the way of steam activity but, intermittently, amongst the frenetic coming and going of the endless stream of electric units, the odd steam engine appeared. As well as noting a few workings involving empty stock movements, there was the occasional steam-hauled passenger train, too. 'West Country' Pacific No. 34013 Okehampton was noted in charge of a southbound express and Ivatt 2-6-2T No. 41312 appeared with the unadvertised 4.36pm ex-Kensington Olympia to Clapham Junction service for the Post Office Savings Bank staff. Diesel locomotives had operated this service in previous summers, but once again it was in the hands of steam power. This would be the last inner-London steam suburban service to regularly cross the River Thames and would continue until the Southern Region withdrew the remaining members of its steam fleet on 9th July.

The loco in charge on this day had already made history by hauling the last steam branch line train between Brockenhurst and Lymington Pier on 2nd April. After photographing the Ivatt tank, I caught one of the four-car suburban electric units to Waterloo, and the tube to Euston calling in at Kings Cross and St. Pancras on the way. Dennis's train was on time, and we were back on Waterloo Station by about 8.30pm. Before catching the 9.22pm to Guildford, where we would stop overnight in a guesthouse, six steam were noted: No's. 41298, 41319, 35003 Royal Mail, 73065 and 73093. For the second time during the week, on Wednesday 28th June, reports eventually surfaced to suggest that 'Merchant Navy' No. 35003 Royal Mail reached over 105mph near Fleet - see page 110 for details regarding an earlier run on Monday 26th.

Built at Crewe in May 1952, Ivatt 2-6-2T No. 41312 enters Clapham Jnct. station with a post office passenger train from Kensington Olympia. Two days later the tank would be withdrawn from service, but, fortunately, would be bought and preserved.

Left. 'West Country' class No. 34013 Okehampton hurries through Clapham junction with a Southampton bound express. After being withdrawn on 9th July, the engine would be moved to Cashmores, Newport and be broken up during the following month.

Evening arrivals at Waterloo, 30th June 1967: clockwise - Merchant Navy No. 35003 Royal Mail, standard 5MT 4-6-0 No. 73093 and sister engine No. 73065. All three engines would be withdrawn nine days later.

July

Saturday 1st July

The morning dawned with a suggestion that the day ahead would most likely be a fair one. After breakfast we bunked Guildford Shed and noted five engines in steam: USA 0-6-0 Tank No. 30072, 'West Country' Pacific No. 34095 Brentor and standard locos No's. 73092, 73118 King Leodegrance and 77014. Once we had photographed all five engines, we climbed aboard my Lambretta and set off for Basingstoke to see what was on shed there.

Initially destined to spend a number of years allocated to sheds in the northeast, standard 3MT No. 77014 was built at Swindon and entered traffic in July 1954. Following approximately eighteen months based at Northwich, the 2-6-0 was transferred to Guildford in March 1966, where it is seen above the shed's ash pit, together with standard 4-6-0 No. 73092, on 1st July 1967.

Basingstoke MPD had been demoted to a stabling point in March 1963 and at the same time lost its shed coding. Its engines had been transferred to Nine Elms, Guildford and Eastleigh. We knew, therefore, that there might not be any steam on what was now no more than a signing-on point. However, its loss of status had little influence this day, and we recorded five standard engines on shed: No's. 73018, 73029, 73043, 76031 and 80151. All three 4-6-0 5MT's were in steam. The smokebox numberplate of 73029 (see opposite) had been made and fitted by Ron Cover, a diesel fitter employed at Eastleigh at this time. While in the shed yard, we also noted 'West Country' Pacific No. 34025 Whimple heading a passenger train for Waterloo.

Top. Standard 5MT No. 73018, with a non-standard front number plate and altered top lamp bracket position, makes its way on to Basingstoke shed on 1st July 1967. Previously allocated to Nottingham, Shrewsbury, Swindon and Weymouth the 4-6-0 was now a Guildford-based engine. Above. On the same day, sister engine No. 73029, also with a wooden replacement front number plate, but somewhat more elaborate, is found resting at the side of the shed building.

Next stop Eastleigh shed. Here a total of 20 steam were in residence representing 6 different varieties. Seven of the eight engines in steam must have been camera shy as they were all to be found inside the shed building. Photographed endless number of times during the final few days of steam working, the one engine in steam, and happy to be in the lime light, was unrebuilt 'West Country' Pacific No. 34102 Lapford. So, not to disappoint, I've included another picture of her here.

Eight more days to go before withdrawal: unrebuilt 'West Country' Pacific No. 34102 Lapford in the yard of Eastleigh MPD (top), and USA 0-6-0T No. 30064 (above) inside the shed building.

We had not been the only enthusiasts wandering round the three sheds we had bunked so far. A good number of others were to be found freely roaming around and noting and photographing the engines present. No one, as far as I was aware, had been challenged, and it appeared that the shed staff, foremen and other 'officials' at each of these depots had decided to turn a blind eye to our presence; they had most likely resigned themselves to the fact that over the next few days there would be a steady stream of people wanting to experience being close to resting engines, and to savour for one last time the sounds, smells and atmosphere of a steam shed environment.

Continuing our journey south we soon reached the outskirts of Bournemouth. On this our last but one visit to the shed, representing 6 different classes, we logged 9 locos: No's 34004 Yeovil, 34021 Dartmoor, 35030 Elder Dempster Lines, 41224, 73020, and 80146 (all in steam), together with 76005, 76026 and 80134 appearing to be surplus to requirements and sitting cold. We made the short walk to the station and had lunch while spending about half an hour there; disappointingly, it was devoid of any steam movements during this time.

Travelling via Poole and Wareham we arrived at Weymouth late in the afternoon. It was a warm summer's day and we had enjoyed the journey, with my Lambretta running well. This would be our last shed visit of the day, but before heading to the depot, we called in at the station. No steam to be found here, only Birmingham R.C. & W. Type '3' diesels and dmu's. The shed, however, housed 16 steam representing 6 different classes. Three locos were in steam No's. 34089 602 Squadron, 34093 Saunton and 35023 Holland-Afrika Line. Tonight we would stay with my great aunt again and during the evening make plans for the following day.

The attention being given to 'Merchant Navy' No. 35030 Elder Dempster Lines while in Nine Elms shed yesterday had obviously been successful, and had ensured the engine could continue in service. Being made ready for a return to Waterloo, she is seen here being oiled by her driver in Bournemouth MPD on 1st July 1967. Fittingly, the last of the class to be built, she worked the final steam hauled train from Weymouth (2.11pm) to Waterloo on 9th July 1967.

Sunday 2nd July

After enjoying another of my great aunt's excellent breakfasts, we were on our way again to Weymouth shed where, in the bright morning sunshine, we noted its residents for the last time. As with previous visits, there were far more steam (17) than diesels (2) present, but many of them stood cold and forlorn in the yard. Including one new arrival, 'West Country' Pacific No. 34021 Dartmoor, five engines were noted in steam. Before leaving the site, we turned to have one last look at the shed and, tinged with sadness, we started off for Bournemouth.

Taking some thirty photographs in the process, I made my last visit to Weymouth MPD on the morning of 2nd July. The one above is of an engine that had already completed over a million miles since entering service in September 1941, 'Merchant Navy' No. 35003 Royal Mail. Regarded by a number of drivers as the freest steaming member of its class, six days earlier, with the late Fred Burridge on the regulator, the Pacific reached 106mph between Winchfield and Fleet. In time to come, this would be regarded as the last authenticated speed in excess of 100mph achieved by a steam engine in the UK.

On the same morning 'Battle of Britain' class No. 34089 602 Squadron rests inside Weymouth MPD shed building. In the background, next to the single diesel unit, is 'West Country' Pacific No. 34093 Saunton.

Above. The most travelled member of the 'Merchant Navy' class: No. 35007 Aberdeen Commonwealth at the side of the shed building, Weymouth MPD on 2nd July 1967. Entering traffic in June 1942, the engine would be withdrawn on 9th July 1967 having completed 1,318,765 miles. Below. On the same day, having worked the BR 12.15pm 'Farewell to Steam' special from Waterloo to Bournemouth, Bullied Pacific No. 35028 Clan Line has moved on to shed to be serviced.

Immediately after arriving at Bournemouth Central we were greeted by the sight of 'West Country' pacific No. 34025 Whimple slowly entering the station with its train from London (possibly 8.30am ex-Waterloo). Once photographed, we left the engine resting in the station and made for the depot. In the yard we found two engines in steam, standard 4-6-0 No. 73020 and Ivatt 2-6-2T No. 41224 and in steam, too, inside the shed building, were 'West Country' No. 34037 Clovelly, and standard 2-6-4T's, No's. 80011and 80146. After the arrival of Clan Line on shed, a total of 11 steam locos were present representing 6 different classes.

1967 (Farewell to Oliver Bulleid's Pacifics)

The next two hours or so were spent on Central station. Amongst a number of movements, we witnessed the arrival of two BR sponsored 'Farewell to Steam' specials headed by 'Merchant Navy' class engines No's. 35008 Orient Line and 35028 Clan Line. The former loco proceeded to Weymouth while Clan Line terminated at Bournemouth and moved on to the shed where I photographed her in the yard. They both carried the normal headcode arrangement with no additional headboard announcing that they were commemorating the end of steam, albeit a week early. The final entry in my notebook reminds me that the down Bournemouth Belle was hauled by Brush Type '4' No. D1926 and, amongst the Pullman cars I noted, were Aquila, Lucille, Phyllis and Ursula. We packed our cameras and notebooks away and left for Salisbury to experience our very last visit to a Southern Region steam shed.

Once allocated a wide range of locomotives of the LSWR and Southern Railway, including several of the well-known 'King Arthur' class, Salisbury now had only a handful of working steam on which to call. Even at this late hour, it did remain, according to reports, as having the cleanest Pacifics on the South Western Division of the Southern Region. And, as if to confirm this, we found four or five such engines in extremely presentable external condition. The pick of the bunch, though, was 'Battle of Britain' class No. 34052 Lord Dowding, a Salisbury engine since 1951. Needless to say, she was photographed from several angles and also with Dennis and yours truly on the footplate. Her final passenger turn would occur five days later when she would be in charge of the 7.06pm Basingstoke to Eastleigh. Amongst a total of 9 steam representing 3 different varieties, three engines were in steam: No. 34052, which would be the last SR steam loco in normal service I would capture on film, standard 2-6-0 No. 76007 and 'Battle of Britain' class No. 34060 25 Squadron.

Waterloo's steam sunset would come a week later but, for me, this day would represent the end of another chapter in the decline of steam.

Salisbury MPD, 2nd July 1967. 'Battle of Britain' class No. 34052 Lord Dowding is the main subject of this and the following two pictures taken during our final visit to the shed. Dennis is peering out from the cab (next left) while I can be seen in a similar pose (next right). The locos spotless appearance was testament to the commitment, dedication and determination of the shed's staff to turn out their engines in such superb condition, despite the fact that the end of steam was so near, and, more importantly for some, the fact that redundancy was only the matter of a few days away.

It was now time for Dennis and me to go our separate ways. After dropping him off at Salisbury station, I headed north, now of course without any good reason to break my journey - there were no steam sheds left en-route; Dennis, however, would record a few more steam workings on his way to and during a brief stay after his arrival at Waterloo. Contrary to speculation that some of its more serviceable engines might be transferred elsewhere, steam would have its final fling on the SR over the next few days; all remaining steam stock would be withdrawn by the start of the new timetable on 10th July.

After returning from our southern steam bash, I developed the black and white films I'd taken, and waited eagerly for the return of the colour films deposited with the local chemist. I also prepared myself for starting work full-time at Fordigraph Ltd., the company mum worked for and which, through its relocation, had acted as the catalyst for moving from Birmingham to Droitwich. While this would enable me to pay for more trips either by scooter or train, it also meant that, like Dennis, I would not have the freedom to travel when I wanted to. I was also playing cricket regularly at weekends and of course seeing my girlfriend. Even so, about five weeks after the Southern Trip I would manage to get a couple of days off work and tag them on to a weekend. This meant I could fit in another steam trip, see Jackie and play cricket on the Sunday!

With thoughts of tomorrow witnessing the last day of steam on the Southern Region never far away, I visited both Saltley and Tyseley MPD's on the evening of 8th July. Still looking very much like a steam shed, the former now catered for diesels only, the last three remaining '8F's having now made their final journey to the scrapyard. Tyseley in contrast, was still playing host to preserved 'Castle' 4-6-0 No. 7029 Clun Castle and 0-6-0PT No. 1638 and, on this occasion, providing a welcome for several other steam locos that had been despatched from their home territory for wheel re-profiling. The full compliment of steam present was as follows: No's 1628, 7029, 44902, 45368, 45382, 45437, 48107, 73128, 73135 and 75048. 'Black 5' No. 44902, a Kingmoor engine, was inside the diesel depot occupying the WTL.

August

The few areas where BR was still employing steam were now all north of Birmingham. Having planned my itinerary a few days earlier, I set off initially for Oxley, on the morning of Thursday 10th August. Even though it had closed to steam five months earlier, I discovered 'Black 5' No. 44805, last seen on steam heating duties in Oxley carriage sidings in early March, and '9F' No. 92088 in the company of a 'Warship' and two Brush Type '4's. The steam locos, although cold, were both still active and listed in capital stock, so I presume they had recently worked freights into the area.

From Wolverhampton I took the A449 first to Stafford and then on to the potteries town of Stoke on Trent. The shed here had officially closed to steam on Monday 7th August, but there were still 21 steam present representing 4 different varieties. Standard 4MT 4-6-0s were most evident with a total of nine of this class awaiting removal to the breakers yard. 'Black 5' No. 45270 was noted in steam and within a couple of days would become a Crewe South engine, only to be withdrawn about a month later.

'Black 5' No. 44661 started its revenue earning service in June 1949. Now, on the closure of its home shed, Stoke, where it is pictured, its days of employment have finally come to an end.

10th August 1967.

On the same day, while smoke drifts lazily from 'Black 5' No. 45270, former North Staffordshire Railway shed, Stoke, witnesses another sunset. Its original 1935 shed code, 5D, was retained up until official closure on 7th August 1967.

The sun was sinking low in the sky when I left the depot. There would be just enough time to cover the eighteen miles to Crewe South and bunk the shed before nightfall. Indeed, by the time I arrived, what little light was left was fading fast. Care was needed while moving around the depot, noting the locos present and trying to take a few pictures. The shed was full of steam, however, with 7 classes represented amongst the 80 engines logged (see appendix 20). Most evident were Stanier 'Black 5's (39) and '8F's (27). Only three standard class engines were present, '8P' No. 71000 Duke of Gloucester, 'Britannia' Pacific No. 70029 Shooting Star and 4MT 4-6-0 No. 75029.

Twenty-three movements were observed while I spent the night of $10^{th}/11^{th}$ on Crewe Station. Except for two freight trains with 'Black 5' No. 44962 and '8F' No. 48742 in charge, all of these involved diesel or electric locos. By 5.30am, after visiting North Stabling Point and the Diesel Depot, I was once again taking pictures in Crewe South and recording four overnight arrivals, one of which was 'Britannia Pacific' No. 70035 Rudyard Kipling.

'Britannia' Pacific No. 70035 Rudyard Kipling in Crewe South MPD soon after sunrise on the 11th August 1967. First allocated to Norwich Thorpe when new in December 1952, the Pacific remained an Eastern Region loco until its move from March shed to Kingmoor in December 1963. Withdrawal would come at the end of the year on the closure of 12A. Disposal would take place at T.W. Ward, Inverkeithing, in March 1968.

Heading north for a further eighteen miles I reached my next destination, Northwich. Prior to visiting the shed I looked in at the station and noted Stanier 2-8-0 No. 48727 with a freight train. The depot had never had a big allocation of steam motive power, especially since the early 60's, and this had now settled at approximately fifteen, so it was encouraging to find a total of 25 on shed. The variety of motive power wasn't great, though, with only '8F's (21), Ivatt 2-6-2's (3) and a solitary '9F' present. Eight engines were in steam and one of these, '8F' No. 48151, was recorded with a footnote describing her as being very clean.

Manchester was next in my sights and its three remaining steam sheds. The first on my programme, Trafford Park, was host to 35 steam, but with only five prepared and ready for duty. Three varieties were noted, '8F' (10), 'Black 5' (20) and Fairburn 2-6-4T (5). The shed had had a reputation for unkempt and dirty engines in the past, but now it's standard of engine cleaning pretty much applied to all other remaining steam depots too.

Representing 4 different classes, a total of 48 steam were logged on shed at Patricroft. Exactly one third of the engines present were in steam. Thirty-two standard 5MT 4-6-0s were noted, together with 'Britannia' Pacific No. 70023 Venus, not looking at all as beautiful as her name once suggested! Another 'Britannia', No. 70004 William Shakespeare, was one of the 39 steam I found on shed at Newton Heath, the last of the Manchester depots I visited. Here I recorded 5 varieties with Stanier's '8F's (12) and Black 5's (19) dominating. Two more of his 4-6-0's, No's. 44734 and 45076, were observed while waiting at Dean Lane station and, on arrival at Victoria, another 'Britannia', my fifth of the day, No. 70024 Vulcan, at the head of a passenger train.

Leaving Victoria I set off for Bolton on my scooter. This would be the last but one shed visit for the day. Here I logged 4 different classes amongst the 31 steam present. Two locos, 'Black 5' No. 45110 and standard 5MT 73014 had recently been spruced up and noted as being very clean. Predictably, Stanier locos were in the majority - a trend that would become more familiar as the year wore on. The final shed, Springs Branch, housed 47 steam: there wasn't a lot of diversity here either; only two standard 2-6-0's and two Ivatt 2-6-0's together with eighteen '8F's, and nineteen 'Black 5's making up the 4 different classes represented. Sixteen engines were recorded in steam.

Stanier '8F's No's. 48151 and 48063 next to Northwich shed's turntable on 11th August 1967. Destiny would differ greatly for the two 2-8-0's; the latter, following what would be its final reallocation (to Heaton Mersey) would be withdrawn in March 1968 and be cut up, while the former, after being rescued from Barry scrapyard in November 1975, would eventually be restored and passed to work on the mainline again in 1987.

Left. At one time a local engine for me, Stanier 'Black 5' No. 44807, once allocated to Monument Lane and Aston, Birmingham, rests under the lamps in Trafford Park shed on 11th August 1967. Having been in Crewe works for five weeks from 1st September 1966 undergoing a non-classified overhaul, the 4-6-0 would not quite make it until the end of steam on BR and would be withdrawn in March 1968.

First allotted to Old Oak Common when new, 'Britannia' No. 70023 Venus is seen here in Patricroft MPD on 11th August 1967. From entering traffic in August 1951 until withdrawal in December 1967, the engine would be reallocated no fewer than fifteen times to eleven different sheds, including the Southern Region shed, Salisbury (see caption next to picture on page 144).

Transferred for the final time, from Stoke to Patricroft, the previous March, Stanier '8F' No. 48453 is seen in her home shed on 11th August 1967. The engine would continue in service for another eight months before being withdrawn.

Sunlight and shadow: standard 5MT No. 73160 sits inside Patricroft, its home shed, on 11th August 1967. Originally allocated to Blaydon when new in January 1957, the loco had been transferred from Oxley to Patricroft in April 1965 and would remain working from here until withdrawal in November.

Ashford-built Stanier '8F' No. 48620 was found resting in its home shed, Newton Heath, on 11th August 1967. The 2-8-0 would cease working on the closure of the depot on 1st July 1968.

Inside Newton Heath on the same day was 'Black 5' No. 45234 having just finished a turn of duty. There would not be many more: within two weeks the 4-6-0 would be condemned.

Not quite as it appeared when working The Golden Arrow! 'Britannia' No. 70004 William Shakespeare waits to be coaled while on Newton Heath shed on 11th August and (below) following servicing, about to leave the depot. What a pity the last few of this class were not being kept in the same condition as Bullied's Pacifics had been while working out of Salisbury, as witnessed only last month. Interestingly, following collision damage, the loco was the last Pacific to be overhauled at Darlington works being outshopped in February 1965.

'Black 5's No's. 44822 and 44891 in Newton Heath MPD, their home shed, on 11th August 1967. The former would be withdrawn about two months later, while the latter would continue working until the closure of the shed to steam the following June.

On the same day, standard 5MT No. 73156 is seen standing in the yard of Bolton shed. Built at Doncaster Works in December 1956, the engine would be eleven years old when taken out of service on 27th October. Fortunately, it would be sold to Woodham Brothers, Barry, and after being rescued from there in 1986, would eventually move to the Great Central Railway where, at the time of writing, it is undergoing restoration.

Front ends: Bolton MPD, 11th August 1967.

1967 (Farewell to Oliver Bulleid's Pacifics)

Clockwise. With a fine array of signals in the background, standard 4MT No. 76077 is ready to move off Springs Branch (Wigan) MPD on the afternoon of 11th August 1967. Still looking refreshed, the 2-6-0 had been cleaned a week earlier ready to take charge of an LCGB (North West Branch) Brake Van Railtour on 5th August. Also on shed the same day was Stanier '8F' No. 48715. Built in 1944, this 2-8-0 would remain in service until the end of steam on BR. Standard '9F's No's 92152 (nearest the camera) and 92050 inside the shed building, Warrington MPD, on 12th August 1967. First allocated to Saltley, but now based at Birkenhead, the former engine was completing what would prove to be its final year in service. Transferred to Warrington during the previous week, No. 92050 would be withdrawn in the matter of a few weeks.

Stanier 'Black 5' No. 44674 and '8F' No. 48373 in Warrington MPD on the same day, 12th August. The depot would close on 2nd October, and the yard would be cleared, but the shed building would remain standing for at least a further seven years. Note the date (1957) on the front of the shed roof, which was inscribed after BR had completed its replacement.

On the Saturday morning, after spending the night under canvas, I made an early start for St Helens and Sutton Oak Shed. Closed about three weeks earlier, it still harboured 12 steam belonging to 3 different classes. At least nine of the engines would be found further work at other depots such as Speke Junction and Springs Branch. My second and last shed visit of the day, Warrington, had about six weeks to go before closure. The depot was host to 15 steam representing 3 different classes, with five engines fired and ready for work. From here I set out for Birmingham. I had logged a total of 363 steam and in the process seen 13 different varieties of locomotive. Stanier designed engines totalled two hundred and sixty-three; almost 75% of the steam locos recorded.

I made my last trip to Derby for its Works open day on Saturday 26th August. Once the hub of the Midland Railway it had gone through lots of motive power changes like many other great railway centres. Seven years earlier I had recorded a total of 133 steam in the works and shed, but the replacement of steam had gathered pace since the BR/Sulzer 'Peaks' had taken over the work of the 'Jubilees' and 'Black 5's' during 1962 and was now complete. As the shed had closed over six months earlier, on the same day as Saltley, I didn't expect any steam to be present and indeed this proved to be the case. Derby station had continued to see the isolated steam passenger working however, and as recently as 10th August Trafford Park 'Black 5' No. 44851 had hauled the 8.35am Manchester-St. Pancras as far as here.

Nowadays these workings were most unusual, and the general paucity of steam was further emphasised by 'Britannia' Pacific, No. 70013 Oliver Cromwell, being the sole representative of this form of motive power on display. As well as photographing the engine, I queued with lots of other visitors to access the footplate and gain a driver's view from the cab. Two years after my visit the steam shed would be demolished, leaving only the offices, although part of the site would be converted to a diesel refuelling/stabling point. Interestingly, one of four withdrawn diesels noted in the works this day was Derby designed and built No. 10000. This engine, withdrawn in December 1963 after being active for sixteen years, had been earmarked for preservation, but would be sold for scrap in 1968.

September

Dennis had been holidaying in Scotland during the last two weeks of August, but on his return home we were soon considering another trip north. Reports of plans to curtail the use of steam in the West Riding suggested that certainly by the end of October sheds such as Holbeck, Low Moor and Royston would no longer be using this form of traction. We had heard, too, that the omens weren't good for steam to continue much longer in the northeast, so we decide to fit in visits to West Hartlepool and Sunderland the last two sheds with an active steam allocation in this area.

Travelling by scooter again, I met Dennis at Derby Station on the evening of Friday 15th September after he finished work. We camped close to Royston, north of Barnsley, and made the short journey to the shed early on the Saturday morning.

Royston would be the last shed on the Eastern Region with an allocation of steam power - about 20 Stanier '8F's. A total of 25 steam were recorded during our visit, twenty-four of which were not unexpectedly of the 2-8-0 variety, with nine of these in steam. The other engine present was '9F' No. 92082. The depot would provide one of the '8F's noted inside the shed building, No. 48276, to carry out the final duty for an ER-based steam engine on 4th November. She would work the 3.00pm freight turn from Carlton North Sidings, near Barnsley to Goole, and return light engine. Once back home, she would face immediate withdrawal. Two days later, on 6th November, the shed would close and dieselisation of the Eastern Region would be complete.

Fitted with a small snowplough, Stanier '8F' No. 48622 stands inside Royston MPD on 16th September 1967. Except for a brief period working out of Toton, from September 1948 the 2-8-0 was based at Stourton, and was transferred to Royston, its present home shed, earlier in January. Withdrawal would come later in November on the closure of 55D.

With its duties now in the hands of the new diesel depots at Knottingley and Healey Mills, the next shed on our itinerary, Wakefield, had closed on 3rd July and its steam allocation put into store. Surprisingly, over two months later, there were still 42 steam on shed representing no fewer than 9 different classes, including a solitary 'Jubilee' No. 45675 Hardy. This engine, withdrawn at the end of May, was reinstated a week or so later and managed another three weeks or so in revenue earning service before its final farewell. Oh, and this time Dennis didn't split his trousers getting into the shed!

Top. On 16th September 1967, 'B1' No. 61123 was still waiting to be removed from Wakefield shed to be broken up. The engine had come to the end of its working life eight months earlier in January.

Above. Transferred, for the last time, from Tebay to the Eastern Region in April, and then specifically to Low Moor MPD in May, Fairburn 2-6-4T No. 42251 is seen in the yard of its home depot on the same day. Two weeks later the shed would close completely and the tank, together with several others of its class, would be withdrawn.

From the silence exuded by the stored engines of Wakefield shed we set off for Normanton. Here, amongst the 21 locos present, we found two in steam both 'Black 5's'. Other classes represented were WD, Fairburn 2-6-4T, Stanier 2-6-4T and Ivatt 4MT 2-6-0. En-route to Leeds we called in at Low Moor and found 22 steam on shed representing 5 different classes. Three engines were in steam No's. 42072, 42251 and 45208.

After a brief stop at Leeds City Station, revealing 'Black 5' No. 45428 waiting for its next turn of duty, we were soon making our way round Holbeck. A total of 30 steam were on shed and eight of the thirteen 'Black 5's' present were found fired ready for duty. Worthy of note was the presence of the following: 'Britannias', No's. 70004 William Shakespeare, 70023 Venus, 70025 Western Star and 70029 Shooting Star, two 'Jubilees', No's. 45593 Kolhapur (in steam) and 45562 Alberta and 'K1', No. 62005. Altogether 7 different classes of locomotive were recorded with a total of 16 engines in steam.

York MPD, our next destination, had been closed to steam for three months by this time but luckily we found four engines here: inside the shed building was preserved 'A4' No. 60019 Bittern and in the yard 'K1' No. 62048, 'Q6' No. 63455 and WD No. 90200. For me this was once one of the most appealing sheds to visit and three years earlier I had logged sixty-eight steam representing thirteen different classes. How things had changed. This would be my final visit to the shed before it became the main part of the National Railway Museum.

Closed on the day of our visit, the next two sheds on our itinerary were the last to survive with an active steam allocation in the northeast district. West Hartlepool, the first we successfully made our way round, was home to 18 steam. Two classes were represented, Raven's 'Q6' 0-8-0 and Riddles' 'WD' 2-8-0 of which there were 15.

Sunderland the second depot had a total of 14 steam on shed representing 3 different classes. It had the same varieties seen at West Hartlepool plus five members of the 'J27' class, all of which had been transferred from Blyth earlier in May. Every one of the engines at both depots was cold. Leaving Sunderland we skirted Newcastle, and joined the A69, which would take us to Carlisle. We camped overnight north of the city at Blackford, the same site we had used before our tour of Scotland began last summer.

In steam and looking in pristine condition, 'Jubilee' No. 45593 Kolhapur is seen standing next to 'Britannia Pacific No 70023 Venus inside Holbeck roundhouse on 16th September 1967. Shortly after this date the 4-6-0 would move south to Tyseley - see page 151.

Home sheds in the past for 'K1' No. 62005 included Darlington, Ardsley, Heaton and York, but its final transfer, to Holbeck, was officially due to take place during the first week of October. Seen here inside Holbeck on 16th September 1967, the 2-6-0 appears to have arrived early. Withdrawn three months later on 30th December, the engine would gain further employment as a stationary boiler at ICI's North Tees Works. Purchased by a consortium, the 2-6-0 would eventually be donated to the NELPG for overhaul by the group's volunteers.

Contrasting front ends: Stanier '8F' No. 48399 and 'Britannia' No. 70025 Western Star standing in the yard of Holbeck shed on 16th September 1967. The 2-8-0 had a few days of its working life left while the Pacific would soldier on for a further three months working out of Kingmoor. Minus its original nameplates, someone had taken the time to preserve a little dignity for the engine by resurrecting its name neatly in chalk on the side of its smoke deflectors.

Raven 'Q6' 0-8-0 No. 63395, the last of its class to be overhauled at Darlington Works in September 1965, sits in the yard of Sunderland MPD on 16th September 1967. Together with sister engine No. 63387, the 0-8-0 had been withdrawn a week by the time this photograph was taken.

No. 63395, far left, has the company of two 'J27's No's. 65811 and 65894, both withdrawn at the same time as the 'Q6'. The latter, having worked the last diagrammed turn from the shed, would join the 0-8-0 in preservation after being purchased by the North Eastern Preservation Group.

Sunday 17th September. We were both looking forward to seeing the biggest collection of steam locos on one depot since we left the Midlands. Once again Kingmoor came up trumps and we recorded 101 steam on shed with 8 different varieties on view. Classes noted and number of engines of each type were as follows: Fairburn 2-6-4T (1), Ivatt 4MT 2-6-0 (3), 'Black 5' (48), 'Jinty' 0-6-0T (2), '8F' (10), 'Britannia' (22), standard 4MT 4-6-0 (2) and '9F' (13). Twenty-six engines were in steam. Included in the assembly of 'Black 5's was No. 45274, which had been withdrawn four months earlier on 13th May. This engine had been in one of the worst accidents involving this class of engine when it derailed at Sutton Coldfield station on 23rd January 1955. Two days later, following its removal to Aston shed, the 4-6-0 was towed to Crewe Works where extensive repairs were carried out, the engine returning to traffic three months later on 19th April.

Despite the fact that it had closed at the end of 1966, we decided to see if Upperby shed had any steam in store. And interestingly it did. A collection of 14 engines stood in the yard and between them represented 5 different classes. We thought that they were destined for the cutter's torch, but it transpired that six of them (No's. 44932, 45262, 45447, 48400, 75019 and 75027) would not be officially withdrawn until the end of steam on BR. It would appear, however, that 'Black 5's No's. 44932 and 45262 didn't actually return to traffic and, although allocated to Rose Grove on paper, remained in store at Kingmoor shed. I certainly didn't witness them working or laid-up at any time during my visits to the northwest during the final months of steam operation.

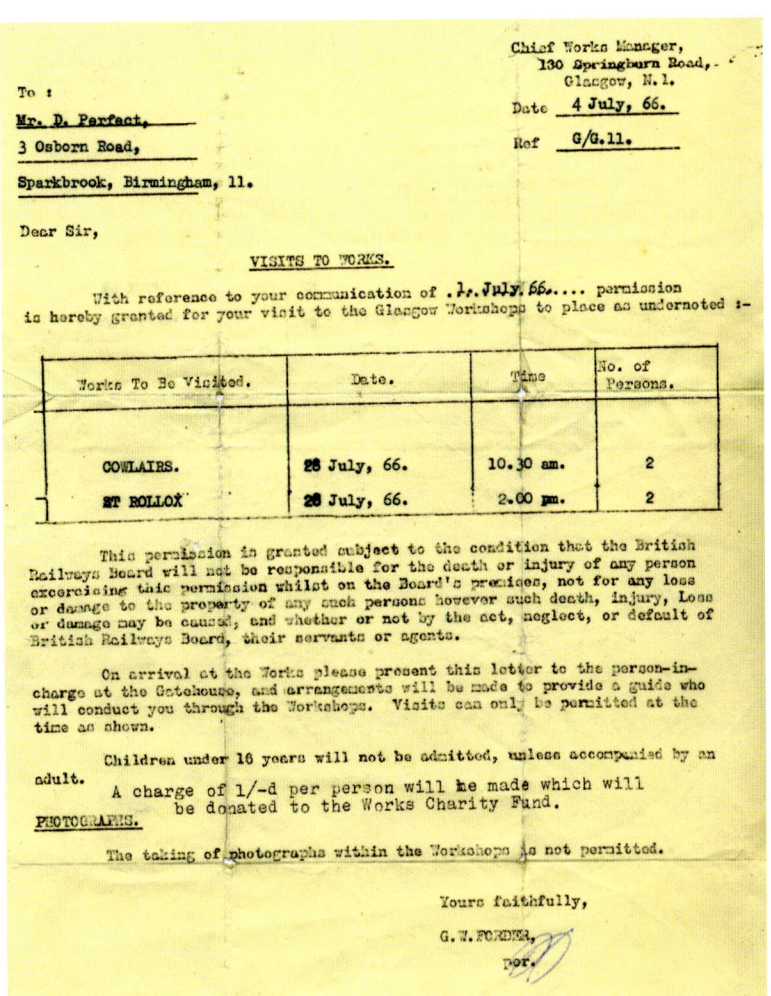

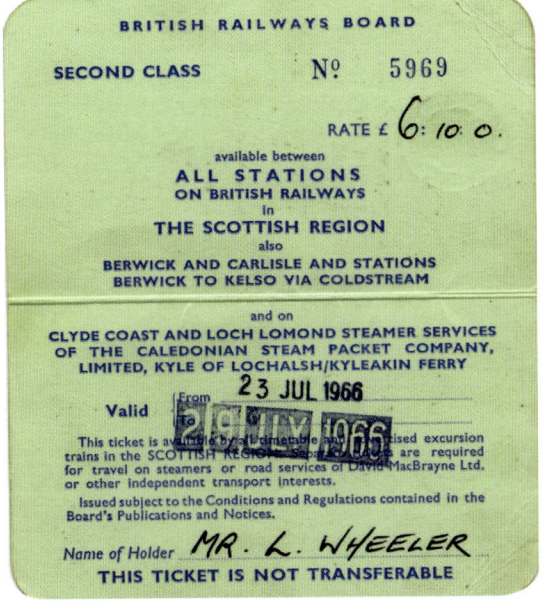

Top. The letter granting permission to visit Cowlairs and St Rollox Works while in Scotland at the end of July 1966 and (above) my Freedom of Scotland ticket valid for seven days of unlimited travel. Today (2016), such a ticket would cost approximately £114.

'A2' Pacific No. 60528 Tudor Minstrel takes a breather in St Margarets shed yard on 9th October 1965. Allocated to Dundee Tay Bridge at the time, its final home shed would be Aberdeen Ferryhill. The 4-6-2 would be withdrawn about a month before our visit to Scotland in July 1966 (see picture page 27). G. W. Sharpe. Author's collection.

Following the failure of 'V2' No. 60919, 'Black 5' No 45493 was called upon to substitute for the 2-6-2 on the LCGB Railtour on 3rd July 1966. Together with sister loco No. 44942, the Stanier engine had dominated the duties for the Poole-York service during April and May (see part one page 212) and, presumably, the Banbury-based 4-6-0 was still in the area and deemed a suitable replacement. Piloting 'West Country' Pacific No. 34100 Appledore the loco is seen with the Yeovil Pen Mill - Weymouth Junction leg of the tour. Author's collection.

Above. 'A4' No. 60024 Kingfisher moves off Aberdeen Ferryhill shed and will soon begin her journey to Glasgow with another 3hr express. It is now very late in the day for this and the only other 'streak' still in employment, No. 60019 Bittern. With a shortage of motive power at Ferryhill, the Pacific had remained in service as standby and would be called upon after its official withdrawal on 3rd September to head two further expresses (see page 63) Unlike the Glasgow allocated 'A4's, which were left somewhat neglected by comparison, the staff at 61B continued to look after their Pacifics right up until the end. Below. On a lovely summer's day, Kingfisher takes on water in Forfar station while in charge of one of the Aberdeen - Glasgow expresses. Both August 1966. Author's collection.

Gresley 'J38' No. 65914 sits below Thornton shed's imposing coaling stage on a bright summer's day in August 1966. The 0-6-0 was allocated to Edinburgh St Margarets for many years, but from November 1964 would see out its days as a 62A engine. Withdrawal would come three months after this photograph was taken. Below. Photographed on Perth shed on 25th July 1966 (page 31), 'Black 5' No. 44997 is seen standing at the side of St Margarets on 8th July 1967. The Stanier 4-6-0 had been officially withdrawn two months earlier, in May, while allocated to 63A, but further observations noted in Railway Magazine confirm that the loco was still working out of Perth at the end of May, and that it was being used as a stationary boiler at 64A at the end of June. By August, however, the loco was recorded on Perth shed carrying a board marked 'To Motherwell Machinery Scrapyard'. Interestingly, the RCTS book A Detailed History of the Stanier Class 5 4-6-0's suggests its disposal taking place at J. Mc Williams & Sons, Shettleston. Both Author's collection.

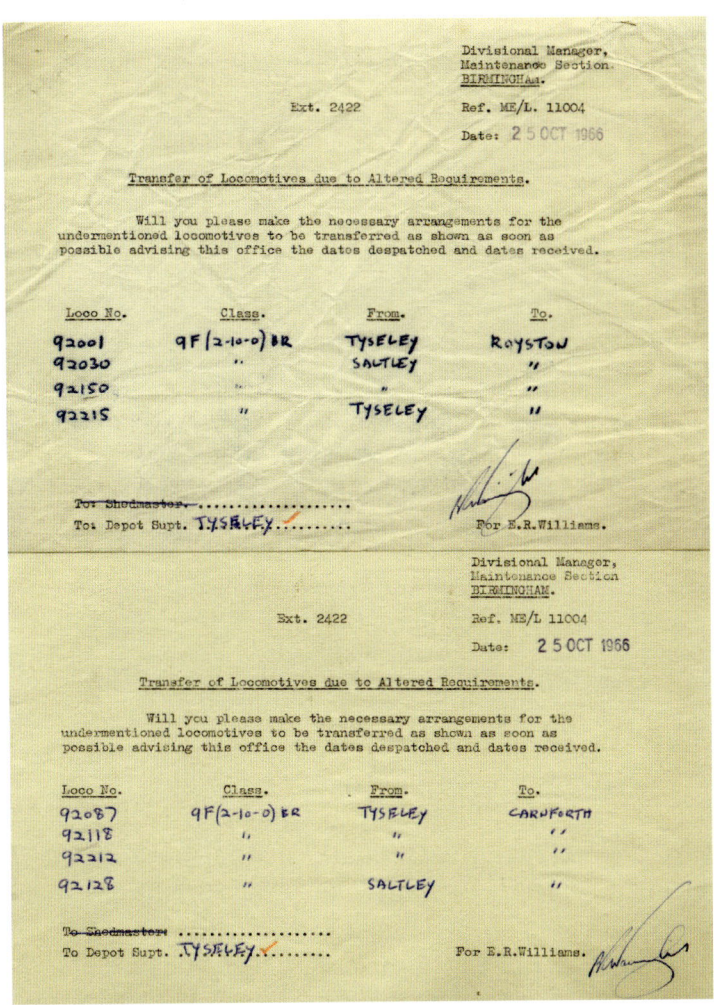

The two items of correspondence shown opposite were sent to Tyseley MPD two weeks before it was due to close to steam. 'Paper transfers' were often suspected of happening over the years, and I believe the top communication may be an example. Royston MPD of the N.E.R. is clearly the next proposed home shed for the four '9F's, but this depot was due to close at the same time as Tyseley on 6th November. According to the Motive Power Report in Modern Railways (January 1967), all four engines by this date were allocated to Wakefield. When the engines were eventually despatched from Tyseley, it seems quite likely that arrangements for their transfer had changed and they would never reach Royston, but go directly to 56A.

Another circular that would arrive weekly on the shedmaster's desk at this time would be the alteration list to The Locomotive Stock Book dated 14th September 1963. Opposite is an example received at Tyseley dated 30th September 1966, which includes information regarding engine transfers, new locos into service and those withdrawn for breaking up. Mentioned in my October report for visits to the shed, the first two engines listed under deletions, No's 9610 and 9630, have their fate officially confirmed.

The Final Few Years of British Steam Part Two (Colour Section)

Above. Just days after being out shopped from Crewe Works following a Heavy General overhaul, standard 2-10-0 No. 92029 is seen in Kettering MPD in August 1962. Two months later the loco would become a Saltley engine - the first of three periods allocated to 21A/2E. Converted from a Franco-Crosti boilered engine in August 1960, the '9F' would be transferred to Birkenhead from 2E in December 1966. Withdrawal would come at the beginning of November 1967. Below. Completed on 21st January 1967, form BR 9214, shows that standard 5MT No. 73130 (picture page 71) returned to service on 29th December 1966. Both engine and tender wheels had been turned on the profiling machine without, it would appear, any problems. However, what is interesting is for how long the engine remained in traffic, if indeed it was put back to work at all. Records show that the ten-year-old 4-6-0 was withdrawn sometime the following month, around the time the repair sheet had been completed, and was disposed of by J. Cashmore of Great Bridge.

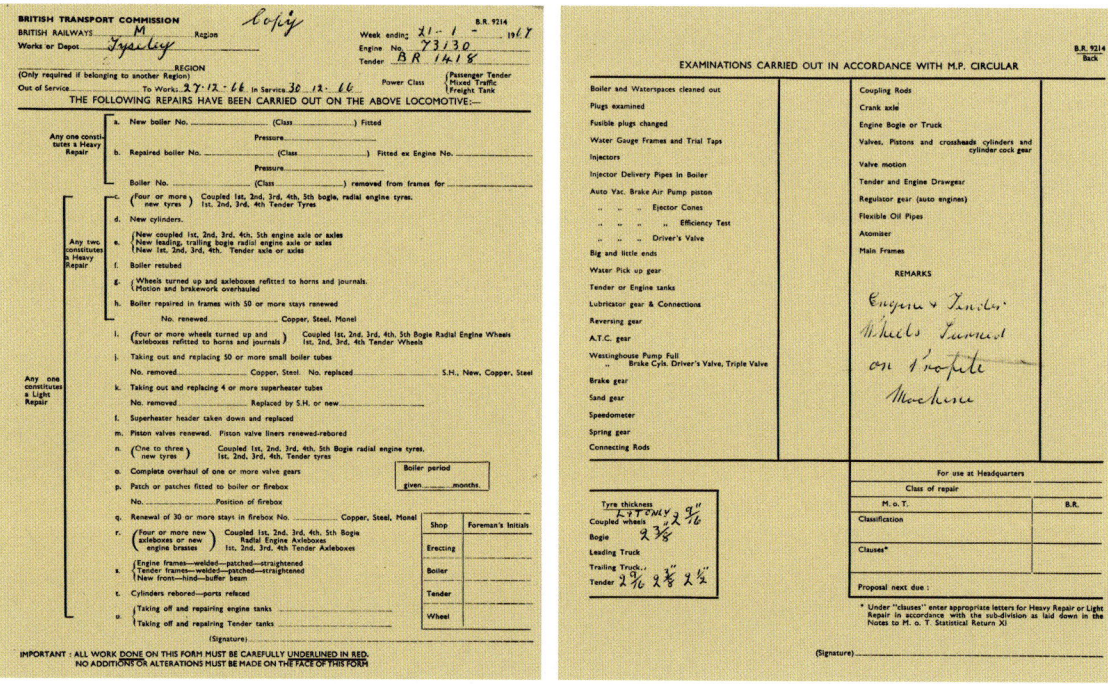

134 The Final Few Years of British Steam Part Two (Colour Section)

Having earlier worked The Jubilee Preservation Society special 'The Border Countryman' from Leeds, 'Jubilee' 4-6-0 No. 45562 Alberta rests in the yard of Carlisle Kingmoor on 25th February 1967. As the last representative of the class, she would be involved in at least five more specials before being withdrawn on 4th November 1967. Below. Standard 5MT No. 73065 takes a break from duties in the yard of Salisbury MPD on 27th June 1967. The 4-6-0 entered traffic in October 1954, and was allocated to Millhouses. After twelve months working out of Canklow, the loco headed south to Eastleigh. Further reallocations to Feltham, Nine Elms, Guildford and finally 70A again, would take place before withdrawal twelve days after this photograph was taken. Both Author's collection.

Top. 'West Country' Pacific No. 34024 Tamar Valley waits for the 'right away' to leave Southampton on 25th March 1967. Above. 'Merchant Navy' No. 35028 Clan Line featured regularly in my notebooks during my trips to the Southern Region. Here on 31st May 1967, she is seen preparing to depart from Weymouth for Waterloo.

Following the departure of No. 35028 Clan Line for Waterloo (above), Birmingham R.C. & W. Co. Type '3' diesel No. D6536 leaves with a similar service (below). Fortunately, I was in the right place at the right time to capture at the same instant the arrival of 'West Country' Pacific No. 34040 Crewkerne coasting into Weymouth station at the head of a down service from London.

The Final Few Years of British Steam Part Two (Colour Section)

On a splendid summer's day, 'West Country' Pacific No. 34040 Crewkerne returns to Weymouth shed after bringing in its express train seen above. After watering and coaling, the engine is slowly moved on to the depot's turntable (below) to be repositioned ready to take up her next turn of duty. Withdrawn four weeks later on 2nd July she would be disposed of at Cashmore's, Newport in March 1968.

Top. While standard 4MT 2-6-0 No. 76009 relaxes in Weymouth MPD, 'West Country' No. 34024 Tamar Valley passes by with an up passenger train. Above. Horwich-built standard 4MT No. 76011 simmers on Bournemouth MPD, the last of its shed allocations. With a light axle loading, these engines had wide route availability. Withdrawn approximately six weeks after this photograph was taken, the engine would be hauled to Birds of Morriston to be broken up. Both 31st May 1967.

Top. Ivatt 2-6-2T No. 41224 is caught resting between duties in the yard of Bournemouth MPD on 1st July 1967. Previously allocated to more northerly depots such as Bangor, Warrington Dallam and Monument Lane, the tank gradually moved south, arriving at Eastleigh in December 1962. Further transfers followed until it found itself allotted to Bournemouth in November 1964. Above. Allocated to Eastleigh in September 1964 (its last home shed), 'West Country' No. 34093 Saunton stands in the yard of Weymouth MPD later on the afternoon of the same day.

'West Country' Pacific No. 34021 Dartmoor was found very much in steam in the yard of Weymouth MPD on 2nd July 1967. A bright red glow can be seen emanating from the open firebox door - the well-prepared fire has ensured the production of plenty of steam, resulting in the engine's safety valves lifting.

Left. Built at Swindon in September 1955, and first allocated to Dover, standard 5MT No. 75068 seems to have inherited the ability of the chameleon and taken on the colour of the ground in the yard of Weymouth shed. Fitted with a double blastpipe and chimney in January 1961, the 4-6-0 would be withdrawn a week after this picture was taken and so not quite achieve twelve years service. Disposal would take place the following February at Birds Commercial Motors, Risca, near Newport, south Wales.

The Final Few Years of British Steam Part Two (Colour Section)

Top. A sight to lift the spirits of any steam enthusiast: Crewe South MPD, spring 1967.
Above. First allocated to Stratford in January 1953, 'Britannia' No. 70038 Robin Hood finds itself at the head of the SLS (Midland Area) special on 2nd July 1967. It is seen passing the famous Rippon Brothers Works, Huddersfield, where Britain's oldest coachbuilder would remain for a further four years. Noted for making bodies for such companies as Bentley, Daimler and Lanchester, Rippon Brothers most prestigious association was with Rolls Royce for whom it built nearly all of the bodies of its cars until 1958. The Pacific would be withdrawn six weeks later and be cut up before the end of the year. Both author's collection.

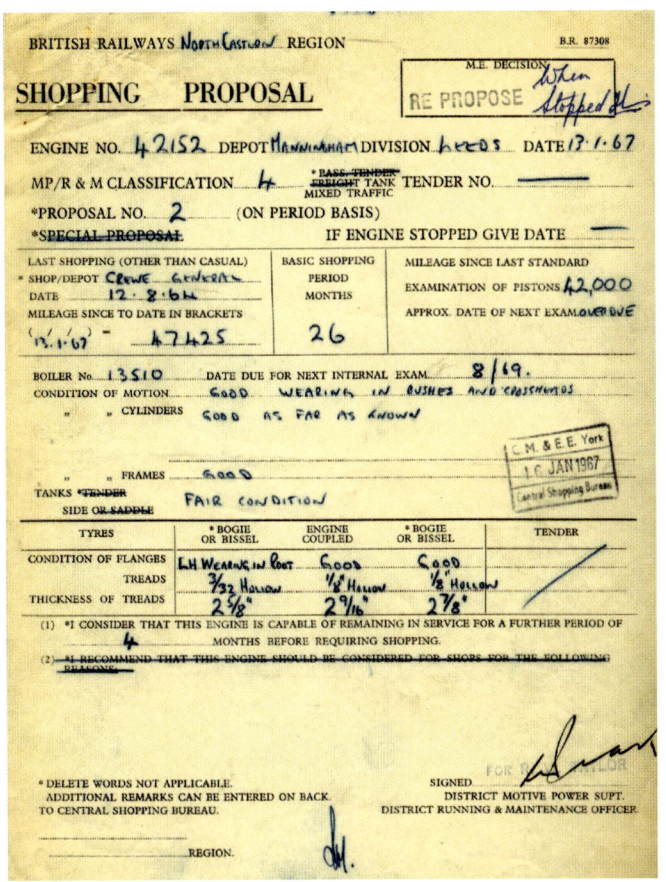

By 1st October 1967, when Fairburn 2-6-4T No. 42152 headed the last steam hauled Bradford-Leeds service, its days of usefulness were at an end. Its last shopping proposal form and safety valve certificate issued at Crewe works are shown left and below. Interestingly, the date given for its next internal boiler exam, August 1969, would prove to be exactly a year after steam had finished on BR.

According to the 1969 RCTS Locomotive Stock Book, 'B1' No. 61337 was the last of its class to be withdrawn. Built by North British Locomotive Company, Glasgow, in August 1948, the 4-6-0 had its final overhaul at Darlington in November 1964. With its imminent demise (it was withdrawn by the end of September 1967), it is surprising that it should be deemed necessary to carry out a boiler inspection at the beginning of the month. However, the report opposite confirms this, and states that the boiler is fit for service for a further six months and that its next internal exam would not be due until November 1969. Both the 'B1' and the Fairburn tank can be seen pictured standing in the yard of Low Moor MPD on Saturday, 14th October 1967 on page 150.

The Final Few Years of British Steam Part Two (Colour Section)

Built at Crewe in August 1951, 'Britannia' Pacific No. 70023 Venus begins her attack on Shap Fell. In May 1953, while allocated to Old Oak Common, the engine had been called upon to work on the Southern Region to assist with the shortage of 'Merchant Navy' class locos while they were inspected for possible crank axle cracks. Following its brief allocation to Salisbury, the 4-6-2 moved back to the Western Region. Transferred to the London Midland Region in September 1961, the Pacific would remain an LMR loco until withdrawal at the end of the month

Assisting the 'Britannia' with its mixed freight train is standard 4-6-0 No. 75030. Built almost two years after the Pacific and first allocated to Bletchley, it, too, would cease working at the end of December following the closure of its home shed, Tebay. Both 9th December 1967.

September contd.

Travelling down the A6 we soon arrived at the small village of Tebay. The shed here provided assistance in the form of banking engines for freight and passenger trains needing help up Shap Fell. The frequently used class 4 2-6-4Ts had now been replaced by standard class 4MT 4-6-0's, and we found four of these (No's. 75024, 75030, 75037 and 75038) on shed during our brief visit.

By this time many steam sheds were cluttered and untidy, but Tebay seemed to have an air of orderliness about it when we visited on 17th September 1967. Inside the building, with chalked numbers in place of their original cast ones, are standard 4MT's No's. 75059 (left) and 75030. The former had been withdrawn earlier in July but the latter would remain working until the shed's closure at the end of December.

An hour or so after leaving Tebay we were making our way round Carnforth MPD where we recorded 9 different varieties of steam amongst the 67 locos present. Engine totals for each type were as follows: Fairburn 2-6-4T (1), Ivatt 4MT 2-6-0 (1), 'Black 5' (32), Ivatt 2MT 2-6-0 (4), Stanier '8F' (7), 'Britannia' Pacific (3), standard 5MT 4-6-0 (1), standard 4MT 4-6-0 (13) and standard '9F' (5). Twenty-five locos were in steam.

Continuing our journey south along the A6 we eventually reached Preston and Lostock Hall. This shed, like Carnforth, would last almost another twelve months before closure. We logged fourteen locos in steam amongst the 46 present with a reasonable spread of different classes totalling 8 in all. Over a quarter of the steam present appeared to be out of use, with thirteen engines in store in the open. Included in these were four standard 2MT 2-6-0's No's. 78020, 78021, 78037 and 78041 and 2-6-4T's No's. 42187 and 42611.

Our last shed visit for the day, Springs Branch, had 40 steam in residence representing 6 different classes. I recorded eight engines in steam and seven appearing to have been put into store. Stanier '8F's (18) and 'Black 5's (16) dominated. When looking at the grand total of 434 steam recorded during the weekend, Stanier designed engines accounted for 224 of them. Considering how late it was in the day for steam power, we had been fortunate to see, no doubt for the last time, more than twenty varieties of locomotive design (see appendix 21 for locos noted on shed).

Above. Derby built Stanier 4-6-0 No. 44822, of Newton Heath shed, waits for its turn to be serviced while standing in the yard of Carnforth MPD on 17th September 1967. In the background, about to be coaled is Edge Hill based '8F' No. 48012. The 'Black 5' had roughly a month to go before withdrawal, but the 2-8-0 would not cease work until April 1968.
Below. On the same day, 'Black 5' No. 44905, was found dead, deep inside the shed building. Seen earlier in the summer, very much in steam and working hard, the 4-6-0 has just passed through the remains of Farington station (closed in March 1960) with a mixed freight. Following withdrawal at the beginning of December, Albert Draper & Sons of Hull would eventually dispose of the engine. Author's collection.

October

I promised myself that I would return to south Yorkshire as soon as I could and four weeks later on 14th October, I caught the 6.40am from Birmingham New Street to Bradford Forster Square. I knew the trip wouldn't produce many working engines - it would be more of a glimpse of mainly stored locos in sheds now closed to steam. Indeed, the first steam locos noted had been condemned and were standing in a siding outside Chesterfield, presumably en-route to Garnham, Harris & Elton a nearby scrapyard. I may not have logged them all, but did manage to record the following: No's. 61002 Impala, 61255, 61289, 62023, 62048, 63426, 75055, 77002 and 77012.

I alighted at Normanton where my shed bash would begin, and by 10.30am had recorded 26 steam representing the following classes: Fairburn 2-6-4T (7), Stanier 2-6-4T (1), 'WD' (4), 'Black 5' (10), Ivatt 4MT 2-6-0 (3) and '9F' (1). Engines noted in steam were No's. 43043, 44861, 44902, 45299 and 92073. This depot had officially closed on 2nd October and had been the last in the Eastern Region to provide facilities for servicing visiting LMR steam locos. As with a number of other 'closed' depots, the shed would in fact continue to service such motive power until 1st January 1968.

Sitting on Normanton station waiting for the 11.30am service into Leeds, I knew that the next shed, Holbeck, had closed its doors to steam on 30th September, and would in all likelihood have only a few, if any such engines still to be found on shed. However, I'd heard on the grapevine that a couple of 'Jubilees' were still tucked away inside the shed, so I was hoping I would get a final glimpse of them during this visit.

The first engine I came across was '8F' No. 48399 in the yard, but a further 15 were under cover inside the shed building and amongst these I found one in steam. Gently simmering next to a very presentable 'Black 5' No. 45428, was spotlessly clean 'Jubilee' No. 45562 Alberta. Also present, and equally well groomed, was sister engine No. 45593 Kolhapur. Fairburn 2-6-4T No. 42251, Stanier 2-6-4T No. 42616, 'Black 5's' No's. 44826, 44852, 44896, 44943, 44983, 45080, 45219, 45273, '8F' 48158, and a very clean 'K1' 2-6-0, No. 62005 made up the compliment of engines on shed.

Five days after noting her in Holbeck, No. 45562 Alberta would be rostered for Royal train duty after the Queen had opened the Tyne tunnel. Used initially for steam heating purposes at Newcastle, sometime later the 'Jubilee' would head the train from Central station to South Gosforth cutting, where she would remain overnight keeping everyone warm. Six days later on 20th, sister engine No. 45593 Kolhapur, would travel under its own steam to Tyseley following its purchase by 7029 Clun Castle Ltd., and 'K1' No. 62005 would be bought by a consortium for its boiler to be kept as a spare for preserved 'K4' No. 61994. However, good fortune meant it wouldn't be needed, and the 'K1' would become another lucky engine and be saved and restored. Stanier 4-6-0 No. 45428, which had worked the 2.18pm Bradford - Kings Cross as far as Leeds on the final day of steam working on Sunday 1st October, would also be preserved.

Stanier 'Jubilee' 4-6-0 No. 45562 Alberta simmering inside Holbeck shed on 14th October 1967. The last two 'Jubilee's to be given a general overhaul were No's. 45589 Gwalior and 45697 Achilles in the summer of 1965, but Alberta would be the last to remain in service, and the last steam loco to haul the Royal Train in BR days.

It was always uplifting, especially so late in the day for steam, to come across engines that had been cleaned and polished, with sunlight being reflected from their paintwork rather than being absorbed by the dirt and grime now normally associated with this form of motive power. Here is another view of Alberta, together with a very smartly turned out 'Black 5', No. 45428.

As I made my way back to City station, I couldn't help but think about how Holbeck had changed since my last visit only a month earlier. Gone was the shed's liveliness and vibrancy; its familiar sounds, smells and noises replaced by a foreboding stillness that prompted me to further realise that steams decline had reached the point where its days of usefulness were swiftly coming to an end. No steam workings were noted while I waited for 2.58pm to Bradford or any observed en-route.

My day out was coming to an end, too, and following a bus ride to Low Moor I began my last shed visit. Closed twelve days earlier on 2nd October, I noted only stored engines all of which were in the yard. Classes represented amongst the 14 steam now no longer needed were 'Black 5'(3), 'B1' (2), Fairburn and Stanier 2-6-4T's (2 of each) and 'WD' 2-8-0's (5). Two hours after 'Black 5' No. 45428 had worked the 2.18pm departure, one of the Fairburn tanks present, No. 42152 (pictured overleaf), had had the honour of heading the last steam-hauled Bradford-Leeds train, the 4.18pm, reportedly achieving 74mph down Kirkstall bank.

During my journey home, three withdrawn standard engines were logged, No's. 90644, 90722 and 92065 and, in Nunnery carriage sidings near Sheffield, Departmental loco No. 30 (formerly BR No. 61050) on steam heating duties. When I added up the engines representing the twelve different classes I had seen during the day, the total had reached seventy-two. With the above shed closures came the withdrawal of the last of the 'B1's, the Stanier and Fairburn 2-6-4T's and the 'WD's. The two remaining 'Jubilees' would not be officially withdrawn until later in the month. The northwest was now undoubtedly shaping up to be steam's last outpost.

Previously recorded and photographed at Low Moor MPD on 16th September (page 125), Fairburn 2-6-4T No. 42251 had found its way to Holbeck shed where it is seen on 14th October 1967.

Top. Fairburn tank No. 42152 stands next to the turntable in the yard of Low Moor MPD on 14th October 1967. Further along the row of condemned locos was 'B1' No. 61337 (above). Copies of official paperwork concerning maintenance and repairs (shopping proposal and boiler inspection respectively) for both these engines can be seen on page 143.

Also stored pending removal from Low Moor for scrap on 14th October was 'B1' No. 61030 Nyala. Keeping the engine company is Stanier 2-6-4T No. 42587, which would go to Drapers of Hull to meet its fate; the 4-6-0 would be destined to be broken up at Garnham, Harris and Elton, Chesterfield.

About this time it was rumoured that Crewe South and Birkenhead would cease to have a steam allocation within the next two to three weeks. Before making plans to head in that direction however, I visited Tyseley on Wednesday 25th October. Six steam were found on shed, including one of the 'Jubilees' I had travelled north to see only eleven days earlier; No. 45593 Kolhapur had taken up residence and was sharing the roundhouse with No. 7029 Clun Castle. In the diesel depot yard three steam locos (No's. 44938, 45328 and 73035) were waiting to have their wheels re-profiled, while '9F' No. 92088 was occupying the wheel turning lathe. According to official records, No. 45328 had already been withdrawn by this time, and No. 44938 was taken out of service sometime the following month, so it seems extremely unlikely that either of them saw the inside of the diesel depot. This was my last visit to the shed while it was still receiving engines for such attention. Ironically, it was also twelve months since the shed had 'closed' to steam!

On 20th October 1967 No. 45593 Kolhapur travelled under its own steam from Leeds to Tyseley, its new home, where it is seen five days later. The 4-6-0 was no longer a BR engine; 7029 Clun Castle Ltd. now owned the 'Jubilee'.

November

BR Type 'A' No. E3060 made its way silently out of New Street, accelerated quickly and headed north early on the morning of 1st November; I was on my way once again to Crewe behind electric traction. Four withdrawn engines were noted as the train approached the town's station, No's. 43112, 45241, 45264 and 48275. As I looked across to the shed, conspicuous by its absence, it was apparent that there was very little, if any, smoke rising from the yard or the shed building. Normally, I would have expected to see the obvious signs of life where so many engines were gathered; but these were not normal times and Crewe South depot was clearly within a hair's breadth of closure.

The statistics speak for themselves: only three engines were in steam - No's. 45349, 48402 and 92218 - out of a total of 51 noted (see appendix 22) on shed. Including a very presentable standard 4-6-0, No. 75029, which had been purchased by David Shepherd, all of the remainder appeared to have ceased work and been put into store. However, there was one exception. The preserved 'A4' No. 4498 Sir Nigel Gresley, although sitting cold inside the shed, was immaculate and as far from the cutter's torch as no doubt the vast majority of its stable mates wished they could have been too. There was a reasonable variety of motive power in evidence, but considering the circumstances it didn't really mean very much. The shed would officially close five days after my visit, and the unthinkable would soon become a reality: Crewe without steam. For younger trainspotters it may have continued to be a Mecca; for the older, earnest steam enthusiast its appeal and magic, even though severely diminished over the previous few years, would be gone forever.

Birkenhead would be joining Crewe on 6th November in dispensing with its steam power, so hauled again by an electric loco (No. E3197), I headed north from Crewe to Liverpool Lime Street, walked across to St. James station and caught the Wirral and Mersey service to Birkenhead Central. I was soon inside the shed busily noting down the steam engines still taking up residence. The depot was certainly livelier than South shed had been, with ten locos (No's. 92022, 92025, 92088, 92094, 92108, 92165, 92166, 45280, 48252 and 48305) out of a total of 26 in steam. Only three varieties were represented with twenty-one locos belonging to the standard '9F' class.

'9F's No's. 92165 and 92166, initially Saltley engines had created quite a stir when they had been allocated to the Birmingham shed when new in 1958. Both they and sister engine No. 92167, had been fitted with Berkley mechanical stokers and all three weren't really tested with this modification until diagrammed for the freights from Water Orton to Carlisle via the Settle and Carlisle line. With their inefficient use of fuel, and problems with the screw when moving the coal from the tender to firebox, they were soon converted back to using traditional firing methods. Terry Essery, in his book More Firing Days at Saltley, gives an excellent first-hand account of the difficulties he encountered when he was introduced to what, for all intents and purposes, should have been a labour saving device. However, some ex-Saltley men such as John Hill, recollects the stokers differently. Once the special deliveries of household coal for the three '9F's began to arrive, he recalls his experience on the footplate more positively. The only problem that he recalls encountering was the occasional build up of fire under the brick arch, which was soon levelled out with a fitting fire iron.

Albert Ford began his railway career at Saltley in April 1958 and well remembers the engines for different reasons. He was part of the cleaning team and, together with several other young cleaners, assisted in preparing the three engines for their trips to Carlisle. Under the watchful eye of deputy foreman cleaner, Arthur Atkins, they had the unenviable task of having to break up the larger pieces of coal once the '9F's tender had been half-filled and again after its full compliment had been achieved on its second visit to the coaling stage. It would seem that although this effort reduced the risk of the screw jamming, the method was not foolproof and some oversize lumps of coal still managed to go unnoticed. Once promoted to fireman, Albert recalls that these difficulties were not repeated when the engines were serviced in Carlisle, with a much more suitable, uniform size of coal being supplied.

Retracing my route across the Mersey I was soon walking down the cinder path from the end of Tiverton Street to Edge Hill. Once overflowing with 'Patriots', 'Jubilees', 'Royal Scots' and 'Princess Royals' the shed was now only able to muster a few of the less glamorous Stanier 'Black 5's' and '8F's. I noted 27 of these engines with seventeen of them belonging to the former class. Two '8F's and nine 'Black 5's', including No. 44878 fitted with a snowplough, were in steam.

My final destination, Speke Junction, housed a total of 37 steam, with 'Black 5's No's. 44873 and 45232, '8F' No. 48745 and '9F's No's. 92117 and 92204, ready for their next turn of duty. The remaining thirty-two engines were cold. Three classes were represented, 'Black 5', '8F' and '9F'. Almost half of the engines present were noted as being withdrawn or in store.

Standing in the next platform to my train home, I had the opportunity to see first-hand the new Liverpool Pullman while awaiting departure from Lime Street to Birmingham New Street. This was a first-class only service to Euston and it struck me how opulent and modern it appeared. As I began to look through my notebook and the locos I'd noted, I couldn't help but wonder how such coaching stock would look behind a steam engine, not a scruffy one, of course, but one that had been well-groomed. I had already added up the engines I had seen during the day by the time my train seemed to effortlessly ease its way out of Lime Street. The steam total stood at 145, with 9 different varieties represented. Thirty-four, fewer than a quarter, had been noted as fired and ready for work. While sitting back and enjoying the journey home, I made plans for my next trip north. I decided on Stockport and Manchester, and to visit at least three sheds during the day. While more expensive, I also made my mind up to use the train rather than my scooter - the journey on two wheels at this time of year didn't really have quite the same appeal as in the summer months.

Above and previous. Withdrawn by BR on 1st February 1966, but fortunately preserved, 'A4' Pacific No. 4498 Sir Nigel Gresley is seen inside Crewe South MPD on 1st November 1967. Following its involvement with the RCTS special 'The Border Limited' four days earlier, the engine seems to have problems with its boiler, its twelfth since new in 1937, and has several shed staff in attendance. In the view of the loco above, water can be seen dripping from below the smokebox, while a fitter appears to be in the process of replacing one of its tubes.

Birkenhead MPD, 1st November 1967. Found standing out in the gloom and rain, Swindon built '9F' No. 92094 and '8F' No. 48305, a Speke Junction engine, seem only to add a greater depth to the dimness of the day, while Stanier 2-8-0 No. 48252, with a marginally cleaner smokebox and white painted numberplate, manages to look that little more presentable. Both the 2-10-0 and 48252 would remain in service for a further six months, whereas 48305 would cease work at the start of the New Year.

Top. Allocated to Saltley on four separate occasions over the years, 'Black 5' No. 45280 is kept company by EE Type '4' No. D308 in Birkenhead MPD, the 4-6-0's final home shed. The Stanier engine would be withdrawn a few days after this photograph was taken.
Above. With the rain persisting, the dismal day hadn't improved as I made my way round Edge Hill MPD. Also with only the matter of days left before withdrawal, Stanier '8F' No. 48119 stands over the ashpit while it has its grate cleared of ash and clinker.

As glamorous and engaging as steam power could appear to be, a stark reminder of the reality of working with such engines is clearly evident in the picture above. Stanier 'Black 5' No. 44878, a Carlisle Kingmoor engine, was part way through its disposal routine when I took this photograph during my visit to Edge Hill shed on 1st November 1967. Having opened the smokebox door for his fireman, the driver seems deep in thought as his loco has the ash removed from the front of its smokebox. The 4-6-0 would be transferred to Lostock Hall after Kingmoor's closure at the end of December, and would then see out a further seven months before being withdrawn at the end of steam on BR.

On 1st November 1967, with cylinder cocks open and steam to spare, Springs Branch allocated Stanier 4-6-0 No. 44873 moves off Speke Jnct. MPD to take up its next job. Built at Crewe in March 1945, the 'Black 5', despite looking so full of life, would be condemned a few days later. Often confronted with dismal and depressing weather conditions, this and the previous four pictures serve to highlight how any window of opportunity had to be made the most of for taking photographs, even though the results might leave a lot to be desired.

On Saturday 11th November, after staying overnight at Jackie's, I travelled to New Street by scooter, paid 2/6d for the privilege of parking it there for the day, and set off on the 8.00am to Stockport hauled by BR Type 'A' electric No. E3069. Rather than listing the customary good number of active steam in and around Crewe station and MPD, I inserted instead a brief note in my logbook: 'Crewe South shed closed, all remaining steam in store.' The few dead engines I noted, as far as I could tell, hadn't moved since I'd seen them ten days earlier.

Remaining seated, I looked out through the carriage window while the train stood in Crewe station only too aware that there were no longer any steam engines vying for my attention - no need anymore to move quickly from one side of the carriage to the other to record as speedily as possible the locos that had been so much part of the scene here. The train left without any indication as to how hard the engine up front was working, but it got into its stride quickly and I stepped down on to the platform at Stockport Edgeley spot on time at 9.25am. It was a short walk to the depot, and by quarter past ten I had logged the 15 steam present and taken several photographs. Two classes were represented, 'Black 5' (10) and '8F' (5) with five engines, No's. 44916, 44940, 45046, 45316, and 48532 in steam.

After a long walk from Edgeley, I finally arrived at the next shed on my itinerary, Heaton Mersey. The variety of locomotives here reflected the determined effort by BR to confine its steam power to a handful of reliable classes, and once again only Stanier's 'Black 5's and '8F's were represented. Honours were even with six of each present, with one of the former, No. 44663 (photographed at Tyseley MPD in the queue for the WTL on Christmas Day 1966) and two of the latter, No's. 48365 and 48551, in steam.

While waiting for the train to Manchester Piccadilly the opportunity presented itself to photograph Stockport-based 'Black 5' No. 44855 standing in Edgeley station on empty stock duty; two young boys were looking up into the cab and talking to the driver, probably in the hope of being invited on to the footplate, which was always a bonus during a day's trainspotting.

After arriving at Piccadilly, I took the bus to Trafford Park. The last of the shed's allocation of Fairburn and Stanier tanks had now gone, and it was now left with Stanier 'Black 5's' and '8F's. A total of twenty-one engines were logged, with three out of the fourteen 4-6-0's and two of the seven 2-8-0's in steam. The pattern of seeing only these two classes on shed had persisted, and I wondered if the next depot I was about to visit, Newton Heath, might break the mould.

Stockport Edgeley MPD: the fireman of 'Black 5' No. 44940 has just finished moving coal forward in its tender and can be seen clearly above the cab roof. He would soon be organising the replenishing of the locos water supply before the 4-6-0 is placed next to sister engine No. 45046 (left foreground), already prepared for its next undertaking. 11th November 1967.

Allocated to Willesden for many years before being transferred to Crewe South, Stanier '8F' No. 48551 had moved for the last time to its present depot, Heaton Mersey, earlier in March. Seen here in its final home shed on 11th November 1967, it is receiving attention from two fitters. The shed appears to be bereft of engines and ready for closure, but would in fact continue servicing steam until May the following year.

On the same day, class AL6 No. E3195 with a northbound passenger train, and 'Black 5' No. 44855 at the head of a parcels train, wait in Stockport Edgeley station for the 'right away'. The 4-6-0 would remain in service for a further six months before being despatched to Wards, Beighton, for scrapping.

Stanier 4-6-0 No. 45150 at rest in its home shed, Trafford Park, on 11th November 1967. Built by Armstrong Whitworth in June 1935 at a cost of a little over £5,000, its working life would come to an end in March 1968. Its final journey would take it to Drapers of Hull where it would be broken up three months later in June.

As I began to note the steam locos in the northern half of Newton Heath, I soon realised that Stanier's engines would once again dominate. Indeed, the mould wasn't broken at all, and I recorded the same two varieties once more at this shed. The 'Black 5' contingent numbered 20, with fourteen in steam, and the body of '8F's totalled 14, with seven of these fired and ready for work. The weather had been gloomy and wet all day and my pictures mirrored the fact, especially those taken of 'Black 5' No. 45046 (seen earlier on Stockport shed) passing the depot heading a mixed freight and being banked by sister engine No. 44818.

From nearby Dean Lane station I caught the next train to Manchester Victoria and spent the remainder of the afternoon on this and Exchange station. What little light that managed to penetrate the thick grey clouds was barely sufficient to show up the numbers of the locos involved in the not infrequent steam turns. By the time the ever-deepening gloom enveloping both stations had given way to nightfall, I had noted the following engines: 'Black 5's No's. 44734, 44803, 44818, 45202, 45390, and 45436, standard 5MT's No's. 73035 and 73132 and 'Britannia' No. 70004 William Shakespeare. A total of 94 steam had been logged by the day's end with 5 different classes noted as follows: Ivatt 4MT 2-6-0 (1), 'Black 5' (57), '8F' (33), standard 5MT (2) and 'Britannia' Pacific (1).

Being ably assisted by sister engine No. 44818 at the rear (see below), Stanier 'Black 5' No. 45046 heads a mixed freight train past Newton Heath MPD on 11th November 1967.

Newton Heath MPD, 11th November 1967: grimy and wet 'Black 5' No. 44899, based at Carlisle Kingmoor, stands under the coaling stage ready for its tender to be replenished with more fuel. Early in the New Year it would head south to a new home, Rose Grove, where it would remain until withdrawal in July 1968.

Still good for steam: with only a matter of months to go, Manchester Victoria could be relied upon to regularly produce such motive power in and around its confines. There was a chance that a steam engine could be found anywhere amongst its seventeen platforms. The first of five photographs taken here on 11th November shows 'Black 5' No. 44803 at the head of a parcels train.

Both. Also in charge of a parcels train was 'Black 5' No. 45436. Thirty years after entering traffic in November 1937, the 4-6-0 was by now a Lostock Hall engine, but in spite of the depot remaining open until the end of steam, the 4-6-0 wouldn't be kept in employment quite so long and would be withdrawn the following April.

Originally allocated to Normanton when new in June 1946, 'Black 5' No. 44803 was transferred to Belle Vue in May 1945. It remained at this depot until its closure (the first in Manchester) on 16th April 1956, and subsequently spent the rest of its working life allotted to Newton Heath. Seen somewhat in a hurry leaving Manchester Victoria with a parcels train, the 4-6-0 would continue in service until 25th May 1968.

Having assisted No. 45046 with a heavy freight earlier (see page 162), Stanier 4-6-0 No. 44818 is back in Victoria station ready for its next banking task. This engine entered traffic in November 1944 and spent its first fifteen years allocated to Derby. After two and a half years working out of Saltley, the 'Black 5' moved on to Burton and then Bolton, and would be withdrawn on the closure to steam of its final home shed, Newton Heath, in June 1968.

Journeying home in the dark meant fewer distractions. I had time to reflect on the day's events and the engines I had seen. Inevitably, as on previous occasions, I thought too about steam's sad downfall and where its tenuous presence was under further threat. The year's end was fast approaching, and the depressing prospect that another great railway centre, Carlisle, would cease to have an active allocation of steam power within a few weeks only served to highlight the remorseless removal of steam power from our railway. Its Kingmoor depot, once the New Year was underway, would close to steam, which in turn would mean the end of regular steam workings over Shap Fell and the closure of Tebay shed, too. Long before I reached New Street station, I knew where my next trip would be taking me.

Within a few days, I got in touch with Dennis to see if he would be willing to brave the elements and venture up to the well-known incline the following month to witness steam working out its last winter in this wild and rugged area of the northwest. He didn't need any persuading, and we agreed to spend Saturday 9th December at Tebay. We would experience, while the opportunity still existed, the sights and sounds of steam locos striving to move their northbound trains up over Shap Fell. Weather and opportunities permitting, we would reel off a few photos, too.

December

Four weeks after the Manchester trip, on the evening of 8th December, we caught the 11.20pm sleeper from New Street to Carlisle and arrived at a very cold and windy Citadel station at about 3.45am. To welcome us was 'Black 5' No. 44868 at the head of a parcels train. A warm glow emanated from her firebox and lit up the cab, and her safety valves were fully lifted readily proclaiming she had an abundance of energy - a lot more than the task in hand would probably require. Bathed in the station lights she created an ethereal atmosphere and I decided to try and photograph her as best I could - no tripod or any other support, the camera just hand held. As can be imagined, the result wasn't brilliant, but the picture (below) goes some way to capturing the sort of striking images and mood only steam can produce during freezing conditions in the dead of night.

Carlisle Citadel station, 3.45am Saturday 9th December 1967: with plenty of steam to spare, Stockport Edgeley-based 'Black 5' No. 44868 is seen at the head of a parcels train. The 4-6-0 began its working life in February 1945 and by this time had approximately a further five months of employment left before being withdrawn.

With cameras tucked safely away, we left the 'Black 5' and made for the nearest waiting room to try and get some rest. We both slept fitfully; the room was not as warm as we expected it to be, and the wooden seats, as always, made it very difficult if not impossible to achieve any level of comfort. Nevertheless, it was much better than remaining outside on the platform. After about four hours of fidgeting, we bought a hot drink and boarded a pleasantly warm dmu forming the 8.20am local train to Tebay.

During the fifty-minute journey we encountered a couple of snow flurries but nothing of any significance. As we got closer to Tebay, however, the sky had taken on a more threatening appearance and the prospect of further and heavier snow seemed more and more likely. On reaching the junction with the old line to Kirkby Stephen, we could see that the shed housed several engines in steam and, as if on cue, no sooner than we had set foot on the platform, we spotted the approach of 'Britannia' Pacific No. 70025 Western Star with a northbound freight. She halted in the station to take on water and then, with banking engine (standard 4MT No. 75030) at the ready, she started the hard slog up the incline. Initially 1 in 146, the real climb started about a mile further on when the gradient became almost twice as steep at 1in 75 and lasted for almost four miles.

After watching sister engine No. 70012 John of Gaunt follow hard on the heels of No. 70025 into the station, we walked down the platform and into the depot. Three 'Black 5's No's. 44898, 45013 and 45236 together with five standard class 4MTs No's. 75015, 75030, 75032, 75037 and 75039 were noted on shed. During the day we divided our attention between the station, depot and lineside, taking as many photographs as possible. The weather remained bitterly cold with the sky varying from bright blue through shades of grey to almost black. The snow showers became more frequent and heavier as the morning wore on, but the wind finally eased a little and made things marginally more bearable as we stamped our feet and plunged our hands deep into our pockets while waiting to photograph each northbound steam working. Our enthusiasm and resolve resulted in some reasonable photographs of engines seeing out their final days of having to fight their way up this formidable fell.

This and the following nine photos were taken on 9th December 1967. Shrouded in steam, 'Britannia' Pacific No. 70025 Western Star leaves Tebay to begin her ascent of Shap. Built in September 1952, the engine had been allocated to Kingmoor since September 1966. On the closure of her home shed at the end of the month, the Pacific would be condemned and despatched to G.W. Campbell of Airdrie for breaking up. Closed in January 1962, the lines branching off to the left of the picture are those of the former 'Stainmore Line', made famous by the ten minute long British Transport Film 'Snowdrift at Bleath Ghyll' made in 1955.

Following in the footsteps of sister engine No. 70025, 'Britannia' No. 70012 John of Gaunt, is about to have its thirst quenched before it, too, takes on Shap Fell with its mixed freight train. First allocated to Norwich when new, No. 70012 spent a number of years on the Eastern Region before moving to Willesden in March 1963. The 4-6-2 would remain a London Midland Region engine until withdrawal at the end of the month. Its final journey would be to T.W. Ward of Killamarsh where it would eventually be disposed of in March 1968. Below. 'Black 5' No. 45236, of Kingmoor shed, stands out in the snow in Tebay MPD. This engine, like so many others allocated to the Carlisle depot, would be condemned at the end of the year when 12A ceased servicing steam. Note the railway workers' cottages in the background.

Standard 4MT No. 75032 is seen resting in Tebay MPD. The 4-6-0 entered service in June 1953 and had become a 12E engine earlier in May. For a number of years after entering traffic, it could regularly be seen working out of Llandudno and Chester Midland sheds.

Transferred from Newton Heath to Kingmoor in May 1965, '9F' No. 92110 is seen just before leaving Tebay, light engine, for its home depot. Having completed just eleven years service, the 2-10-0 would be withdrawn on the closure of the Carlisle shed.

While the snow falls, standard 4MT No. 75032 gives a helping hand to a northbound diesel headed freight train. For what would prove to be a short-lived reprieve from the cutter's torch, the 4-6-0 would move to Carnforth early in January after the closure of Tebay shed.

Opened by the Lancaster & Carlisle Railway on 17th December 1846, Tebay station would close completely on 1st July 1968. With the time approaching 11.30am, smoke drifts lazily from the stove situated below the watering tower at the end of the down platform. No evidence of the station remains today, but the nearby terraced houses built for the railway workers are still standing

1967 (Farewell to Oliver Bulleid's Pacifics)

While the snow flurries continue and 'Britannia' No. 70012 John of Gaunt gets ready to set about tackling Shap Fell (top), Newton Heath-based Stanier '8F' No. 48200 appeared with an up freight and proceeded to reverse into the siding adjacent to the station. Soon to be transferred to Bolton MPD during the first week of the New Year, the 2-8-0 would be withdrawn very shortly afterwards - certainly before the beginning of February.

After walking a reasonable distance up the incline under an ever-darkening sky, I managed to take several shots of No. 44899 as it began its journey up Shap. Built at Crewe works in September 1945, the 'Black 5' was allocated to Kingmoor where she would remain for a little over 22 years. On the closure of 12A at the end of December, the 4-6-0 would be transferred to Rose Grove shed, from where she would continue to work until the end of steam on 4th August next year.

By 4.00pm we were on our way back to Carlisle. Appreciative of the warm dmu carriage, we slowly started to sense that we did have fingers and toes after all! No steam movements were noted during the journey or while waiting on Citadel station for the 6.04pm to Crewe. Indeed, it wasn't until we reached the outskirts of Preston that we saw our next steam loco, Ivatt 2-6-0 No. 43106. This would prove to be the last of the day, and gave us a final total of 18 steam representing 6 different classes. After a change of trains at Crewe, we arrived back in Birmingham at about 10.00pm. In three weeks time the hills around Shap would no longer regularly echo to the familiar sounds of steam; Kingmoor, Tebay and Workington MPD's would close, and a further chapter in steams downfall would have been written. Despite the historical significance of what was about to happen, we had had an enjoyable and productive trip, providing memories that would remain with us to this day. It would also prove to be our last expedition in search of steam for the year.

In retrospect, steams continuing demise during 1967 meant different things to different enthusiasts. For some, steam was now working so far away from where they lived it was too time consuming and expensive to travel to see and experience; a number probably preferred to remember the engines and locations they were familiar with from their trainspotting days; for others it didn't matter, they had simply lost interest and given up looking at ill-kempt engines. And, for many of those whose interest was of a more photographic nature, there was no longer any pleasure or satisfaction to be gained from photographing filthy and poorly maintained engines. Certainly for me, the loss of Saltley, Birmingham's last working steam depot, featured highly on my list of the most significant changes over the year - it was the last place locally where I was able to achieve close contact with engines that were still involved in the day-to-day running of the railway. However, having been fortunate enough to be able to travel far and wide to see steam, I couldn't help but relate to the many other transformations that had occurred all around the country during the previous twelve months.

Throughout the year BR's withdrawal of its steam locomotives had continued unabated, with a further 1,329 engines being condemned. This heavily impacted on all remaining classes, as one would expect, but for twenty-seven it proved fatal. Express passenger varieties that had gone for good included, 'West Country', 'Battle of Britain', 'Merchant Navy' and 'Jubilee'. Mixed-traffic types that suffered a similar fate included 'B1', 'K1', Hughes-Fowler 'Crab', and Stanier 'Mogul'. Various suburban passenger and freight designs, too, had become extinct and included 'J27', 'J36', 'J37', 'J38', Stanier, Fairburn and standard 2-6-4T's and Ivatt 2-6-2T's to mention only a few. The 'Britannia' Pacific's had all gone except for one, No. 70013 Oliver Cromwell, which had been kept in service to take charge of some of the many steam specials that lay ahead.

From 5th March the Shrewsbury - Chester - Birkenhead service had been dieselised, ending what had been the last scheduled steam diagram to be timetabled at an average speed over 60mph. The last two surviving class 'O2' 0-4-4-tanks No's. 24 Calbourne and 31 Chale were withdrawn shortly before the isle of Wight electric services began on 20th March; by the end of the same month, following further deliveries of EE Type '1' diesels to replace the last steam locos used on local freight work, York shed closed to steam in June. By 9th July steam had made its final statement on the Southern, and come the autumn its presence in the northeast had waned and eventually expired. By the start of October steam had been eliminated from the Leeds, Bradford and Normanton areas, and Holbeck's 'Jubilees' would no longer be called upon to haul any summer Saturday trains over the Settle - Carlisle route. Crewe had lost its allocation of steam power in November and, at about the same time, the trickle of steam engines reaching Tyseley for wheel re-profiling had dried up.

Serving the Liverpool, Manchester and Preston areas, there were thirteen sheds left with an allocation of steam power by the year's end. At the beginning of 1961 there had been over two hundred varieties of steam engine on BR's books; excluding the three narrow gauge Vale of Rheidol locos, this figure had been reduced to just seven. Towards the end of December I recorded in my notebook that, by my reckoning, there were approximately 375 steam locos still working. The undoubtedly more accurate RCTS Locomotive Stock Book gave the total as 362 at 31st December 1967. So, taking January 1961 as a reference point again, the figures lay bare the fact that BR had disposed of close to 13,000 steam engines in the space of seven short years. Not including sub-sheds, during the same period, it had also closed completely, or to this form of motive power, no fewer than 267 main depots.

1968 (The Final Farewell to British Steam)

January

The first steam locomotives I saw during their final year of operation on BR were from the lounge window at home. On 11th January standard 4MT 4-6-0's No's. 75002, 75006 and 75013 and '9F' No. 92138, passed through Droitwich hauled by a diesel in the direction of Worcester. I noted at the time that, in all probability, they were bound for Barry scrapyard, but later found out that they had not been so fortunate and had been taken to Birds of Long Marston to be broken up.

Further shed closures were now inevitable and early in the New Year the depressing news filtered through that three of the remaining steam depots, Buxton, Northwich and Trafford Park, would cease to have an allocation of such motive power from early March. Determined to visit these sheds at least once before they closed in the early spring, I rearranged my planned trip to Stockport and Manchester before the end of the month to allow a visit to Buxton first.

It was a dull and overcast start to the morning of Saturday 20th January. Thankfully the weather forecast for the day was reasonable, and there hadn't been any frost overnight, so I travelled as intended as far as Buxton by scooter.

There wasn't a great deal of activity at the depot, and only five Stanier '8F's were on shed. No's. 48190, 48336, and 48495 were dead while No's. 48424 and 48471 (fitted with a small snow plough) were in steam and ready for work. After parking my scooter outside the station, I caught the first available dmu service to Stockport.

Stanier '8F' No. 48424 was once a Saltley engine in the early 50's. After returning for a second stint in the Midlands, based at Tyseley and Stourbridge, during the early 1960's, the 2-8-0 was transferred to Buxton in February 1965, where it is seen inside the shed building on 20th January 1968. This would prove to be its final home before being withdrawn the following month.

No steam workings were witnessed on the way, but Edgeley shed had 26 steam in residence, sixteen of which were 'Black 5's and the remainder '8F's. Ten engines were in steam and one, Edgeley-based 'Black 5' 4-6-0 No. 45312, had undergone a good wash and brush up and was duly noted as being very clean. Considering the shed had never had an allocation of more than about thirty-four steam locos since 1950, seeing as many as I did on this visit suggested that they had a little while to go yet before being displaced for good.

With ash still lying below its smokebox door, snowplough-fitted '8F' No. 48471 waits to leave Buxton MPD to take up its next turn of duty on 20th January 1968. The Stanier 2-8-0 would be granted a stay of execution on the closure of the shed in early March, and would be transferred to Heaton Mersey. This would prove to be the engines last re-allocation, and withdrawal would eventually come on the closure of 9F early in May.

Following the short journey from Stockport to Manchester Piccadilly, I caught the local service from Victoria to Dean Lane, close to Newton Heath MPD. Three steam were noted during this second leg of the journey and, after the short walk from the station to the shed, I was soon noting its compliment of engines. Once a twenty-four-road shed, it now used half this number for housing steam, and all its allocation could, if necessary, be comfortably kept under cover. A total of 48 representing 5 different classes were present, with fifteen engines in steam. Interestingly, three weeks after withdrawal, 'Britannia' Pacific No. 70023 Venus, looking very much the poor relation, remained in store in the yard. I had last seen and photographed this engine in December working up Shap Fell in the snow with a mixed freight. The pictures I took of her now would prove to be quite a contrast and tell such a different story to those I was fortunate to take while she was still in action only a few weeks earlier.

Top. Former home sheds for Stanier 4-6-0 No. 44855 included Bristol Barrow Road, Kentish Town and Sheffield Grimesthorpe. On 20th January 1968 the loco is seen simmering inside Stockport Edgeley, the last depot it would be allocated to. The 'Black 5' would be deemed surplus to needs following the closure of the shed at the end of the first week in May. Above. Equally alive and kicking is classmate No. 45046 nearest the camera. Ten years older than 44855 and built at the Vulcan Foundry, Newton le Willows, she would move on to Bolton MPD on the closure of Edgeley before being withdrawn in June.

Towards the end of what had been a thoroughly drab and dismal day, I made my final shed visit. With a total of 44 engines representing 4 different varieties, Patricroft had almost as many steam to cater for as Newton Heath. Stanier engines were very much in the minority, especially his 'Black 5's'. The predominant form of steam power here was the standard 5MT 4-6-0 class totalling twenty-eight in all. I also logged another stored 'Britannia', No. 70012 John of Gaunt, standing inside the shed building with connecting rods in place and looking as though it could still be fired-up and made ready for work if called upon. Seven standard 4-6-0's and three '8F's were noted in steam.

Stanier 2-8-0 No. 48740, fitted with small snowplough, pounds past Newton Heath MPD with a train of empty coal wagons late on the afternoon of 20th January 1968. Formerly allocated to Crewe South, Buxton, and Northwich the '8F' was now a Bolton engine. Withdrawal would come just over a month after this photograph was taken.

During the hour-long train ride back to Buxton one steam working was logged, '9F' No. 92218 at the head of a freight train. Reviewing the day's jottings revealed that a total of 120 steam had been recorded (see appendix 23 for steam noted on shed) representing the following classes: 'Black 5' (45), '8F' (42), 'Britannia' (2), standard 5MT (29) and '9F' (2). Forty-three, a little over a third, were in steam. Leaving the warmth and comfort of the carriage I collected my scooter and headed off into the cold night, looking forward to reaching home and developing the three films I had taken during the day.

Top. 'Black 5' No. 45420 receives attention from a Newton Heath fitter. Entering traffic in October 1937, the loco was a Crewe engine for six months before moving to Patricroft where it would be based for about twenty years. Its final transfer from Agecroft to Newton Heath in June 1965 would prove to be its last and, following the closure of 9D later in June, the 4-6-0 would be condemned. Above. Standard 5MT No. 73136 is seen resting in the yard of Patricroft MPD on 20th January. Fitted with British-Caprotti valve gear, the 4-6-0 had been transferred to 9H in May 1964 and would be withdrawn in March. Disposal would take place at J. Cashmore, Great Bridge.

Top. Patricroft at this time had 21 active standard 5MT's on its books, plus several such engines stored after withdrawal. It is not surprising, then, that in this view the only engines to be seen are 73xxx 4-6-0's. Above. Following a year in store (May 1966 to May 1967), standard 5MT No. 73000 was eventually found work again as a Patricroft engine, where it is seen here. Built in 1951 at a cost of £17,603, it would be deemed surplus to requirements in March and sent to J. Cashmore's, Great Bridge for cutting up.

February

Further news about the impending closure of Buxton, Northwich and Trafford Park MPD's confirmed that they would cease to service steam from Monday 4th March. Wishing to visit these sheds once more, I contacted Dennis to see if he would like to join me and he was keen to make a weekend of it so we could fit in a few other sheds, too. Provided the weather was okay, we agreed to travel by scooter on the weekend of 16th, 17th and 18th February and to camp to help economise. If the weather forecast was at all questionable, we would travel by train and reduce the number of planned shed visits as necessary.

On Friday 16th, with chilly but favourable conditions for travelling on two wheels, I left Birmingham at about 8.00pm and met Dennis at Derby station an hour later. In due course we reached the outskirts of Northwich and pitched the tent well after 11.00pm in what we thought was a reasonably flat field. We didn't sleep very well, however. The night proved to be a bitterly cold one, and the field we had picked in the dark was nowhere near as even as we had first thought. We were more than content to be up and about as soon as it got light and, after sharing sandwiches and a small flask of coffee for breakfast, we started off for the first shed visit of the day.

17th February

Stanier '8F's were well in evidence as we recorded the engines on Northwich MPD. Indeed, it first appeared that this would be the only variety occupying the shed, but in addition to the sixteen 2-8-0's present we discovered standard 2-10-0 No. 92088, in steam and being topped up with coal. Three of the 2-8-0s were prepared and ready for work – No's 48294, 48340 and 48493. Another of the '8F's on shed, No. 48151, which I had photographed during a visit the previous August, had been withdrawn in early January. The 2-8-0 would eventually reach Barry scrapyard in September where she would remain for ten years before being purchased privately and moved to the Yorkshire Dales Railway.

From Northwich we continued on to Runcorn and then, after crossing the River Mersey, to Speke Junction. Here we noted three steam classes amongst a total of 68 engines on shed (see appendix 24). A healthy number of steam or so it would appear. But a closer inspection of my records revealed that seventeen '9F's, fourteen 'Black 5's', six '8F's and one 'Britannia' Pacific, No. 70024 Vulcan, appeared to be awaiting removal for scrap. Showing signs of life and in steam, however, were: '9F's No's 92054, 92069, 92160 and 92249, 'Black 5' No. 44663 and '8F' No. 48551.

Half an hour after leaving Speke we were listing the locos present in Edge Hill. A total of 49 steam were on shed with 3 different classes represented. Stanier 'Black 5's (23) and '8F's (18) were most prevalent, with the other eight engines belonging to the standard '9F' class. Eleven engines were in steam - No's 44711, 44804, 44897, 45282, 48012, 48045, 48294, 48308, 48467, 48665 and 48687. Worthy of note was the presence, deep inside the shed building, of Stanier '8F' No. 48297, which had had more than a minor mishap. It had lost its buffer beam and two leading wheels making it, in effect, an 0-8-0 prior to being taken away for breaking up (see picture page 185).

With sacking over its chimney, 'Black 5' No. 45388 finds itself stored inside Speke Junction MPD on 17th February 1968. With the distinct prospect of being withdrawn, or so it would first appear, the 4-6-0, on the closure of this depot, would be transferred to Lostock Hall during the second week of May, and would continue in service until the end of steam on BR.

On the same day, Stanier locos No's. 48687 and 45376 are found tucked away from the elements inside Edge Hill, their home shed. The former engine would continue in employment until July, but the class '5' 4-6-0 would only survive until the end of March.

Built at Horwich, 'Black5' No. 44711 entered traffic on 21st October 1948. Allocated initially to Crewe North, the engine moved on to a further five depots, including Rugby, Holyhead and Shrewsbury. Seen inside its last home shed, Edge Hill, on 17th February 1968 the 4-6-0 would officially be withdrawn on the depot's closure on 4th May.

Skirting the city centre, we journeyed north from Liverpool along the A59 through Ormskirk, where we had camped two summers earlier during our journey to Carlisle, and on to Lostock Hall MPD near Preston. In residence here were 27 steam (see appendix 24), sixteen of which were 'Black 5's'. These were accompanied by five '8F's and six Ivatt 4MT 2-6-0's. Five 4-6-0's, No's. 44761, 45149, 45212, 45345 and 45353, one 2-8-0 No. 48646 and Mogul No. 43027 were in steam.

Progressing further north we set our sights on Carnforth, and what would be our last depot visit of the day. On shed we found 6 different varieties amongst the 41 steam noted as follows: 'Black 5' (20), '8F' (3), Ivatt 2-6-0 (1, preserved), 'Britannia' Pacific (2), standard 4MT 4-6-0 (10) and standard '9F' (5). 'Britannia' No. 70013 Oliver Cromwell was covered in tarpaulin, while sister engine No. 70021 Morning Star continued to wait for her final fateful journey. Eleven locos in were in steam - No's 44709, 44758, 44874, 45095, 45134, 45390, 45394, 45424, 45445, 48533 and 92110 - most of them resting outside the shed building in the north yard.

Withdrawn sometime in August/September 1965 while based at Lancaster Green Ayre, '8F' No 48297 is seen inside Edge Hill MPD on 17th February 1968. With bogie wheel assembly having been removed after sustaining a badly damaged front end, quite why she had not been despatched to a breakers yard for disposal is a mystery.

A very grimy and work weary looking Ivatt 2-6-0 stands in the yard of Lostock Hall on 17th February 1968. To its left is '8F' no. 48646 and immediately behind 'Black 5' No. 44761. No. 43027 had been based at a number of depots in the past, including Nuneaton, Derby, Saltley and Kingmoor, but 10D was now its final home. Built at Horwich works in 1949, the 2-6-0 would face withdrawal at the beginning of May and soon afterwards its final journey, to Arnott Young scrapyard, for breaking up.

Top. Its late afternoon and the winter sun produces a little brightness and highlights the smokeboxes of 'Black '5s' No.'s 44800, 45353 and 44761 standing in the yard of Lostock Hall MPD. Only No. 45353 (centre) would remain at work until the end of steam. Above. Lostock Hall MPD as viewed from Watkin Lane. In the foreground is withdrawn (December 1967) Ivatt 4MT No. 43088. For many years a New England engine, the 2-6-0's final transfer, to Lostock Hall, had taken place in August 1967. Both 17th February.

We reached Carnforth shed late in the afternoon and the light was fading fast. By the time we had noted all the locos present it was almost dark. Illuminated by the sheds lighting, 'Black 5' No. 44894 waits for a fire to be laid and to raise steam ready for its next turn of duty. In the foreground, and in steam, is sister engine No. 44709, a Carnforth engine since moving from Crewe North in January 1949. Both locos would continue in service until the end of steam on BR. 17th February 1968.

18th February

Our journey home would take in several sheds on the way. The first of these, Rose Grove, was once the Burnley depot of the L & Y railway, with its main undertaking to supply suitable motive power for the many coal trains operating in this part of Lancashire. Of the 31 steam noted during our visit six were in steam, including '8F' No. 48448 fitted with a snowplough. Four different classes were represented: 'Black 5' (6), '8F' (23), standard 4MT (1) and '9F' (1). The lone standard 2-10-0, No. 92167, was in steam and rekindled memories of Saltley once again and the excitement and fascination that this engine, together with sister locos No's 92165 and 92166, had generated amongst the 'top link' footplate crews of the shed when they first arrived. The anticipation and excitement, especially for the fireman who would not have to face the arduous job of manually satisfying the demands of the engine and driver, were now a distant memory as soon would be the engine, too. Looking worn out and grimy after much mistreatment and neglect, she had only about three months of her short life left.

Stanier 2-8-0 No. 48375, seen here in Rose Grove on 18th February 1968, looks as bruised and battered as sister engine No. 48297, recorded in Edge Hill the previous day. Allocated to Bescot for most of its post-war life, the 2-8-0 was transferred to Rose Grove in August 1967. When and how the damage to its front end was sustained is unclear, but could well have happened quite soon after moving to 10F as it was withdrawn approximately six weeks later.

Next on our itinerary was Bolton. Three years earlier this L & Y shed had increased its steam allocation to fifty-seven, but since April 1965 the trend had been reversed and it had now fallen to twenty-seven. With several visitors to bolster numbers, we logged a total of 32 steam (see appendix 24) representing 3 different types - 'Black 5' (14), '8F' (15) and standard 5MT (3). Engines noted in steam were No's 44802, 44947, 45104, 45110, 45260, 45290, 45294, 45318, 45435, 48026, 48652, 48773 and 73069. Photographs taken here remind me what a gloomy and miserable day it was. Beneath the leaden sky the gently swirling mist produced an ethereal feeling and mood to the shed throughout the visit.

Interestingly, we came across what was now a most unusual practice. Allocated to Bolton after the closure of Kingmoor shed, 'Black 5' No. 44802 was being cleaned! Holding on to her handrail was a gentleman, presumably an enthusiast, trying his best to persuade months of grime to part company from the boiler? He was making a rather good job of it under the circumstances, so not wishing to disturb him we took a couple of photographs and left him to it. As the year progressed, an increasing number of spotless steam engines began to appear on different trains (other than specials) and at several of the surviving steam sheds. As time moved on, we wondered if there was any connection, was the cleaner at 9K a member of a group of enthusiasts that were to make their mark by sprucing up a good number of engines before steam faded into history? More will be said about the last (unofficial) steam engine cleaners on BR later.

Top. Noted inside the shed building on 18th February 1968, withdrawn Stanier '8F' No. 48559 was transferred from Crewe South the previous August, the 2-8-0 is seen in her home shed (9K) about a month earlier while still being usefully employed. Author's collection.
Above. An extraordinary sight: 'Black 5' No. 44802 stands in the yard of Bolton MPD being cleaned! The engine moved to the shed after its previous home depot, Kingmoor, had closed at the beginning of January. As a result the 4-6-0 would continue in service for a further six months, and would not be withdrawn until the closure of Bolton depot on 30th June.

Having left the 'cleaner' hard at work, we proceeded to Manchester and the next depot on our programme, Patricroft. The weather improved a little as we travelled further south, and the mist had lifted by the time we reached the shed. Once again standard 5MT 4-6-0's were dominant with 22 present. Making up the total of 35 steam on shed were ten '8F's, two 'Black 5's and 'Britannia' Pacific No. 70012 John of Gaunt, still in store inside the 'new' shed building. The following nine engines were in steam: No's 48033, 48325, 48453, 48491, 48700, 73000, 73067, 73132 and 73134.

Inside of the cab of '8F' No. 48700. When Burton shed closed, the '8F' was transferred for its final time to Patricroft in October 1966. On 15th February, three days before these pictures were taken, the engine had had a boiler examination, and as a result required just the replacement of a fusible plug. Nevertheless, the 2-8-0 would only continue working for another three weeks before withdrawal.

Trafford Park, the second of the city's depots on our agenda, had 21 steam on shed - thirteen 'Black 5's and eight '8F's (see appendix 24). Only three engines were in steam - No's 44665, 48317 and 48319. Newton Heath, the last of the Manchester sheds we visited, had 4 different varieties amongst the 52 steam noted. Fifty of the locos comprised Stanier 4-6-0s (35) and 2-8-0s (15). The other two engines were 'Britannia' Pacific No. 70023 Venus, continuing its period of storage in the yard, and '9F' No. 92109, last allocated to Birkenhead and withdrawn together with forty-three of its classmates during the previous November. Seventeen, almost a third of the engines logged, were in steam.

Above. Stanier '8F's No's 48345 and 48763 are seen inside Trafford Park MPD on 18th February 1968. The former engine would be withdrawn on the shed's closure while the latter would move on to Lostock Hall only to face withdrawal the following month. Left. Also inside 9E, their home shed, are three 'Black 5' 4-6-0's that would remain resolute until the end: No's 45269, 44735 and 45096 would continue in service until 4th August.

Sporting the name of their home shed, Trafford Park, on their buffer beams, Stanier '8F' No. 48317 and 'Black 5' No. 44807 stand side by side inside the shed building on 18th February 1968. The former engine arrived in February 1967 and the latter in December 1966. Both locos would be withdrawn on the closure of the depot on 4th March 1968.

The two 'Black 5's seen here in the yard of Newton Heath MPD on the same day, No's. 45202 and 45203 (one of five of the class to have three changes of frames) had spent all the years since nationalisation allocated to this depot. I suppose it was fitting that they ended their working lives here when they were taken out of service on the shed's closure on 30th June.

Left. Someone with a stick of chalk handy had decided to 'rename' 'Britannia' Pacific No. 70023 Venus while she remained in store at Newton Heath MPD, pending delivery to T.W.Ward's scrapyard, which would be effected sometime in April.

Below. It wouldn't be long before the lamps above 'Black 5's No's 44855 (nearest the camera) and 44836 would be turned on to provide some illumination to help Stockport Edgeley shed staff see their way around. Both the 4-6-0s entered traffic towards the end of 1944; both would be withdrawn on the closure of Edgeley, their home depot, on 6th May.

18th February 1968.

We were making our way round Stockport Edgeley, the penultimate shed of the day, less than an hour after leaving Newton Heath. The depot was home to 25 steam with three classes represented. Needless to say, Stanier 4-6-0 (16) and 2-8-0 (8) engines were most evident with twenty-four in all. The other engine making up the total was ex-Saltley '9F' No. 92165 mentioned earlier when seen at Rose Grove. She was in steam as was seven of the 'Black 5's and two '8'F' 2-8-0s.

Buxton MPD was reached late in the afternoon, with barely enough light left to take a few pictures. Here we found only '8Fs', nine altogether, and except for one, all were in steam. With cameras and notebooks safely stored away, we climbed on to my Lambretta ready to face the elements and undoubtedly a cold ride home.

Looking spruced up and very presentable, Stanier 2-8-0 No. 48775, of Patricroft MPD, is seen standing partly inside the shed building of Buxton on 18th February 1968. The '8F' would be kept in employment until the end of steam, moving from 9H on its closure to Lostock Hall. Buxton depot would close in two weeks time.

The following evening while developing the films I had taken, I checked the entries in my logbook and produced the usual statistics for the trip. A grand total of 402 steam engines had been noted representing 8 different varieties as follows: Ivatt 4MT (6), 'Black 5' (176), Ivatt 2MT (1, preserved), '8F' (136), 'Britannia' (5), standard 5MT (25), standard 4MT (11) and standard '9F' (42). A total of 104 engines, approximately one in four, were recorded as being in steam - 50 'Black 5's, 42 '8F's, 5 standard 5MT 4-6-0's and 7 standard '9F's. Stanier designs accounted for three out of every four engines noted.

March

On Saturday 2nd March I travelled by train to visit three sheds in the northwest. This weekend would see the final steam turns provided by Buxton, Northwich and Trafford Park MPD's before closing to steam two days later. However, for some reason, I chose to see what Stockport Edgeley, Lostock Hall and Carnforth sheds would have to offer instead.

My train left New Street twenty minutes late at 7.35am and after making up some of the lost time arrived at Stockport Edgeley at 9.14am. The first steam engines of the day had been noted shortly after passing through Macclesfield - two 'Black 5's' and two '8F's all in steam.

I had about thirty minutes to get to the depot, record the engines present, take a few photographs, and then get back again, before the train I planned to catch to Manchester left at 9.48am. I very hastily noted 17 steam on shed, comprising thirteen 'Black 5's' and four '8F's. All of the latter were in steam with eight of the 4-6-0's also ready for their next call of duty. Stanier 4-6-0 No. 44940 was noted as being very clean and under repair.

Following a quick sprint back to Edgeley station, I was just in time to catch the 9.48 train to Piccadilly. After a brisk walk across the city centre to Victoria, I had about twenty minutes to wait before departing on the 'stopper' for Preston. I didn't see any steam workings while on the station, but during the journey several engines were noted going about their business, including 'Black 5' No. 45104 at Miles Platting station and standard 5MT No. 73040 in a siding next to Bolton station. On arrival at Preston, 'Black 5' No. 45025 was found standing in the station with a parcels train.

'Black 5' No. 44940 stands inside Stockport Edgeley MPD on 2nd March 1968. Its left hand cylinder valve is receiving attention, with a number of parts left lying at the side of the loco. Withdrawn only days later, the repairs must have been too involved to warrant proceeding with any further.

Above. On a very wet and miserable 2nd March 1968, 'Black 5' No. 44871 has its coal stocks replenished while in its home shed, Stockport Edgeley. Following this depots closure in May, the 4-6-0 would move first to Bolton and then, finally, in early July, to Carnforth from where it would be withdrawn after working the BR 'Fifteen Guinea Special' on 11th August.

Left. On the same day the fire burns slowly in the brazier by the water tower in the yard of Stockport Edgeley: it would not be needed again after this winter.

'Black 5' No. 45025, at the head of a parcels train in Preston station, attracts the attention of a group of spotters on Saturday 2nd March 1968. Later in the year the engine would find itself looking rather smarter than it appears here.

Lostock Hall, the next depot on my itinerary, had been given extra responsibilities, together with Carnforth and Warrington, as a result of the closure of Preston, the former L&NWR shed, in September 1961 after a devastating fire there on 28th June 1960. Subsequently, Lostock Hall's motive power allocation had increased slightly to cope with the extra duties asked of it. However, its present steam allocation reflected the changes that had taken place during the intervening years but, having said that, it still had thirty steam locos to call upon - only three fewer than at the end of 1961.

With 30 steam noted on shed during this visit, the total reflected exactly its allocation of this form of motive power. Twenty-five of the engines present were assigned to the depot, including all of the remaining Ivatt 4MT 2-6-0s. The other two varieties present were Stanier's 'Black 5' (15) and '8F' (8) designs. Nine engines were noted in steam, and although she would be caught up in this month's batch of withdrawals, 'Black 5' No. 44800 was recorded as being very clean.

Arriving back at Preston station at about 1.30pm, I had a little over an hour to wait before catching the 2.38pm to Carnforth. While sitting and tucking in to my sandwiches, I caught sight of a steam-hauled freight train heading slowly towards the station from the south. As it got nearer I could make out that it was a standard '9F' with a train of hoppers. Once in the station it was evident that it was sporting a headboard and on closer inspection the inscription read: 'Farewell to Steam Northwich'. This was obviously to commemorate the shed's closure and had most likely been made and attached to the loco by enthusiasts. The engine in charge was No. 92218 and, according to the 8C shed number painted on the bottom of the smokebox, belonged to Speke Junction MPD. The 2-10-0 remained next to the platform for a few minutes until it got the signal to continue its journey north; our paths would cross again later the same afternoon.

1968 (The Final Farewell to British Steam)

Above. Stanier 4-6-0 No. 44713 simmers gently inside its home shed, Lostock Hall on 2nd March 1968. The 'Black 5' would continue working up until the end of steam on BR.

Below. Looking through the space above the frames of one Ivatt 2-6-0, No. 43106, to the cabside number of another, No. 43019, while both engines rest in the yard of Lostock Hall MPD on the same day.

As my train reached the approaches to Carnforth, the smoke rising from the shed area adjacent to the station was a clear indication that the depot had a fair number of engines ready for employment. I logged a total of 50 steam on shed with 6 varieties represented (see appendix 25). Interestingly, as well as the last surviving working 'Britannia', No. 70013 Oliver Cromwell, being present in the yard, sister engine No. 70021 Morning Star was still to be found in store close by. Was she I wondered being kept for spare parts for No.70013 should she require any? Ten of the twenty-three 'Black 5's were noted in steam and, even though there were twelve standard 4MT 4-6-0s logged, only No's. 75039 and 75048 were fired and ready for duty. Eight '9F's' were present with one in steam - the newly arrived No. 92218 seen earlier at Preston - and a solitary '8F' No. 48323.

A grand total of 109 steam had been logged by the end of the day with 38 engines fired ready for duty - less than thirty per cent. Come Monday 4th March there would be ten depots left employing and servicing the few surviving steam locos on BR's books.

While noting the locos in the yard of Carnforth shed later in the day, '9F' No. 92218 was found being serviced. The 2-10-0 entered traffic on 18th January 1960 and was initially allocated to Bristol St Philips Marsh. Although now based at Speke Jnct., the headboard it carried was a tribute to Northwich MPD and the fact that it was about to close. The '9F' would be withdrawn on the demise of its home shed on 6th May and subsequently disposed of by Arnott Young, Parkgate, two months later.

Left. 'Black 5' No. 45096 passes underneath the footbridge leading to Carnforth MPD on 2nd March 1968. The 4-6-0 entered traffic in April 1935 and spent many years based in the northwest. During the final few months of its working life it would be transferred from Agecroft to Trafford Park and, finally, to Rose Grove, from where it would continue to see service until the end of steam on BR.

Below. On the same day, Stanier 4-6-0 No. 44942, once a familiar engine around the Birmingham area in the 1950's and early 60's, stands over the ash pit in Carnforth MPD. By January 1966 the 'Black 5' had moved to Banbury and later in September to Shrewsbury. From early March 1967 the northwest had become her stamping ground and Lostock Hall her final home shed, from where she would be withdrawn in July.

Four weeks would elapse before I set off on my travels again. Steam was now well and truly shackled and confined almost exclusively to Lancashire. Elsewhere, for many, only Alan Pegler's Flying Scotsman, which had BR's permission to travel virtually anywhere on the system, would provide a brief opportunity to see a steam locomotive in action. However, adverts for steam specials in the northwest were beginning to appear and a plethora of these would run regularly throughout the spring and into the summer. The odd passenger turn diagrammed for steam haulage on the LMR still survived, including Lostock Hall's weekday and Sunday turns from Preston to Liverpool Exchange. These duties, which should have been taken over by Brush type '4's from 4th March, remained in the hands of Stanier's 'Black 5's because of a shortage of these diesels. Reports were suggesting, though, that the only consistently steam-hauled passenger train was the Belfast Boat Express between Manchester Victoria and Heysham.

On 30th March, I once again chose to go in search of steam by train rather than by scooter. I caught the 7.15am from New Street to Stockport as I had earlier in the month and not travelling any further north than Manchester and Liverpool this time, my schedule would allow me to make five shed visits if all went to plan. The first of these, Edgeley, had had both 'Flying Scotsman' and 'Oliver Cromwell' plus privately preserved 'Jubilee' No. (4)5596 Bahamas on view at the depot on 16th, the day prior to the Pacifics working a William Deacon's Bank Club special. My visit produced the more commonplace Stanier '8F's of which there were four and 'Black 5's totalling nine. Two of the former and five of the latter were in steam.

Heaton Mersey, reached after a very sprightly twenty-minute walk, had 24 steam on shed (see appendix 26), nineteen '8F's and five 'Black 5's. Six of the 2-8-0's were in steam but the 'Black 5's were all cold. On the way back to Edgeley, I stopped to admire the viaduct and photographed two unidentified steam locos crossing the impressive stucture. While on Edgeley station, 'Black 5' No. 44855 passed through light engine and during my brief wait for the train to take me from Manchester Exchange to Liverpool, I noted standard 5MT No. 73128 at the head of a parcels train as well as Stanier 4-6-0 No. 45203 acting as station pilot. A further three steam were noted during the journey.

Sitting inside Stockport Edgeley MPD on 20th March 1968 are Stanier 'Black 5's No's 45269, 45046 and 45312. All are in steam and ready for their next turn of duty.

Stanier 2-8-0 No. 48437, fitted with a snowplough, stands alongside EE Type '4' No. D381 inside Stockport Edgeley MPD on 30th March 1968. Records show that the '8F' was withdrawn around this time and may have already carried out her last duty.

Above and next. Stockport Edgeley viaduct. Standing 111ft. high it was officially opened on 4th June 1840. Bridging the valley of the river Mersey, 11,000,000 bricks were used in its construction over a period of 21 months. Next to the shop displaying the Guinness advert the Mersey slowly flows by while a steam loco and emu pass on the viaduct. The second view has a 'Black 5' crossing the structure, and, parked on wasteland in the foreground, an array of popular cars of the time. The structure would undergo a programme of restoration in 1989 costing £3,000,000.

From a steamless Lime Street I set off for Edge Hill shed. The presence of only two classes of engine repeated itself once again, with seventeen Stanier 2-8-0s and sixteen of his 4-6-0s on shed. Four of each variety were in steam and one of the 'Black 5's, No. 45284, I found and photographed under the coaling stage. The structure and method used to re-fuel engines here always fascinated me as I couldn't recall seeing it employed in any of the other sheds I'd visited up and down the country. Indeed, I didn't realise until many years later, when I read about how efficient and speedy its method of operation was, that it had become the shed's policy to book most visiting engines to take coal as a matter of course before returning home.

Stanier 'Black 5' No. 45284 rests beneath the coaling stage (mentioned above) in the yard of Edge Hill MPD on 30th March 1968.

The second of the Liverpool sheds on my itinerary, Speke Junction, produced 52 steam representing 4 different varieties as follows: 'Black 5' (22), '8F' (16), '9F' (13) and a 'Britannia' in the form of No. 70024 Vulcan, having completed its third month in store after withdrawal. The vast majority of the locos were cold, with only seven noted in steam: No's 44971, 45386, 45388, 48153, 48292, 48356, and 92160. Unlike Edge Hill, the coaling facilities here had never really been improved upon, except if one includes the addition of a portable conveyor belt, which by itself was now more than capable of satisfying the demands of the few engines still availing themselves of the shed's services. Today happened to be Grand National Day and for the first time not one of nine special trains working to and from Sefton Arms station, close to Aintree racecourse, had a steam engine in charge; five weeks later the station would be renamed Aintree.

After returning to Manchester I caught the bus to Dean Lane and walked the short distance to Newton Heath shed. This, the last of the five depots on my programme, was the liveliest of all with thirteen engines recorded in steam out of thirty-five on shed. In the yard another 'Britannia' Pacific, No. 70023 Venus, was also enduring a lengthy period of storage. Making up the total number of steam seen were twenty-four 'Black 5's and ten '8F's.

Altogether 160 steam had been recorded during the day with forty-four in steam. Except for Newton Heath, all of the sheds visited had a little over a month to go before closure.

Vulcan Foundry-built 'Black 5' No. 45096 rests inside Newton Heath. It was late in the day and the light was beginning to fade when I took this picture. Once darkness enveloped the shed, what little illumination the old lamps projected would have to be sufficient to help the shed staff see their way around while going about their duties.

30th March 1968.

April

News of steam locos managing to make inroads into regions that were now fully dieselised had almost dried up. Nevertheless, even at this late hour, this form of motive power was still breaking free of its Lancashire confines. It continued to penetrate the northeast with regular freight workings from the LMR to Healey Mills sidings, and with the Heysham to Leeds oil train, often double-headed by a Type '2' diesel and a class '9F' 2-10-0. Indeed, with the latter diagram, it appears that the rostered steam engine also frequented Neville Hill shed for turning and for somewhere to wait prior to the return working. Interestingly, at least one steam loco was still being employed in Scotland during April. According to information in the Railway World magazine standard 4MT 2-6-4T No. 80002, withdrawn during March the previous year, was regularly being used for steam heating purposes in Cowlairs carriage sidings.

Three weeks passed before I set off for Liverpool and my next trip to the northwest. I left home on the evening of Friday 19th April and travelled on my Lambretta as far as the outskirts of Widnes where I camped for the night. I had decided to see a steam special starting out from Lime Street the following morning, and had to be at the station in time to photograph its departure at 8.53am. The railtour had been organised by the RCTS, and by the day's end would have involved three different steam locos covering a total of 280 miles.

I arrived at Lime Street station at about eight o'clock, and a few minutes later, in the bright morning sunshine, watched 'Black 5' No. 45287 arrive with empty stock. Looking spotless, named 'Black 5' No. 45156 Ayrshire Yeomanry was in charge of the 'Lancastrian No.2 Rail Tour'. Departing right on time from a platform packed with spectators, she would share the day's duties with sister engine No. 45342 and 'Britannia' Pacific No. 70013 Oliver Cromwell. However, while double heading the train with No. 45156 during a later leg of the special, No. 45342 developed a vacuum fault leaving many disappointed line-side photographers with the well-polished 'Ayrshire Yeomanry' in the less photogenic position (see page 243) next to the carriages.

My next stop was the ex-LNWR depot Edge Hill. Now with an undistinguished allocation of a few Stanier '8F's and 'Black 5's, the shed was moving swiftly towards closure. With a total of eleven of his 2-8-0s and thirteen 4-6-0s present, the locos I listed during this visit reflected a far less glamorous collection of engines than those of years gone by. Six engines were in steam: No's 48045, 48206, 44777, 45187, 45287 and 45305.

Leaving Edge Hill I set off for Speke Junction. In the past this depot's main function was the supply of suitable motive power for south Liverpool's freight and shunting requirements. Interestingly, its steam allocation had been reduced from 49 in 1950 to 33 by 1959. But from 1960 on it experienced a gradual increase until April 1965 when its allocation peaked at 57. By the autumn of 1967, however, it had fallen back to 25, comprising '8F', 'Black 5' and standard '9F' varieties. On the conclusion of this visit a total of 43 steam representing 4 different classes had been noted, with just seven engines - No's 45388, 48319, 48493, 48551, 48720, 92160 and 92218 - in steam. Many of the locos present had been withdrawn for some time and one, '9F' No. 92151, had ceased working twelve months earlier. 'Britannia' Pacific No. 70024 Vulcan, withdrawn at the end of the previous year and which I noted here in February, was still enduring a protracted period of storage. Standing next to the 4-6-2 was '8F' No. 48305, which like sister engine No 48151 I mentioned earlier, would also be delivered to Barry for scrapping. However, her incarceration lasted not seven years as endured by 48151, but eighteen before being purchased for and preserved by the Great Central railway.

Top. 'Black 5' No. 45305, last overhauled in March 1966, still looks in good external condition two years later. The 4-6-0, seen in Edge Hill MPD, would be in even better shape by the time the final weekend of steam came around and would be involved with BR's 'Last Days of Steam' special. But her ultimate duty, however, would remain unfulfilled. Rostered to haul the first stage of the BR 'Fifteen Guinea Special' on 11th August, it was found that her fire grate had fallen in and standby engine No. 45110 duly took over the duty.

Above. Following several years allocated to Toton and Nottingham, '8F' No. 48319 moved to the northwest and to further home sheds such as Fleetwood and Springs Branch (Wigan). Her final move, from Patricroft to Bolton, would take place at the beginning of May, with withdrawal coming after the closure of 9K in July. Standing next to the engine in the yard of Speke Jnct. shed is my Lambretta scooter JOP 753 E. Both 20th April 1968.

No one could have predicted that the next shed on my itinerary would attract as many visitors as it did before the end of steam on BR. Once of the Lancashire & Yorkshire Railway, Lostock Hall enticed more and more trainspotters and enthusiasts to experience its daily servicing and preparation of steam engines for duty as the year wore on. Every time I visited the shed there were always lots of other steam fans eager to note and photograph the engines present. On this occasion, together with several other people making their way round the depot, I noted 30 steam representing 4 different classes. 'Black 5's were most evident totalling fourteen, followed by nine '8F's, six Ivatt 4MT 2-6-0s (only three of which remained in capital stock - No's 43019, 43027 and 43106) and, making up the mix, a solitary '9F', No. 92054, one of eight engines in steam.

With smokebox hinges, shedplate and number painted white, it looks as though 'Black 5' No. 44713 has been prepared for a special turn of duty. Built at Horwich, the loco entered service in November 1948. Just shy of its twentieth birthday, the 4-6-0 would be withdrawn at the end of steam on BR. Lostock Hall MPD, 20th April 1968.

From Lostock Hall I continued up the A6 to Carnforth for my final shed visit for the day. The depot occupied the site of the ex-Furness Railway shed and, with the use of Italian prisoners of war during its construction, was opened in the December of 1944. Little did I realise that the depot would be preserved and continue to maintain and service a number of steam engines lucky enough to keep well clear of the breaker's yard. Four weeks earlier on 17th March, the depot had had an 'Open Day', which attracted in excess of 2,500 visitors. On this day, with no more than a handful of other enthusiasts about, I logged a total of 32 steam representing 6 different varieties as follows: Fairburn 2-6-4T (1, preserved), 'Black 5' (16), '8F' (1), 'Britannia' Pacific (1), standard 4MT 4-6-0 (7) and '9F' (6). Eleven engines were in steam including No. 70013 Oliver Cromwell. She had worked the RCTS rail tour from Fleetwood to Windermere and back to Morecambe Promenade earlier in the day and was now ready to travel to Preston to head the special train on the final leg of its journey to Liverpool Exchange.

After photographing the RCTS special, now with two 'Black 5's in charge, No. 45342 piloting No. 45156, I spent a short while on Carnforth station before setting off for the camp site at Bolton-le-Sands. Once I had eaten, I walked down to the station and sat on one of the benches from about 7.30pm until dusk hoping to see one or two steam workings. None materialised, however, and I had to be satisfied with noting three Brush Type '4's and an 0-6-0 diesel shunter travelling light engine back to Carnforth its home depot.

For two months at the end of 1964 '9F' No. 92088 underwent a heavy intermediate overhaul, including a boiler change. Collected since these repairs were carried out, the grease and grime on its motion is a stark reminder of the neglect that many of the last working engines of the BR steam fleet had to endure. Carnforth MPD, 20th April 1968.

On the same day, No. 70013 Oliver Cromwell, looking far more cared for than the '9F', is about to leave Carnforth MPD and head the ten coach RCTS special from Preston via Farington Curve Junction, Burscough North Junction, Burscough Bridge, Southport, and Freshfield to Liverpool Exchange.

On the morning of 21st I was up early and after breaking camp checked the route I planned to take to reach the first of the four sheds I would visit on my way back home. I had decided to travel on a minor road from Lancaster through the wild and rugged area of Bowland Forest, through the Trough of Bowland, across the River Ribble and on to Clitheroe and, finally, Burnley and Rose Grove shed. I remember how desolate the area was and, contrary to expectations, almost completely devoid of trees and indeed traffic. With mobile phones many years away, quite what I would have done if my scooter had broken down I don't know.

Fortunately, my Lambretta behaved itself and I arrived safely at Rose Grove around 9.30am, quickly noting a total of 29 steam representing three different classes (see appendix 27). With twenty-two on shed, Stanier '8F's were predominant, followed by his 'Black 5' design of which there were five. Adding a little more variety to the scene were two standard 4MT 4-6-0s No's. 75023, withdrawn in February, and 75048, which would continue working until steam finished on BR. I recorded a solitary engine in steam, '8F' No. 48476. Sister engine No. 48448 was continuing to sport a small snow plough and, as a grim reminder of the fate facing most of these engines, I noted and photographed lying on the ground the cabside of No. 48375. This engine, once briefly allocated to Saltley, was transferred from the Birmingham shed to Stoke towards the end of 1966 and then after this depot's closure in August 1967, to Rose Grove. Only a few weeks after her arrival at 10F she was condemned. Unfortunately, I didn't make any notes about the engine at the time, so I can only assume she had been cut up on site, or prior to its disposal for scrapping, someone had employed an acetylene torch to remove the cabside for a memento.

A weighty and cumbersome keepsake, if that is what it was intended to be. The cabside of '8F' No. 48375 lies on the ground in Rose Grove MPD on 21st April 1968, almost seven months after the engine's withdrawal from service.

Built at Swindon in October 1953, standard 4MT No. 75048, seen here in Rose Grove on the same day, was originally allocated to Accrington. By now the engine was based at Carnforth but, together with 75019 and 75027, would work from Rose Grove to cover the Rylstone Quarry roster along the Grassington Branch.

Climbing into the cab of the only engine in steam on Rose Grove MPD, I captured this view from the footplate. Stanier '8F' No. 48476 had been allocated to Willesden for about twelve years after Nationalisation, but was then transferred to the northwest, eventually becoming a Lostock Hall engine. The Swindon-built loco would evade the cutter's torch right up until steam finished on BR, and would be amongst the final batch of steam withdrawals. The view of the 2-8-0 below shows how clean the loco was at the time, although it is puzzling why the number on its cabside had had the grime only partially removed from two of the five digits. 21st April 1968.

Recently cleaned for its leg of the previous day's Manchester Rail Travel Society/Severn Valley Society Special, Stanier 2-8-0 No. 48773 rests in the yard of Bolton MPD on 21st April 1968. I couldn't resist taking a photo of the now clearly visible and easily recognisable 1956 "ferret and dartboard" crest on its tender, used on BR locos prior to the introduction of the corporate (blue) livery.

Stanier line-up on Bolton shed on 21st April 1968: from nearest the camera - 'Black 5' No. 45394, '8F' No 48773 and 'Black 5's No's. 44929 and 45318. Only No. 44929 wouldn't make it until the end of steam on BR, the 4-6-0 would be withdrawn after the closure of Bolton MPD on 30th June 1968.

Resuming my journey south I soon covered the twenty miles or so to reach my next destination, Bolton. From 1950 until the spring of 1965, this former L & Y Railway shed invariably had an allocation of at least seven varieties of steam locomotive. Now, of course, its allotment of steam reflected the dearth of classes remaining, and, with the transfer the previous week of its last two standard 5MT 4-6-0s to Patricroft, the depot was left with 'Black 5's and '8F's to cover its duties. So, it was no surprise to find fourteen of each of these Stanier types present. However, out of the 28 engines on shed twelve were in steam and consequently the depot felt a lot livelier than Rose Grove had.

Heaton Mersey, the penultimate depot on my itinerary, produced a total of 35 steam. Twenty-seven of these were '8F's and the remainder 'Black 5's. Nine of the former and two of the latter were in steam. It would appear from my notes that at least fifteen (three 'Black 5's and twelve '8F's) had either been withdrawn or placed in store. A walk of half an hour was reduced to a few minutes by scooter to reach the last shed I would visit, Heaton Mersey's neighbour, Stockport Edgeley. Here I found a total of 18 steam - five '8F's and thirteen 'Black 5's with the following engines ready for duty: No's 48170, 48267, 48549, 44836, 44868, 44781, 44871, and 45046. An analysis of the steam recorded during the weekend revealed seven different varieties amongst the total of 244 engines noted, with 67 engines in steam.

May / June

On 1st May, and more than deserving a special mention, was the Alan Pegler / Locomotive Club of Great Britain special celebrating the 40th Anniversary of the first non-stop run from Kings Cross to Edinburgh. In charge, of course, was arguably the world's best known steam engine, Flying Scotsman, just as she had been on the same day 40 years earlier on Tuesday, 1st May, 1928. Less well-known sister engine No. 2580 (BR No. 60081) Shotover was the other engine involved in the up working of the famous train all those years previously.

The 40th Anniversary run proved to be a bit of a cliff-hanger with plenty of drama, including speed dropping down to walking pace when put into the goods road outside Berwick. But the train arrived, without stopping, at platform 10 Waverley greeted by an enormous crowd, the Lord Provost and a pipe band playing 'Scotland the brave'.

By this time Royston and Normanton sheds had been cleared of all remaining stored steam engines and further LMR depot closures were looming; the news was that another four steam sheds would close on 5th May. Determined to make a final visit to each one before they ceased operating, I decided to travel by train to Stockport and Liverpool to see steam for the last time at Edgeley, Heaton Mersey, Speke Junction and Edge Hill. All of these sheds would close completely; there would be no further use made of them for servicing diesels or storage, and they would be demolished within a relatively short space of time.

Steam was still, but only just, infiltrating supposedly all-diesel areas. A few freight services with steam in charge were continuing across the Pennines from Bolton to places like Hull and Healey Mills. Reports were also occasionally filtering through, too, of isolated steam-hauled freight workings from Patricroft and Liverpool to the Chester area.

On 4th May I caught the 8.00am service from New Street to Stockport. A little over an hour and a half later I was busily noting and photographing the last few steam engines using the depot's facilities. A total of 16 steam were present representing 3 different classes. In steam was '8F' No. 48546, 'Black 5's No's. 44871, 44888, 44940 and 45312 and '9F' No. 92069. I photographed the '9F' several times and included in one of the shots is a Brush Type '4' (No. D1996) a class of diesel I had not recorded here before.

Heaton Mersey had twenty-two '8F's and six 'Black 5's on shed. Like Edgeley this depot would close for good the following day. Two engines were noted in steam: '8F' No. 48191, next to the coaling plant, and sister engine No. 48723 inside the shed building, both of which were photographed. These two locos would, for the time being at least, escape the withdrawal net and move on to new home depots of Rose Grove and Lostock Hall respectively. All of the other engines had either already been withdrawn or would be so after the shed's demise.

Built at Crewe in December 1955 and first allocated to Doncaster, standard '9F' No. 92069 stands in the yard of Stockport Edgeley MPD on 4th May 1968. After spells based at Annesley and Birkenhead, the 2-10-0 moved to Speke Jnct. in November 1967. Withdrawal would come the day after this photograph was taken when 8C closed.

Before taking the train into Manchester, 'Black 5' No. 45269 was noted in Stockport Edgeley station with two young trainspotters talking to the driver and succeeding in being invited on to the footplate. The engine was at the head of a parcels train, and later my picture of her prompted me to realise how quickly this scene would become just a memory. I walked across the centre of Manchester from Piccadilly to Central station and was soon on my way to Allerton and Speke Junction MPD, hoping that the weather would keep as bright and cheerful as it had when the day started and not to begin to go downhill as so often seemed to happen when I visited this area.

Three different classes were represented amongst the 25 engines on Speke shed. Four locos were in steam: 'Black 5's No's 45386 and 45388, Stanier 2-8-0 No. 48493 and '9F' No. 92160. The '8F', after taking on water, immediately left the shed, while No's 45386 and 92160 remained over the ash pit having their fires attended to. The two Stanier 4-6-0's would be transferred to Lostock Hall, whilst the '8F' would move on to Rose Grove. These three engines would not face withdrawal until week ending 10th August. The '9F', after being taken on board by Carnforth MPD, would cease work some time later in June.

Built by Armstrong, Whitworth, No. 45386 entered traffic in July 1937. Seen here in Speke Junction MPD on 4th May 1968, the 4-6-0 would remain in service until steam finished working on BR. Allocated to Mold Junction at the time of the Second World War, this engine was the first 'Black 5' to be damaged during enemy action while at Kentish Town on 10th October 1940.

The last of the four sheds closing this weekend, Edge Hill, was home to eighteen '8F' 2-8-0s and nine 'Black 5's. Six of the '8F's and three of the 'Black 5's were in steam. Unlike the previous three depots where most of their engines would be withdrawn on closure, over half of Edge Hill's locos would be transferred between the six remaining steam depots. Named 'Black 5' No. 45156, following initial re-allocation to Patricroft, must have been in pretty good shape as she would be transferred once more on this depots closure at the end of June to her final home, Rose Grove. Other engines that would steer a similar course as the 'Black 5' and still be active up until the last weekend of normal steam working included No's. 45231, 48665 and 48715.

Before setting a course for home I visited one further depot, Newton Heath. In addition to the expected Stanier varieties I also noted sole surviving 'Britannia, Pacific No. 70013 Oliver Cromwell and a solitary '9F' No. 92054 on shed. Both of these engines were in steam, together with three '8F's and twelve 'Black 5's. The '9F', allocated to Speke Junction, would not return home; this was most likely to have been the last time she was in steam, as it appears she was withdrawn during this weekend.

A total of 130 steam locos, many already or about to be taken out of service, had been noted during the day, with forty engines in steam (see appendix 28 for steam locos recorded on each shed).

'Black 5' No. 45156 rests in the yard of Edge Hill MPD, on 4th May 1968. Although not quite as stylish as the original nameplate, someone had decided that it should at least carry a presentable reminder of the fact that it was still regarded as a named engine.

Above. Stanier 4-6-0 No. 45046 receives coal in Newton Heath MPD on 4th May 1968. Built by Vulcan Foundry, the 'Black 5' entered service in October 1934 and spent a number of years post 1948 in the northwest. Allocated to various sheds, including Carlisle Upperby, Barrow, Longsight and Carnforth, she would be transferred during the following week, for the final time, to Bolton, and would be withdrawn on this shed's closure on 30th June.

Left. One can almost smell the mix of oil, steam and smoke! 'Black 5' No. 45310 sits inside its home shed, Newton Heath on the same day. Further pictures of and details about this loco can be found in the colour section, page 247, and on page 258.

The end of steam's history book was drawing ever closer, and the conclusion of yet another significant chapter had been reached. Monday 6th May, however, was noteworthy for reasons other than the closure of a further four steam depots. It was an important date in terms of employing steam power for ordinary service train operation. To coincide with the start of the new timetables on this day, BR intended to stop using steam on such diagrams and so end almost 140 years of steam-hauled passenger trains. But, as was soon discovered, it didn't quite happen. Even though BR formally announced that steam motive power was no longer being used, a few such turns continued in the hands of this form of traction right up until 3rd August.

The old routine of visiting Tyseley and Saltley was difficult to shake off, and on 11th May I made what would be my last visit to these depots before steam finished on BR. The need for steam locos to use the diesel depot's lathe facilities had now long since ceased, but once again Tyseley produced one or two such engines in the form of 'Jubilee' No. (4)5593 Kolhapur and 'Castle' No. 7029 Clun Castle, both of course preserved. Intriguingly, also sharing the roundhouse was 'Black 5' No. 45279 minus, amongst other parts, its connecting rods and tender. Transferred to Heaton Mersey from Kingmoor after the depot's closure in January, I last recorded the engine as withdrawn while at its home shed on 21st April. Disposal would take place at J. Cashmore, Great Bridge, so quite why it had ended up here was a bit of a mystery. Perhaps it was being cannibalised for spares, although I never found out if this was in fact the case.

Tyseley MPD, 11th May 1968. Allocated to Aston from June 1961 to November 1963, preserved Stanier 4-6-0 No. 5593 Kolhapur shares the roundhouse with Collett 'Castle' No. 7029 Clun Castle, also preserved. These two fine engines had a bright future, but the same couldn't be said for the other 4-6-0 on shed at this time. Minus its tender, 'Black 5' No. 45279 was in what appeared to be a cannibalised state, with lots of parts missing, including its connecting rods and numerous cab fittings. A Kentish Town engine for many years, it gradually made its way north with further allocations, including Llandudno and Kingmoor, and finally Heaton Mersey from where it had been withdrawn in March 1968.

Saltley had lost its steam allocation over twelve months earlier and now had what had become the regular mix of diesels associated with the shed. As I moved from one empty roundhouse to the next, there was a ghostly silence permeating each building. I stood for a few moments while memories of the days when the smells and sounds associated with a working steam depot came flooding back; moving into the yard, I looked past the diesels present and pictured the last three stored '8F's that had defiantly remained here long after the shed had closed to steam.

I would return to a completely different Saltley almost thirty years later to display some of the photographs I had taken at the shed between 1965-1967. The access was exactly as it used to be, but the depot itself had changed almost beyond recognition. Nearly all of the buildings had been demolished and many tracks had been uprooted; I suppose a tenuous link with the past remained - at least part of the site was still being used for diesel servicing.

Prior to making my next trip to the northwest, I joined a West Country 'shed bash' organised by The Worcester Locomotive Society during the weekend of 17th, 18th and 19th May. My main reasons for joining this tour were the inclusion of visits to Buckfastleigh, where a number of ex-GWR steam engines were stored ready for use on the Dart Valley Railway, and to Dibbles Wharf, Southampton, where a special little engine was employed.

I decided to join the party in Hereford, which would enable me to visit Worcester shed on the way. Surprisingly, I saw my first steam engine during my journey from Shrub Hill to Hereford. Quite where I logged 'Black 5' No. 45111 I can't remember, and unfortunately I didn't note the location in my logbook. The engine was last allocated to Rose Grove and had been withdrawn almost six months earlier in November 1967 (I later discovered that it was on its last journey - to J. Cashmore, Town Dock, Newport for breaking up). Nonetheless, I was really looking forward to eventually seeing a charming 75-year-old engine that was a lot more modest in size than the Stanier 4-6-0, but that would not be until Sunday.

By the time we arrived at Buckfastleigh and the Dart Valley Railway on the Saturday afternoon (18th), we had been around seven sheds/stabling points. Here, however, I was reunited with one or two familiar engines, including Churchward 2-6-2T No. 4555 and light 0-6-0PT No. 1638, both of which had previously spent time at Tyseley shed. Unfortunately, the granting of a Light Railway Order would take a lot longer than expected, and it would be almost another twelve months before any of the engines present would be allowed to haul passenger trains.

My patience and resilience were finally rewarded on the Sunday when we reached Southampton Docks, and more specifically Dibbles Wharf. It was here that Corralls Coal Merchants operated steam engines for shunting coal wagons. One of these engines was No. 30096 a 'B4' 0-4-0T designed by Adams for dock shunting. Built in 1893, BR had sold her (with number plate and shed code still intact) to Corralls after withdrawal in October 1963. This was the engine I had so looked forward to seeing, and I have included a picture of the loco not least because of having to endure twenty-five diesel depot visits in order to see her! Towards the end of 1972, after a lengthy period of neglect, the engine was purchased by the Bullied Preservation Society and handed over to the Bluebell Railway on 16th December of the same year.

'Warship' No. D604 Cossack is seen stored in Laira while waiting to be taken to Cashmore's of Newport to be broken up. The engine entered traffic in January 1959 and, after only nine years service had been withdrawn in December 1967.

With less than twelve months of its working life left, North British Type '2' diesel hydraulic No. D6314 stands inside St Blazey MPD. This loco and D604 (top) were destined to be two ill-fated engines and would only manage to muster a total of eighteen years service between them. Both 18th May 1968.

The Warwickshire Railway Society organised a 'North Western Steam Tour' on the same weekend and two of the engines employed on Saturday 18th May, were 'Black 5' No. 44949 and standard 5MT No. 73069, seen above at Wigan station. Author's collection.

Now known as 'Corrall Queen', class 'B4' No. 30096, formerly named Normandy, looks in good shape, while resting in Dibbles Wharf, Southampton, on Sunday 19th May 1968.

Immediately after arriving home on the Sunday evening, I called Jackie and arranged to stay the night. The following day, Monday 20th May, after persuading her mum and dad to let her join me, we set off on my scooter for a day out ... seeing steam in Lancashire! Fortunately the weather stayed fair and we had a pleasant journey to Newton Heath, the first of four sheds we would visit during the day. I recorded a total of 26 steam, all of which were Stanier engines except for one, Riddles' '9F' No. 92054, which had remained here since her withdrawal two weeks earlier. Four of the '8F's present and nine of the eighteen 'Black 5's were in steam.

After a short ride across the centre of Manchester we reached Patricroft station where I parked expecting Jackie to wait for me while I went round the shed. However, she must have been getting into the swing of things and decided to tag along too. We hastily made our way round the depot and logged a total 38 steam. Four different classes were represented: 'Black 5' (4), '8F' (15), standard 5MT (18) and '9F' (1). One of a number of pictures I took while in the depot included Jackie, posing next to standard No. 73040 at rest outside the shed building. Ten engines were in steam, including three standard 5MT 4-6-0s fitted with Caprotti valve gear. I recorded my last ever steam cop here on this day, Stanier '8F' No. 48749. She had been a Mold Junction engine for most of the previous ten years and, after the shed's closure spent a month at Llandudno Junction, before becoming a Patricroft engine at the end of May 1966.

Following sandwiches for lunch on Bolton station (I certainly knew how to treat a girl!), we set off for the depot. We found 23 steam on shed - thirteen 'Black 5's and ten '8F's. There were six locos in steam, No's 48168, 44871, 45073, 45110, 45269, and 45312. Looking very clean and receiving attention from fitters was No. 45110. Briefly, while I was photographing the engine, I noticed that their concentration faltered for a while as they looked at me... or was it the mini-skirted young lady standing by my side!

Sunlight, shadow and smokeboxes, Patricroft MPD, 20th May 1968.

On 20th May, two days after its involvement in the W.R.S. steam special (see page 220), 'Black 5' No. 44949, stands inside Newton Heath MPD ready for its next turn of duty. Built at Horwich, the 4-6-0 entered traffic in February 1946 and would complete a little over twenty-two years service before being withdrawn the following month.

Exactly one month after photographing 45156 on 20th April (see page 241), it is evident that very little, if any, further cleaning of Ayrshire Yeomanry had taken place. Seen here dappled in sunlight inside Patricroft shed, the Stanier 'Black 5' would be spruced up again for its involvement in two further specials. The first, on 28th July, organised jointly by the Severn Valley Railway Society and Manchester Rail Travel Society and the second, on Sunday 4th August, organised by G.C. Enterprises, which the loco would have sole responsibility for throughout. Of the six specials commemorating the end of steam on 4th, 45156 would be the last to arrive back on shed, returning to Lostock Hall MPD at 4.00am on the Monday morning. Driver Andy Hall, would, therefore, go into the history books as the last steam footplate man on British Railways (August 11th special events aside).

1968 (The Final Farewell to British Steam)

Built at Horwich works, 'Black 5' No. 44947 started earning its keep in February 1946. It was allocated to Blackpool Central MPD, formerly of the Lancashire and Yorkshire Railway, for at least fifteen years before being transferred to Bolton in September 1964. The 4-6-0 would remain a 9K engine until closure of the shed on 30th June 1968, after which it would be withdrawn. Seen here inside Bolton MPD on 20th May, it is evident that shed staff or enthusiasts had taken time to ensure that not only both the depot name and its code be printed on its buffer beam and smokebox door respectively, but also added the letters SC to reflect the fact that it had a self-cleaning smokebox.

Taking the more scenic route along the A675 across moorland and past Belmont Reservoir we joined the A6 south of Preston. I had decided to forego a visit to Lostock Hall shed and to continue north to Carnforth so I could show Jackie where Brief Encounter had been shot, although I don't recall her being that impressed about the location, even though it was regarded as a classic film. We had a long return journey to make, so we didn't spend much time on the station or indeed going round the shed. However, I still managed to take a number of photographs while Jackie noted the locos present. Altogether 35 steam were logged with twelve of them ready for their next turn of duty. The number of locos in each class represented was as follows: Fairburn 2-6-4T (2, preserved), Ivatt 2MT (1, preserved), 'Black 5' (16), '8F' (1), 'B1' (1, preserved), 'Britannia' (1), standard 4MT 4-6-0 (5) and '9F' (8). An analysis of the locos recorded, carried out the following day after developing the films I had taken, revealed we had seen 122 steam (including those preserved) representing nine different classes (see appendix 29 for steam logged on shed). Forty-one locos had been noted in steam.

Watched by a fitter, standard 4MT No. 75027 moves on to Carnforth, its home shed, on 20th May 1968. Built at Swindon and finished in BR green livery, the loco entered traffic in May 1954 and was initially based at Laira (Plymouth). The 4-6-0 would be transferred thirteen times before being withdrawn at the end of steam. Good fortune prevailed soon after, however, and the engine was purchased by Charlie Pyne and donated to the Bluebell Railway, East Sussex of which he was a member.

June

Time was fast running out. Steam had only a matter of weeks left to play out its very restricted use in the day to day running of our railway. Once the planned closure of Newton Heath, Patricroft and Bolton had taken place at the end of June, its already minor role would be further diminished. Determined to visit these sheds once more before their responsibilities for employing and servicing steam came to an end, I left home on my scooter on Saturday 22nd June and headed initially for Manchester.

The weather wasn't particularly inspiring and, as so often happened when heading northwest, it got progressively worse. It was 10.30am by the time I reached the former LNWR Exchange station after a miserable journey. The sky was a characterless, consistent grey and it was raining either heavily or very heavily. Nonetheless, while 'soaking' up the atmosphere of the station, I recorded the following steam locos at work - 'Black 5's No's. 45312, 45055, 45318 and '8F' No. 48529. As I walked the 731 yards along the shared Platform 11, to Victoria station, the day started to brighten up a little. Here I saw a few more steam workings all involving 'Black 5's. No. 45255 was acting as station pilot, while No's 44910 and 45203 were in charge of parcel trains. On the closure of Exchange in May the following year, its services would be transferred to Victoria.

Manchester Exchange on a very wet and cool 22nd June 1968.

Watched by a group of enthusiasts, '8F' No. 48529 passes 'Black 5' No. 45312 at the western end of the station, The Stanier 2-8-0 would be photographed again while visiting Newton Heath MPD a little later in the day.

Acting as station pilot, Stanier 4-6-0 No. 44910 is seen in Manchester Victoria adjacent to platform 12. Built at Crewe in November 1945, the 'Black 5', allocated to Newton Heath, would be withdrawn on the depot's closure to steam on 30th June.

A short while later, with the rain continuing to pour from the heavens, 'Black Five No. 45255 had also been positioned in 'Wallside', next to platform 12, ready to carry out its next banking turn. In the foreground, standing in platform 11, is a Derby-built three-car diesel multiple unit.

It was soon time to set off for Newton Heath, one of the three depots due to close in a week's time. This was a big shed and now seemed even more expansive with so few steam engines for it to service and maintain. A total of 36 were present on what would be my final visit here. Except for '9F' No. 92054, which had remained in store since withdrawal at the beginning of May, all of the engines belonged to Stanier's 'Black 5' (21) and '8F' (14) classes. Six of the '8F's and ten of the 'Black 5's were in steam. A few of the engines present would be transferred to Carnforth and included 4-6-0s No's. 44735, 44781, 44809, 45206, 45268, 45310, 45330. Stanier 2-8-0 No. 48665 would continue working until the end of steam after heading further north too (see below). The diesel maintenance part of the depot would remain in use; demolition of the steam shed would begin the following March.

Stanier '8F' No. 48665 stands in the yard of Newton Heath MPD on 22nd June. The 2-8-0 would see further service as a Rose Grove loco and would officially be withdrawn w/end. 10th August.

Pictured earlier in the day at the end of Manchester Exchange station (see above), '8F' No. 48529 had eventually made its way to Newton Heath its home shed where it is seen below. Briefly a Saltley engine, I last noted the 2-8-0 on 2E on 18th February 1967 before it left for Edge Hill depot. Fourteen months later her final transfer, to 9D, had taken place. The cutter's torch would beckon for this and a number of other engines on the shed's closure.

The next depot on my itinerary, Patricroft, produced 33 steam representing four different varieties. Stanier '8F's were in the majority with fifteen noted, closely followed by standard 5MTs of which there were thirteen. Four 'Black 5's and one standard '9F' made up the compliment of locos on shed. Only a handful of engines were in steam: No's 48033, 45156, 45287, 73050 and 73069. Two of these, No's 48033 and 73069 would be employed on the LCGB 'The Two Cities Railtour' the following day. The two 'Black 5's, No's 45156 and 45287, would see a few weeks further service after transfer to Rose Grove, and likewise for No. 73069 after becoming a Carnforth engine. Indeed, this engine would be the last of its class to remain in service. Patricroft shed would be demolished soon after closure and the site cleared.

Bolton, the last of the three sheds about to close was host to 34 steam. They were all Stanier engines: eighteen 'Black 5's and sixteen '8F's. Two of the 4-6-0s' No's. 44871 and 44947 and four of the 2-8-0's No's 48340, 48379, 48652 and 48720 were in steam. Again a small group of engines would be kept busy for a while longer after being given new homes: No's 48340 and 48773 would become Rose Grove locos, while No's 44888, 45073, 45110, 45260, 45269 and 45318 would be allotted to Carnforth. The transfer of engines from the three closing depots would constitute the last of such movements of BR steam power. Ironically, after the final farewell to steam on August 11th and BR's modern motive power image finally achieved, 'Black 5' No. 44888 would turn up as a guest at Derby Works 'Open Day' on 31st August!

From Bolton I headed north through Ramsbottom and Rawtenstall to Burnley and its MPD, Rose Grove. Here I found three varieties amongst a total of 29 steam on shed. In abundance were members of Stanier's '8F' class, with no fewer than twenty-two present. Also in residence were six 'Black 5's and standard 4MT No. 75027. There was no shortage of engines ready for work, and the following sixteen were noted in steam: No's. 44899, 45447, 48191, 48247, 48278, 48400, 48410, 48423, 48448, 48493, 48519, 48666, 48723, 48727, 48730 and 75027. With the occasional glimpse of sunshine to lift my spirits, I set off for the last shed visit of the day.

With its long term future soon to be secured, Carnforth-based Standard 4MT No. 75027, having earlier in the day worked a Rylstone Quarry roster, is found resting inside Rose Grove MPD on 22nd June 1968.

While visiting Carnforth shed later the same day, I climbed up on to the footplate of sister engine No. 75019 and took several photographs, including the driver's side of the cab. The layout for all standard engines was basically the same, and some of the fittings that can be seen include the reversing gear (next to shovel), vacuum and steam chest pressure gauges, water gauge and the driver's brake and blower valves. Built in March 1952, the 4-6-0 was allocated to Southport for eleven years of its short working life, and became a Carnforth engine for a second time in January this year. Following its withdrawal in August it would be taken to Campbell's of Airdrie to be broken up.

Courtesy of owners storing their preserved engines here, Carnforth could boast the best variety of steam power in its care of any of the remaining depots. Indeed, on the occasion of this visit I noted 8 different classes (three of which were preserved) amongst the 37 steam present. Excluding the privately owned engines, the number of locos in each class represented were as follows: 'Black 5' (18), '8F' (3), 'Britannia' Pacific (1), standard 4MT 4-6-0 (4) and '9F' (7). In steam were No's 44713, 44758, 44874, 45095, 45134, 45231, 48062 and 75019. One of the '9F's, No. 92167 (which appeared to be stored) had, according to reports, been seen working the Heysham-Leeds oil tank train on 11th June with its rear pair of driving wheels disconnected. Certainly when I noted the engine they were out of commission, but whether sightings of it running as a 2-8-0 were ever substantiated by way of photographic proof I don't know.

Once again I spent the night under canvas at Bolton-le-Sands. By the time I'd pitched the tent and eaten, it was almost dark, so I didn't bother to walk down to the station to record any possible steam workings. I slept soundly and wouldn't have known if any steam had passed by during what had been a very wet night. Sunday morning (23rd June) wasn't looking at all promising with further rain threatening. Not entirely because of a miserable looking day ahead, I decided to curtail my planned shed visits, except for one, and head back to Birmingham to meet up with my girlfriend.

Lostock Hall was on my route home and on calling in at the depot I found seventeen 'Black 5's, eight '8F's and three Ivatt 4MT 2-6-0s on shed. Only three engines were in steam: No's, 44806, 45212 and 48476. Next month Stanier 4-6-0 No. 45212 would have a surprise of some significance in store for Dennis and me, the importance of which will be explained later.

Reviewing my notes the following day, I found that fifty-eight of the 201 steam engines recorded had been in steam and, including preserved locos, I had seen 10 different varieties of engine over the week-end (see Appendix 30 for steam locos noted on shed). Following the closure of Bolton, Newton Heath and Patricroft a week later, there would be just three sheds left with an active steam allocation: Carnforth, Lostock Hall and Rose Grove.

Surplus to requirements: Lostock Hall MPD 23rd June 1968. Mounds of coal remain at the side of the engines after their tenders have been emptied prior to their disposal. Many years later, a flood of information on the movements of steam locos at this time, and indeed for months after 4th August, would appear to suggest that 10D saw the final engines despatched from a BR shed to a scrapyard. Almost nine months later, three 'Black 5's, No's. 44894, 45017 and 45388, finally left the depot on 28th April 1969 behind a diesel bound for Draper's scrapyard, Hull - the final time non-preserved steam locos travelled over Britain's railways.

Quite late on Sunday 30th June, I left Jackie's for home. Close to midnight, as I was about to pass the first entrance to the Château Impney Hotel, Droitwich, a car pulled out in front of me resulting in a collision while I was travelling at approximately 55mph. Extremely fortunate to survive the impact, I passed out when I landed on the far side of the road. I had sustained only relatively minor cuts and bruises, but my Lambretta had fared less well and eventually cost £127 pounds to repair - about fifty pounds less than the price of a new one! Once out of hospital, I soon discovered that I would not have the convenience of using my scooter to travel freely to see steam during its final few weeks of operation.

July

Very little news of any significance filtered through concerning steams minor part in traffic operations around Lancashire during the next four weeks. There was speculation as to whether the final batch of the D400 EE Type '4' diesels, introduced last year, would materialise in time to ensure steam finished completely on 4th August. And no doubt there were many enthusiasts who wished that such a delay would happen so that steam might continue for a few more weeks. But as was suspected, there would be no last minute reprieve; there would be more than sufficient diesel power available to guarantee the elimination of steam as planned.

19th/20th July

My penultimate trip to steam's last outpost began late on the evening of Friday 19th July. I caught the 11.20pm train from New Street to Crewe and, after spending the night on the station, I made the twenty-minute walk to Crewe South shed as soon as it got light. The majority of the locomotives present belonged to the BR diesel Type '2' class but, inside the shed building, I found 'Britannia' Pacific No. 70013 Oliver Cromwell in steam, and preserved 'A4' No. 4498 Sir Nigel Gresley. Reports I read later about the 'Britannia's' movements confirmed that it had travelled down to Crewe under its own steam the previous day for attention to its boiler. While in the works, someone decided that the engine needed smartening up, so her paintwork was touched up and re-varnished at the same time.

From Crewe I continued along the west coast main line to Carnforth. With steam power now confined almost exclusively to Lancashire, work for the few engines still operating here was in short supply and I logged only three locos in use as my train made its way through the county. Nevertheless, my morale was lifted somewhat when I looked across from Carnforth station towards the shed; the plumes of smoke rising from the depot signified that there were a number of engines prepared and ready for another turn of duty. Once inside the depot, I noted thirteen engines in steam: No's. 44709, 44735, 44809, 44871, 44877, 44894, 45017, 45134, 45206, 45390, 73069, 75048 and 92118. Eight varieties of steam power were represented amongst the 42 engines present. The 'usual' four preserved engines, No's 42073, 42085, (4)6441 and 61306, were noted on the rented section of track opposite the shed building.

As I crossed the footbridge serving the depot and headed back to the station, there was little comfort in knowing that I would be back once more to see steam on shed here. Sitting on Carnforth station while waiting for the local service to Lancaster, I thought of all the hours I had spent pursuing BR steam. It was impossible to comprehend that so very soon this would no longer be possible. Fortunately, I had lots of other interests to occupy my time, and in September I would begin a three-year teacher-training course at the College of St. Mark & St. John, Chelsea. What a pity, or was it a blessing that, except for a few ex-GWR pannier tanks employed by London Transport, there wouldn't be any steam in the capital or elsewhere to distract me from my studies?

During the twenty or so minutes I spent on Lancaster Castle station before travelling on to Preston, I noted and photographed two 'Black 5's - No. 44894 light engine, followed by No. 44709 with a parcels train. On arrival at Preston another 'Black 5', No. 45110 was recorded, but my logbook doesn't intimate what, if any duty, she was carrying out at the time. I didn't remain on the station for long; I was soon off to the docks and the small engine shed that serviced the shunters working there. While never a major port, Preston had, however, pioneered roll-on roll-off ferry transport twenty years earlier. Now, in 1968, approximately five hundred dockers were employed here, traffic had reached its peak, and the port held the record for handling the largest amount of container and ferry traffic in the country. Several of the Bagnall saddle tanks employed in the docks were on shed, including Princess, Perseverance, Courageous (in steam) and Enterprise.

Carnforth MPD, 20th July 1968. Standard 75048 prepares to move off shed while, below, 'Metro-Vick' Co-Bo Type 2 diesel electric No. D5716 stands in the foreground of a view of the north yard. The front of these engines always seemed to me to suggest an air of sadness, which, in the circumstances, seemed appropriate. Time was nearly up for steam, but this class of diesel, built at Bowsfield Works in Stockton-upon-Tees between 1958 and 1959, would last only a matter of weeks after steams demise: all twenty of the class, except for No. D5705 would be withdrawn by the end of September.

On 20th July 1968 'Black 5' No. 44894, light engine, moves through Lancaster Castle station. The 4-6-0 entered traffic in September 1945 and was allocated to a number of depots in the northwest including, Newton Heath, Lancaster, Rose Grove and Lostock Hall. Following a short-lived allocation of three weeks to Fleetwood, the Stanier engine made what would be its final move, to Carnforth, around 10th July 1965, from where it would be withdrawn after working part of the SLS Farewell to Steam No. 1 tour on 4th August.

Preston Dock engine shed, 20th July 1968: Bagnall 0-6-0 saddle tank, 'Princess', is seen resting inside the depot building. Just behind the 0-6-0 is the far older (built 1932 by Armstrong, Whitworth) diesel shunter named 'Duchess'.

While riding on the bus to Lostock Hall, the sun declared its presence for the first time, although only fleetingly. Needless to say I quickly discovered on arrival, that I was one amongst many making notes of the engines on shed. There were spotters everywhere, and it was difficult to take a photograph without someone suddenly appearing 'in shot'. I recorded a total of 35 steam representing three different classes. Two Ivatt 2-6-0's were inside the shed building, No 43019 and No. 43106 the last of the class to be withdrawn and soon to be preserved. The remaining engines were 'Black 5's (25) and '8F's (8). Nine engines were in steam: No's 44806, 44888, 44971, 45110, 45212, 45310, 45388, 45407 and 48723. Two of these, No's 44888 and 45110, would be involved in the following day's Roch Valley Railway Society tour, which would travel over four different routes linking Manchester and Southport.

I often wondered what level of illumination such inadequate looking lamps provided after dark. At least the pathway between the two rows of engines seen in the yard of Lostock Hall looks relatively clear of obstacles and hindrances so that the shed staff and enginemen could go about their business reasonably safely. Heading the left-hand row of locos is Stanier 4-6-0 No. 45212.

Front end variety, Lostock Hall MPD: English Electric Type '4' No. D236 (nearest the camera), new in October 1959; 'Black 5' No. 45269 built in November 1936 by Armstrong, Whitworth, with just two weeks of its working life remaining, and No. D414, a member of the later EE Type '4' class introduced in 1967, which had been in traffic about two months. Someone had already removed the 4-6-0's builder's plates perhaps for safekeeping or, more likely, as mementos.

This and above 20th July 1968.

Above. Through the gap: 'Black 5' No. 44806, twenty years earlier a Saltley engine, moved for the final time in its career from Edge Hill to Lostock Hall, about two weeks before the Liverpool shed closed at the beginning of May. Seen in its home shed on 20th July 1968, the 4-6-0 would be amongst the last group of steam engines to be withdrawn the following month. Below. A close-up of the motion of Stanier '8F' No. 48723 while standing in the yard of Lostock Hall shed on the same day.

Ivatt 4MT No. 43106 stands alongside 'Black 5' No. 44878 inside Lostock Hall MPD on 20th July 1968. The 2-6-0, built at Darlington in 1951, had been withdrawn for about a month by this time, but on 1st August would be on its way to the Severn Valley Railway under its own steam to begin a new life in preservation. For whatever reason, someone had decided to position a piece of steel plate on top of its chimney together with an empty milk bottle, although I don't recall noticing either while taking the photograph. The Stanier 4-6-0 entered traffic in May 1945, and had been taken out of service at the same time as its neighbour. Its future wouldn't be so rosy, however, and it would eventually be broken up at Cohen's, Kettering.

Following a brisk walk to Todd Lane Junction station, I caught the next train to Rose Grove. The depot was situated close to the station and within a few minutes I had joined the throng wandering around the shed. I was in the company of lots of other enthusiasts who were busily taking down numbers and photographing as many of the locos as possible: if someone had informed me that the depot was in the middle of an Open Day, I would have believed them. No fewer than twenty-eight '8F's together with nine 'Black 5's were on shed. The following engines were in steam: 48191, 48247, 48493, 48665, 48666, 48730, 48765, 48775 and 45156 Ayrshire Yeomanry. One would have expected many of the engines present to have already been withdrawn, but interestingly only four locos (No's. 45382, 48115, 48323 and 48384) had been removed from capital stock. The remaining thirty-two engines would not be officially withdrawn until period ending 10th August.

During the 1950's Stanier '8F' No. 48730 could be found in south Wales while allocated to Swansea Victoria and Llanelly from where it was transferred to Lostock Hall in September 1964. The 2-8-0's final move, to Rose Grove, had taken place in early June 1967 where it is pictured above on 20th July 1968. The '8F' would continue to be employed until the 3rd August when it would have its fire dropped for the last time. Below. With lots of ash lying below its smokebox door, Armstrong, Whitworth-built 'Black 5' No 45350 stands inside the shed building of Rose Grove MPD on the same day. The Stanier 4-6-0 would be withdrawn on 3rd August too.

Transferred from Northwich to Rose Grove at the beginning of March, and then to Bolton three weeks later, '8F' No. 48340 returned to Rose Grove during the first week of July, where it is seen above. Still bearing a 9K painted shedcode, it must have been deemed pointless to alter this to 10H with a little over a month to go before the end of steam. With his back to the camera, Rose Grove driver, David Mossop, chats to two enthusiasts, most likely about the demise of this form of motive power and the uncertain future that lay ahead for both him and the other shed staff. 20th July 1968.

My return journey home via Preston and Crewe proved uneventful. No steam locos were seen while travelling through Lancashire or Cheshire. After changing trains at Crewe, I sat and looked through my notebook and produced the usual overview of the day's jottings: a total of 118 locos recorded (for steam noted on shed see appendix 31), representing 11 varieties with 34 engines in steam. Five preserved engines accounted for four of the different classes seen. The next trip, in twelve days time, would be my last to see steam engines working normally on BR.

Throughout the previous three years Dennis and I had said a number of farewells to steam in different parts of the country. The time had now come to say the final farewell to the last few engines flying the flag for steam traction. Fittingly, it would all come to an end in the same county where steam had served notice of its intent to be the prime source of motive power almost 140 years earlier. The 5th August would be the first day without standard gauge steam playing a part in the day to day running of our railway; three narrow-gauge steam locomotives would continue to operate on British Railway's Vale of Rheidol line in west Wales.

July witnessed one or two instances when steam power was called upon to cover for diesel failures. One of these turned out to be quite a comical affair, although I doubt the crew would have viewed their predicament in quite the same way. On 29th July, following 'problems' with Brush Type '4' No. D1855, the 8.15am Preston to Windermere reverted to steam haulage. 'Black 5' No. 45110 was put in charge, and all went well until the train reached Windermere. Having also been given the job of returning with the 11.00am to London Euston as far as Preston, however, the crew found that the turntable was out of commission and, to make matters worse, the watering facilities had been disconnected. Reverting to the use of a hose coupled to the station toilet water supply, at least some water was added to the tender. Of course, nothing could be done with regard to the direction the engine was facing; she would have to work the four-coach train back to Preston tender first, with an emergency stop for water at Carnforth station. It was further reported in Railway World that steam power had been pencilled in for the rest of the week for these duties (rumoured to be proposed by a steam enthusiast in Preston control) although this was promptly changed when the account of the difficulties just mentioned came to light. The following day, another of Carnforth's 'Black 5's, No. 44894, rescued the failed dmu forming the 9.00am from Windermere to Morecambe service and things went straightforwardly compared with the previous day's affair.

Windermere station, 29th July 1968: having deputised for 'failed' Brush Type '4' No. D1855 on the 8.15am Preston to Windermere, 'Black 5' No. 45110 waits to begin the 11.00am return working. As a matter of course, the engine would be turned here, but Driver Peter Norris discovered, much to his surprise, that the turntable was no longer in use; to further complicate matters, no water was available either! As his fireman opens the stopcock, Peter is holding the end of the hosepipe to check if any water is reaching the tender. (Peter Norris collection).

By the middle of July we were ready for another trip to see steam. Just as we had done on numerous occasions before, arrangements had been discussed, but this time the planning, checking of timetables and the drawing up of a programme would be our last; no longer would we be thinking of when or where our next trip would be after this one. This was it, the last foray of all. Nevertheless, once the preparation had been carried out, it was still with a degree of excitement and anticipation - the reality of what we were about to witness would not sink in until sometime after it had happened - that we looked forward to seeing steam again. Dennis had managed to organise some holiday leave, and on Thursday 1st August would catch the 7.20am from Derby to Crewe. I would start my journey from New Street at 8.15am, and we would continue our journey north together from this former Mecca for many trainspotters.

Thursday, 1st August.

Hauled by No. E3138, my train left New Street and arrived on time at Crewe at 9.16am. Here the electric loco was replaced by not one but two diesels to take us on to Preston. Interestingly, behind pilot engine No. D429, and obviously now in better health, was No. D1855, which had supposedly failed (rumour had it that this was just an excuse to revert to steam haulage) two days earlier, when diagrammed to work the Preston to Windermere service mentioned above. Dennis joined me in my carriage, and at 9.25am our train gathered speed quickly as it began its journey north from Crewe: our final trip together to see steam engaged in work on BR had begun.

We sighted our first steam engine of the day, 'Black 5' No. 45318, outside Preston station where, on our arrival, Brush Type '4' No. D1846 was ready to take the train forward to Glasgow. We transferred to the dmu service to Barrow, which called at Bolton-le-Sands where once again we would set up camp. Further engines noted en-route included 'Black 5's No's 45407 light engine, No. 44877 with a parcels train, and also light engine '8F' No. 48715.

Sporting a headboard that appears to be non too complimentary about people hailing from Barrow-in-Furness, 'Britannia' Pacific No. 70013 Oliver Cromwell stands in the south yard of Carnforth MPD on 1st August 1968. In three days time the engine would be involved in one of six specials organised to commemorate the end of steam on BR.

The day was warm with sunny spells becoming more and more frequent. Once we had pitched the tent and had a quick bite to eat we set off for the station. Before catching the 4.13pm 'stopper' to Carnforth we noted standard 4-6-0 No. 73069 and again 'Black 5' No. 44877 both light engine. As we approached the station there appeared to be a fair number of engines on shed with signs of several being in steam. We logged 40 locos, with 12 prepared and ready for duty. In order of being listed the engines present were: 92167, 92223, 92160, 45424, 48124, 92088, 45209, 92077, 92118, 45445, 45435, 75019*, 45342*, 44897*, 45330, 45200, 45394, 44735, 70013, 45025, 45407*, 75027, 73069*, 45231*, 44877*, 75048*, 45310*, 48715*, 45390*, 44781*, 45095, 44758, 75020, 44963, 92091, 42073 (P), 75009, (4)6441 (P), 42085 (P), and 61306 (P). (* In steam, P - preserved)

With such a reasonable number of residents in steam, coupled with movements of engines coming on to and going off shed, the depot was quite busy, and one sensed it still had an air of purpose about it. It was busy with enthusiasts and trainspotters too. As I walked about the depot, taking a good number of photographs (seven of which featured No. 45407 being turned!) 'Oliver Cromwell' came into view looking as clean and presentable as its celebrity status now demanded. She was undoubtedly the engine attracting most attention, and if armed with a camera, as many enthusiasts were, the opportunity to take a shot of her at close quarters could not be resisted. Indeed, such was the appeal of this particular engine, that if the shedmaster had wanted to make an issue of the fact that there were so many people wandering around his depot that ought not to be, he could have done no better than to sit in 70013's cab and occasionally make his presence known - not that I think many of the enthusiasts in question would have been unduly worried if he had!

During the late 1950's and early 1960's, Stanier 4-6-0 No. 45231 was a familiar engine while based in Birmingham at the city's Aston depot. Its final transfer, earlier in May, brought it to Carnforth where it is seen here. With four days to go before withdrawal, the 'Black 5' is in steam and ready for further employment. As things worked out, its last duty, on Saturday 3rd August, would see the engine at the head of a ballast train from Waterslack Quarry to Farington Junction (Preston). After being bought from BR, she would remain at Carnforth long after steams demise on our national railway

1st August 1968.

The 'Britannia' was not the only smart looking engine to be found on shed. Several others had received attention to their paintwork, too, and were sporting a similar well-groomed image. Anyone who actually experienced the final few months of steam on BR will no doubt recall the times when they came across what seemed to be a small but steadily growing number of similarly spruced up engines. Gone was a great deal of the dirt and grime, exposing for all to see the real colour of the loco. Unfortunately, the vast majority were painted black, but at least it became a more striking shiny black! Indeed, with one or two, like Stanier 4-6-0 No. 45110, their long-lost lined mixed traffic livery could once again be seen, giving them a little bit of a lift from their otherwise plain appearance.

What a difference a bit of elbow-grease, followed by some welcome sunshine, makes to the look of 'Black 5' No. 45156 Ayrshire Yeomanry as she stands in Liverpool's Lime Street station at the head of the RCTS 'Lancastrian' No.2 Railtour Special. Much to the delight of the onlookers, a spirited departure followed with lots of attendant steam and smoke. Together with 'Britannia' No. 70013 Oliver Cromwell and fellow 'Black 5' No. 45342, the 4-6-0 would be involved in three separate legs of the rail tour. On this, the first part of the day's journey, 45156 would take the train to Fleetwood via Hyton Junction, Wigan North Western, Preston, Kirkham and Poulton.

20th April 1968.

Four days before 'Ayrshire Yeomanry' carried out its duty at the head of the 'Lancastrian No. 2 Railtour', the special shopping proposal (top) had been completed indicating four concerns. The response (bottom) indicates that the proposal should be resubmitted in October 1968, and that the next internal boiler exam should remain extended to 12th August 1968. This might suggest that there was still some uncertainty as to when steam would finish on BR. Of course, the other possibility could be that the reaffirmed internal boiler inspection date would also allow the engine to be considered for the BR 'Fifteen Guinea' special, planned for the 11th August.

Having completed her first turn of duty on the RCTS Merseyside, Lancs. and N.W. Branches Railtour (taking over from 'Black 5' No. 45156), 'Britannia' Pacific No. 70013 Oliver Cromwell receives a top up coal in Carnforth MPD. The Pacific would later head the last leg of the special between Preston NU, Burscough North Jnct., Southport South Jnct., and Liverpool Exchange.

Above. 'Black 5's No's. 45342 and 45156 Ayrshire Yeomanry at the head of the RCTS 'Lancastrian' No. 2 Railtour pass through Carnforth. They started their journey together from Morecambe Promenade with No. 45342 next to the coaching stock but, on arrival at Preston, it was found that the loco had developed a vacuum fault and, much to the disappointment of the many lineside photographers, the extremely well presented No. 45156 had to take its place. The repositioned engines completed their task of taking the train on to Wennington, Blackburn and Preston, ready for 'Oliver Cromwell' to complete the 280 mile trip in a little less than twelve hours. Both 20th April 1968.

Top. Black '5's No.'s 45110 and 44949 head south past Stockport Edgeley MPD with the Manchester Rail Travel Society/Severn Valley Railway Society North West Tour special on 20th April 1968. Following the completion of this leg of the journey, which would take them through Disley, Buxton, Chinley, Guide Bridge East Jnct., and finally Stalybridge, the train would be taken forward by standard 4-6-0's No's 73134 and 73069, seen above heading for Blackburn and Bolton shortly after passing Rose Grove MPD. From Bolton the penultimate leg would be in the hands of '8F' No. 48773 as far as Stockport. And to prove that not all engines involved in such specials were turned out in pristine condition, filthy '9F' No. 92160 would complete the final leg of the tour to Liverpool Lime Street. Both author's collection.

Stockport Edgeley MPD, 20th April 1968, two weeks prior to closure. Grubby 'Black 5's, No's. 45269 and 44871 are seen in the shed yard (top) and in the process of being turned No. 44871 (above). The loco would feature on the 'Fifteen Guinea' special later in August and would appear somewhat cleaner than it does here. Both author's collection.

Having endured several periods of storage between October 1965 and February 1968, standard 4MT No. 75019 is seen back in employment at Carnforth MPD on 20th April 1968. The 4-6-0 wouldn't be officially withdrawn until the end of steam on BR.

Eighteen years after the repeat of its non-stop run from Kings Cross to Edinburgh, on 1st May 1968 (mentioned above page 212) and looking in fine fettle, Flying Scotsman is seen at Stratford upon Avon with The Shakespeare Limited on Sunday 2nd November 1986. In the background (above left), ready to leave before the 'A3' is No. 4468 Mallard, with the other return working of the same named special to Marylebone (See Part One, 1958-63, page 38).

Top. '8F' No. 48340 is seen below the coaling plant in Bolton MPD, it's home shed, on 31st May 1968. Transferred to Rose Grove following the closure of 9K on 30th June, I would log the 2-8-0 (in steam) for the last time in Lostock Hall on 3rd August.

Above. 'Black 5' No. 45310 in Carnforth MPD on 1st August 1968. The 4-6-0 had last been overhauled as late as November 1966, but details of its visit to Crewe, although dated, are incomplete and the category of repairs carried out not known. The loco would officially be withdrawn two days after this photograph was taken. Both Author's collection.

Above. Each time its home shed closed, 'Black 5' No. 44888 managed to escape withdrawal. The 4-6-0 moved depots on three occasions during the last four months of steam working on BR: from Trafford Park to Stockport, then to Bolton and, finally, to Lostock Hall where it is seen in the shed yard on 2nd August 1968. Below. Standing inside Lostock Hall shed on the same day, Stanier 4-6-0 No. 45017 waits to be steamed ready for its next outing at the head of the SLS (Midland area) 'Farewell to Steam No. 2' special in two days time. The 'Black 5', together with classmates No's 44894 and 45388, would be removed from 10D on 28th April 1969 hauled dead to Albert Draper's scrapyard in Hull. As previously mentioned, this would constitute the final movement of non-preserved steam locos over BR metals.

Above. For many years 'Black 5' No. 45110, worked out of Holyhead MPD. After a year spent at Stafford shed, the engine moved to the northwest and became a Bolton loco during the early part of July 1965. On the closure of 9K on 30th June the 4-6-0 moved for the final time to 10D at the beginning of July. The ex-LMS coach of the shed's breakdown train can be seen in the background. Below. Stanier '8F' No 48476 was a Willesden engine throughout the 1950's but was transferred to Birkenhead in June 1961. It remained in the northwest and became a Lostock Hall loco during the first week in January 1968 and was the depot's last working '8F'. The 2-8-0 also had the distinction of being the final GWR-built standard gauge engine in BR service. Both Lostock Hall 2nd August 1968.

Left. The final boiler report for Stanier 2-8-0 No. 48666, completed on 17th April 1968. The date for its next internal boiler exam is given as 21st April 1970. Interestingly, earlier paperwork from Crewe Works fabrication shop dated 24th March 1965 (below), highlights the fact that the '8F' had had its boiler replaced with that off sister engine No. 48151. The loco is seen in Rose Grove MPD on 2nd August 1968, shortly after being dragged back on to the rails following its untimely derailment while coming on to shed.

Following the derailment and subsequent withdrawal of Stanier '8F' No. 48666, sister engine No. 48773, seen on 2nd August standing in Rose Grove shed, looks ready to take part in the LCGB 'The Farewell to Steam Railtour' in two days time. Together with 'Black 5' No. 44781 she would haul the train on the leg between Blackburn and Carnforth via Clitheroe, Hellifield, Settle Jnct., and Clapham.

On 2nd August 1968 Stanier '8F' No. 48278 of Rose Grove MPD, has just passed through Rose Grove station with the very last steam-worked 2.35pm Wyre Dock to Burnley Central coal empties.

During my final visit to Lostock Hall MPD on 3rd August 1968 I took several pictures of 'Britannia' Pacific No. 70013. This was one of the last and, although I'm unsure about whom the crew are, I believe the driver may be Frank Herdman who previously worked out of Stockport Edgeley. The next day would see the engine feature at the head of two specials: the RCTS 'End of Steam Commemorative Tour' and the LCGB 'Farewell to Steam Railtour'. A week later, of course, the Pacific would take part in BR's 'Fifteen Guinea Special'.

On the same day Carnforth-based 'Black 5' No. 44894 moves from underneath Lostock Hall's coaling stage to proceed to the ashpit to have its fire attended to. The loco had spent its life allocated to sheds in the northwest, including Newton Heath, Fleetwood, Lancaster and Rose Grove. Tomorrow, together with sister engine No. 44871, the 4-6-0 would double head the Stephenson Locomotive Society (Midland Area) Farewell to Steam No.1 special between Manchester Victoria, Huddersfield, Wigan, Rainhill, Manchester Victoria and Stockport.

Top. Shortly after 11.00 am on 11th August 1968, with the crowd under the watchful eye of the police, standard Pacific No. 70013 Oliver Cromwell begins its journey from Manchester Victoria to Carlisle at the head of the BR special commemorating the end of steam. Above. Thrust into the limelight because of sister engine No. 45305 having failed, 'Black 5' No. 45110 waits in Manchester Victoria later the same day, ready to take charge of the final leg to Liverpool Lime Street of what would become known as the 'Fifteen Guinea Special'. (Both D.M. Perfect)

The Final Few Years of British Steam Part Two (Colour Section)

'The Preston Ramblers'- made up of past Preston and Lostock Hall men, plus one or two young recruits and interlopers from other relatively local depots, including Patricroft, are ready to head back to Lancashire after another enjoyable reunion at the NYM Railway on 29th May 2010. The final sunset on steam and Lostock Hall shed may be a distant memory, but the spirit and camaraderie of the footplate men, fitters and other railwaymen of that period continues to flourish.

Above left. Driver Ronnie Clough (left and far right in top picture) and fireman Joe Unsworth wait patiently for the arrival of the first leg of the Roch Valley Society Manchester to Southport Steam Excursion on 21st July 1968. Their engine, Oliver Cromwell, would then head the special from Southport to Manchester Victoria via Wigan and finally back to Southport Chapel Street via Todmorden, Copy Pit, Blackburn and Burscough North Jnct. Bill Ashcroft (R.Clough collection). Above right. Ex-BR steam men: former Lostock Hall driver John Fletcher, on the footplate of 45212, and Jimmy Boyle, a former Preston driver, discuss arrangements for the day ahead while waiting for the 'right away' for 'The Preston Rambler' from Grosmont. 21st May 2011.

Above. The late Peter Norris, former Lostock Hall Driver, on the footplate of 'Black 5' No. 45212 and, right on its tender, checking that there would be no repeat of the Windermere fiasco (see page 238), and that there is sufficient water available to get back to Grosmont from Pickering!

Former Preston driver, Jimmy Boyle (above left), appears as much at home on the footplate of 45212 as he would have been 46 years earlier! Standing next to the tender is John Fletcher, ex-10D, and a regular NYMR driver.

Probably the best-dressed fireman ever to have worked on the footplate of 'Black 5' 4-6-0 No. 45212! Former Lostock Hall fitter, Peter Whalen, finds himself 'on the shovel' for the return journey of 'The Preston Rambler' from Pickering to Grosmont.

All 21st May 2011.

Having headed several trains, including 'The Preston Rambler', the day's work on the NYMR has come to an end for new build 'A1' No 60163 Tornado. Once it's tender has been replenished with coal and water, the engine will retire for the night on Grosmont shed. Three months had passed by since the Pacific had made its first public passenger trip from York to Newcastle and return along the east coast main line. 9th May 2009.

Back out on the west coast main line under its own steam for the first time since 4th August 1968, Stanier 'Black 5' No. 45212, is seen on its inaugural test run on 3rd March 2017. The engine is about to pass through Preston station platform 2 (old platform 4) at 4.27pm and is very close to where I photographed her for the last time on that sad day nearly forty-nine years earlier. Note the authentic position of the top lamp bracket (next to the end of the horizontal smokebox door handle) - exactly where it was all those years earlier, courtesy of Ian Riley and his team.   Peter Fitton.

Thursday 1st August contd.

Referred to briefly earlier, a merry band of enthusiasts, probably regarded as 'nutters' by some of the railwaymen at the time, had decided that at least a few engines would end their working days in a proud and dignified manner. True, of course, there was another reason for the 'oily rag brigade' to ensure that a particular engine was spruced up; a nice, clean engine meant a more camera-friendly appearance and made for a more appealing photograph. Two such gleaming examples - No's 75048 and 45390 - were found on Carnforth shed today and had obviously been the subjects of the groups attention. However, their efforts must be applauded; on a number of occasions they toiled through the night to ensure they rid an engine of layers of muck and grease so it was ready for its photo-call the following day. This group of unofficial cleaners became known as the Master Neverers Association (MNA), although this title appears to have been as much to do with its members trying to avoid buying tickets when travelling by train (otherwise known as 'fare dodging')!

Built by Armstrong, Whitworth in 1937, Stanier 'Black 5' No. 45407 had been allocated to thirteen different sheds by this time. Seen here on 1st August 1968 in Carnforth, her last home depot, the engine would go into the history books the following day as having worked the final steam-hauled parcels train between Preston and Colne return. Fortunately, the 4-6-0 would soon be enjoying a future in preservation.

After leaving the shed we stopped part of the way across the footbridge and spent a few minutes looking back at the depot. Dennis and I didn't speak, but no doubt our thoughts were similar. The scene was a sad and depressing one; some of the engines in view would never steam again, while a handful would continue to be employed during the three remaining days. Those privately stored were safe in the knowledge that they would shortly be moving on to pastures new and a life in preservation.

Also built by Armstrong, Whitworth, 'Black 5 ' No. 45310 entered service in January 1937. Standing next to the 4-6-0 in Carnforth north yard on 1st August 1968 is Clayton Type 1 diesel No. D8514 and '8F' No. 48715. See colour picture page 247.

No steam workings were noted while waiting for our train back to Bolton-le-Sands or during the short journey that followed, but there was still the possibility of an odd steam working before the end of the day. Without leaving the tent we knew we would be able to catch glimpses between the breaks in the bushes and trees of any such engines going about their business along the main line. The evening was a pleasant one and amid the numerous diesel movements 'Black 5' No. 45342 appeared in charge of an oil train and shortly afterwards two similar, but unidentified, Stanier locos (coupled together) travelling light towards Carnforth.

During the night I remember waking once or twice to the sound of steam… or had I been dreaming?

Friday 2nd August.

Three days to go. A cloudy but reasonably bright start to the day would improve as the morning wore on. After breakfast we walked down to the station and while waiting for the 8.53 local to Carnforth, three 'Black 5's passed through - No. 45342 light engine, followed by No's 45025 and 45310 coupled together. A few minutes later our train appeared, hauled by BR Type '2' No. D7575. By the time we reached Carnforth No. 45342 had been found employment and was noted at the head of an oil train once again.

As we were approaching the shed we could see that a few changes to the occupants had taken place overnight, and the depot didn't seem quite so lively. After taking several pictures from the footbridge we began logging the engines present. Newcomers noted were No's 48493, 48665, 44791 and 44894. Locos that had left since the previous evening's visit included No's 44735, 44877, 45025, 45231, 45310, 45342, 45390, 45407, 48715, 75019 and 75048. As a result of these movements, the total number of engines on shed had fallen to 33, with seven locos in steam (No's 44781, 44791, 44894, 44897, 48493, 48665 and 73069). On the evening, Stanier 'Black 5' No. 44781 would work the 8.28pm Barrow to Preston leg of the Royal Mail Parcels train to Huddersfield. This engine, of course, would become a bit of a film celebrity (The Virgin Soldiers - Columbia Pictures) and was so very nearly preserved. However, as a result of being deliberately derailed and left on an unreachable part of the line near Bartlow, Cambridgeshire, it would be cut up where it lay. My camera was once again put to good use and after taking a generous number of photographs we left the depot and made the short walk to the station.

Stanier 2-8-0 No. 48493 stands partly in the shade in Carnforth MPD on 2nd August 1968. The '8F' had been a Northampton engine for over fourteen years before being transferred quickly in succession, firstly to Willesden and then to Bletchley. In July 1965 the engine was allotted to Speke Junction, then to Northwich earlier in February this year and finally to Rose Grove in March. The engine would find itself at Lostock Hall the following evening (3rd) and would remain there, in steam, overnight. One very local shunt duty needed to be fulfilled the next day (Sunday 4th), and as all other '8F's had had their fires dropped, 48493 was the obvious candidate for carrying out the required shunting of ballast wagons in Farington Junction down yard. See page 280 for further comments regarding this engine's final duty

Above. The sunlight is reflected off the smokebox of Stanier 4-6-0 No. 44894 as it waits in the north yard of Carnforth MPD for its next turn of duty. Below. 'Black 5' No. 44781, also standing in the depot's north yard, has been partly cleaned ready for its role in the LCGB Farewell to Steam special due to take place on Sunday 4th August. Later today, however, the engine would work the 8.28pm Barrow-Preston Royal Mail Parcels. Both 2nd August 1968.

Left and below. Built by Armstrong, Whitworth, Stanier 4-6-0 No. 45134 is seen passing below the footbridge to Carnforth MPD. The loco entered traffic in May 1935 and was allocated to Crewe South for a number of years. Following a period of time based at Northampton, the 'Black 5' became a Tyseley engine in September 1965. About a year later, prior to the Birmingham shed closing to steam, it moved to Shrewsbury before being transferred, for the last time, to Carnforth. Its final journey, after withdrawal this month, would take it south once more to Cohen's of Kettering to be broken up.

2nd August 1968.

1968 (The Final Farewell to British Steam)

On reflection, I realised that what we were doing was what we had always done during such trips, but without taking on board the finality and conclusiveness of this our very last excursion of all. So, with little thought of the time left for steam, we were soon back on to the train this time heading south to Preston. Two 'Black 5's were noted on the way, No's 45287 and 44806. Not planned prior to starting out, we decided during the journey to delay our visit to Lostock Hall shed and have a look at the town's dock railway to see what industrial engines were still in use.

Built by the North Union Railway, the branch to Preston Dock was first opened in 1846 to serve Victoria Quay. From the west side of Preston station the line initially descended northwards on a gradient of 1 in 29 before turning abruptly westwards through a cutting and then Fishergate tunnel. As the docks expanded so did the railway and at its peak had over 25 miles of track. Like their counterparts on BR, the steam engines still in service here were soon to be replaced by diesel power. Indeed, the remaining Bagnall-built engines would be withdrawn at the end of the year, and their duties put into the hands of three brand new Rolls-Royce sentinels.

The small three-road shed serviced several Bagnall saddle tanks. The engines were known by their names and those present were: Courageous, Perseverance, Enterprise and Princess, built in 1942 and the only one of them fortunate enough to be preserved. We failed to identify two of the 0-6-0's as their nameplates and builder's plates had been removed. Interestingly, the one diesel we recorded, 'Duchess', was built in 1932 and was older than any of the steam fleet. Close by of course was the Dick, Kerr Works where a far more famous diesel had been built, namely DP1. Plans to give it the same name as that carried by the saddle tank Enterprise, mentioned above, never materialised and the loco became known simply as 'Deltic', the word printed in large letters along its sides (see picture page 17, Part One). After chatting to the driver of Courageous, we were about to leave the shed when he offered us a short ride back towards the station. I can remember how much I enjoyed being briefly on the footplate yet, at the same time under the circumstances, wishing it had been on a 'Black 5' or an '8F'.

We made the short walk to Pitt Street, close to the station, and caught the bus to Lostock Hall. For a change I decided to take a few colour pictures while going round the depot (see pages 248 and 249). The day had brightened up a little and, although sunshine was sporadic, one or two photographs turned out better than expected. A total of 36 steam were present (see appendix 32), with the following engines in steam: No's 44888, 45073, 45260, 45305 and 48476. In addition to the Stanier varieties, one other class of engine, Ivatt's 4MT 2-6-0, was represented by 43019 stored inside the shed building. Later in the day 'Black 5' No. 45260 would work the 9.25pm Preston to Liverpool passenger service and then return light-engine to Lostock Hall.

The last of the three depots on our schedule, Rose Grove, had nine 'Black 5's and eighteen '8F's on shed (see appendix 32). Eleven engines were in steam: No's 45156 Ayrshire Yeomanry, 45407, 48167, 48191, 48340, 48348, 48393, 48666, 48715, 48730 and 48773. 'Black 5' No. 45156, the only other named steam engine still working had, according to the writing on its smokebox, earlier completed steam's last involvement in the Clitheroe shunt diagram. Two of the '8F's had interesting ends to their careers, but for quite different reasons. No. 48167 had the honour of heading the final steam freight along the Blackburn to Bolton line, while sister engine No. 48666, after completing her Copy Pit banking duties, became derailed in the shed yard, was pulled unceremoniously back on to the rails, instantly withdrawn and positioned in the yard next to a line of other stored engines. I took two photographs of the loco, one from the cab, and the other from the more traditional three-quarter perspective (see page 250).

'Black 5' No. 45156 Ayrshire Yeomanry sits amongst piles of ash and all manner of other bits and pieces lying in the yard of Rose Grove MPD on Friday 2nd August 1968. The 4-6-0 has completed its final duties for the day, including heading Target 19, and has on its smokebox written in chalk 'The last steam shunt to Clitheroe 2nd August 1968'. On Sunday the engine would find itself in sole charge of GC Enterprises 'Farewell to Steam Railtour', with several crews, including Driver Ronnie Clough and Fireman Joseph Booth and Driver Colin Hacking and Fireman Dennis Robinson taking to her footplate. Note that the support brackets for the engines nameplates (see page 215) have been removed.

As we finished noting the engines, '8F' No. 48519 plodded past the shed with a mixed freight and, while waiting on Rose Grove station for our train into Preston, another member of the class, No. 48278, trundled through with a freight train and was duly photographed. No other working steam locos were observed during the journey back to Bolton-le-Sands. On the evening two engines passed by the campsite - 'Black 5's No's 44735 and 44877.

By the time we turned in, the eradication of standard gauge steam from British Railways was just 48 hours away.

Saturday 3rd August.

A Saturday, for lots of people, like any other Saturday. Many members of the public travelling through the last outpost of steam would be completely unaware of the significance of this day. For us, however, it was something very poignant. Our avid interest in and continual trips to see such engines would no longer play such an important and time consuming part of our lives. Today would be the last whole day of being able to pursue a hobby that had provided so much excitement and pleasure over a number of years. Tomorrow we would make our way home and, after a final visit to Carnforth shed, our regular jaunts in search of steam on BR would come to an end.

By the time we reached Bolton-le-Sands station several other enthusiasts were already waiting for the local train to Carnforth. Soon after we had joined them two 'Black 5's came through: No. 45390 light engine followed by No. 44735 with an oil train which would prove to be the very last BR steam freight working. The next movement involved three engines coupled together - 'Britannia' No. 70013 Oliver Cromwell, standard 5MT No. 73069 and Stanier 4-6-0 No. 44894 heading south. The arrival of Brush Type '4' No. D1634 in charge of our train gave us a timely reminder that there were still diesels about! Another steam loco, 'Black 5' No. 44709, heading for Kendal, was seen prior to reaching Carnforth. Much to the bewilderment of its crew, this engine would be spruced up while at Kendal by the 'MNA' before heading the last steam working along the Windermere branch.

Carnforth shed was busy with spotters nonchalantly making their way round the depot and scribbling down the numbers of the 28 steam present. Two engines were in steam, 'Black 5's No's 44877 and 45025. Loco movements witnessed after we had left the shed involved three more of this variety - No's 45231, 45342 and 45390 all light engine. Some time later while on Carnforth station we noted that No. 45231 had been found something constructive to do, and was seen at the head of a ballast train from Waterslack quarry to Farrington Junction, Preston. This would prove to be its final duty as a BR engine; following its withdrawal, it would be purchased privately for £3,300 and eventually once again grace the main line.

During the time it had taken us to travel to Carnforth and visit the shed, Lostock Hall had witnessed a steadily growing number of enthusiasts strolling around every part of the depot. In due course the British Transport Police were called upon to remove anyone without a shed permit, which it would seem just about covered everyone they came across. When all this happened I'm not exactly sure, all I do know is that Dennis and I, together with a number of other visitors, walked round the depot during the afternoon without any difficulty. 'Black 5' No. 44806 was not amongst the residents, so our visit must have taken place before 3.48 pm the time it was reported to have arrived back on shed after working a ballast train in the Preston area.

Our very last visit to Lostock Hall produced a total of 47 steam (see appendix 32). Ten of the engines on shed would find themselves involved in the following day's six specials commemorating the end of steam. No fewer than 16 of the locos noted were in steam: No's 44781, 44874, 44888, 44894, 45073, 45212, 45260, 45287, 45305, 45318, 45407, 48340, 48476, 48493, 70013 Oliver Cromwell and 73069.

Carnforth MPD, Saturday 3rd August 1968. Stanier 'Black 5' No. 45025 has a number of unofficial cleaners engaged in enhancing its appearance, some of whom may be shed staff. The next day would see the 4-6-0 join forces with classmate No. 45390 and double-head the LCGB 'Farewell to Steam Rail Tour' leg between Carnforth, Clapham, Settle Jnct., Hellifield, Clitheroe, Blackburn and Lostock Hall Jnct. The engine had a bright future: following its purchase by Ted Watkinson for the proposed Strathspey Railway, a new life in preservation would begin. Initially, it would feature on the Keighley and Worth Valley Railway before moving north in 1974 to Andrew Barclay's Works in Kilmarnock for overhaul. Once refurbished, it would make its debut the following year on the line it was first purchased for between Aviemore and Boat of Garten.

As can plainly be seen, all the hard work was undoubtedly worthwhile. Perhaps not quite ex-works, but not far off, No. 45025 certainly looks a prouder engine than it did before the 'cleaners' set to work. Interestingly, the 4-6-0 might well have been the first of its class to be withdrawn after its involvement in the first train accident, on 13th October 1939, during the blackout. The engine was piloting Royal Scot No. (4)6150 and, after passing six adverse signals in two miles, ran into ex-LNWR 0-8-0 No. (4)9169 while it was shunting in Bletchley station. The 'Black 5' was repaired and put back into service; the passed fireman driving (4)5025, C.W.E. Haynes, was tried for manslaughter but acquitted. 3rd August 1968.

Standing in the north yard of Carnforth MPD on 3rd August 1968 is 'Black5' No. 45206, '9F' No. 92091 and, behind the Ford Cortina, standard 4-6-0 No. 75048. The three locos had reached the end of the road; how long the car would last is anyone's guess.

Two of the sixteen locos in steam on 10D would be involved in historic rosters later in the day. Stanier 4-6-0 No. 45212 would be given the job of taking forward the rear coaches of the 5.05pm ex-Euston from Preston to Blackpool South departing at 8.50pm, while sister engine No. 45318, having been on shunting duties in Farington Yard, would see its final day in traffic culminating in working the very last steam-hauled passenger train, the 9.25pm Preston to Liverpool Exchange, which was a portion of the 5.25pm ex-Glasgow Central.

By all accounts the momentous journey had been a thrilling one. Scheduled to cover a fraction under 29 miles to Liverpool in 33 minutes, reports suggested that 80mph was reached at one point, and that 45318 brought its train to a halt 48 seconds over the booked time. Interestingly, on returning light engine to Lostock Hall, driver Ernie Heyes was informed by fitter Peter Whalen that one of the tender axles had developed a hot box, most likely sometime before reaching its original destination. The 'Black 5's entry into the history books, it would seem, came very close to being recorded in a rather inglorious manner but, as luck would have it, she will always be remembered as the last steam engine to work a BR timetabled passenger service.

It is well documented that sister engine No. 45212, on returning light-engine from her somewhat less exhilarating run (caused mainly by a succession of signal checks), continued her duties at Preston station into the night. Part of the regular diagram involved steam heating the sleeping cars removed from the 11.45pm ex-Euston, which would have arrived at Preston at approximately 3.30am. Various assumptions were subsequently made concerning the engines final movements, and it was suggested in an article in Heritage Rail (November 2008, Issue No.118), entitled 1968 The Last Word, that at about 8.00am the 'Black 5' returned light engine to Lostock Hall and was immediately withdrawn. This supposition, as will be revealed later, was not the case and, in my opinion, the engine's last task would at least match if not surpass the historical significance of No. 45318's final duty.

Lostock Hall MPD, Saturday 3rd August 1968. End of the shift: an engineman walks briskly past Stanier 4-6-0's No. 45287 and, nearest the camera, No. 44874 towards the office to sign off duty. Built nine years apart in 1936 and 1945 respectively, the two 'Black 5's managed a total of fifty-four years service.

Having looked down on Lostock Hall from Watkin Lane for the final time, we walked to Todd Lane Junction to catch the 2.53pm train to Rose Grove. Once again we found lots of other enthusiasts casually wandering around this depot, too, and one could have been excused for thinking it was another 'Open Day at 10F' for anyone and everyone to enjoy. A total of 30 steam were present (full list in appendix 32), twenty-three '8F's and seven 'Black 5's. Engines noted in steam were: No's 48191, 48278, 48348, 48393, 48400, 48519, 48715, 48727, 48773, and 45156. The 'MNA' members had once again been hard at work and two of the locos, No. 45156 Ayrshire Yeomanry and No. 48773, were looking extremely well turned out. Two of the '8F's in steam, No's 48348 and 48393, require special mention, as indeed do fellow classmates No's 48191 and 48278.

Waiting to go into the history books: Stanier 5MT No. 45318 stands in the yard of Lostock Hall MPD on 3rd August 1968. Later in the day driver Ernie Hayes and fireman Tony Smith would take to the footplate and be in charge of the last steam-hauled passenger train on BR. The engine would wait patiently in Preston station for the arrival of the 5.25pm ex-Glasgow, and then convey the through portion to Liverpool Exchange at 9.25pm. The crew would pull out the stops and give the many enthusiasts on board something to remember, and it was subsequently reported that in the process of keeping to the booked time, the train at one point topped 80mph. Unfortunately, the 4-6-0 having earned its rightful place in steams' history book, would shortly be recorded in another - the ledger holding the records of locos bought and broken up by Alfred Draper and Sons, Hull.

According to reports the first pair, No's 48348 and 48393, appear to have been two of the last three steam engines involved in working freight turns. The former had been busy carrying out local trip workings, while No. 48393 had earlier in the day taken a coal train to Huncoat power station from either Rose Grove or Burnley. Its day's work was finished when it took a train of coal empties to Portsmouth Loop, a little way past Copy Pit summit. The latter two locos had been the last steam bankers to operate on BR, both being sent from Rose Grove to Stansfield Hall (Todmorden) to assist as required any freight trains operating over the Copy Pit incline. No. 48191 was the last of the two to return to its home depot.

The end of our third day was fast approaching. We reluctantly left the shed in time to catch the 4.56pm train to Preston, where we waited twenty minutes or so before catching the 6.10pm to Bolton-le-Sands. Rose Grove was demolished not long after closing and most of the site now lies buried under the M65 motorway. There would be one final shed visit tomorrow before heading home. The trip to the campsite was like any other we had made when heading back to base over the years, yet it was so different too. No steam movements were noted during our return journey or indeed during the evening before we turned in for the night. Tomorrow, once back home, there would be films to develop, but no more enjoyable expeditions in search of steam to plan, anticipate and enjoy.

On 3rd August 1968 Rose Grove foreman fitter, Leonard Young, climbs on to the footplate of '8F' No. 48773 while two colleagues make their way alongside the engine. Already earmarked for preservation, the 2-8-0 would be steamed again on 8th August 1968 to travel light-engine to the Severn valley Railway. However, Preston Control learned about this and promptly reminded the remaining staff at Rose Grove that there was a ban on steam locos operating over BR metals (except, of course, those to be involved in its own 'Fifteen Guinea' Special on 11th August!). The '8F' was moved back on shed, had its connecting rods removed and would have to wait to be diesel-hauled to the SVR.

Another view of No. 48773 in Rose Grove MPD on the same day. Driver Arnold Hodgson is in the cab, while deep in thought, sitting at the front of the engine, is his colleague Dougie Wilson.

Sunday 4th August. The Final Day of Normal Steam Working on BR.

Engineering works frequently took place at weekends at this time, and the main line between Crewe and Carlisle was being re-laid with long welded rails to achieve smoother and quieter running. As a result, the number of trains operating between these centres was greatly reduced and would necessitate the use of buses for at least part of our journey home. Bolton-le-Sands station, which would close the following year, didn't have a Sunday service anyway. So after breaking camp, we caught the bus into Carnforth and made straight for the shed.

Far fewer people were about than on our previous three visits. The vast majority of enthusiasts, as well as a considerable number of the general public, had no doubt made their way to various vantage points to witness and photograph the engines working the day's special trains. Excluding those on the 'scrap line' adjacent to the depot, we noted for the final time the following locos on shed: No's (4)6441, 42073, 42085, 44709, 44735, 44758, 44877, 44897, 44963, 45025, 45134, 45200, 45206, 45231, 45310, 45330, 45342, 45390, 45394, 61306, 75009, 75019, 75020, 75027, 75048 and 92091 (for complete list see appendix 32). There were three 'Black 5's in steam, and two of them had had the 'MNA makeover' ready for the day ahead. No's. 45025 and 45390 would leave the shed later in the afternoon to double-head the Carnforth to Lostock Hall Junction leg of the LCGB Farewell to Steam Rail Tour, via Clapham, Settle Junction, Clitheroe and Daisyfield Junction. Partly cleaned ready for duty, No. 45134, appears to have been in reserve, as there is no record of her being employed on any of the six specials operating on this day.

Built at Horwich Works in 1948, Stanier 5MT No. 44709 is seen standing in the yard of Carnforth MPD on 4th August 1968. Having had the 'MNA' treatment at Kendal before heading the last steam working along the Windermere branch the previous day, she looks as if she could be turned out for any of the day's specials. Allocated to Crewe North when new, the 4-6-0 was placed on loan to Carnforth from January 1949. Designated as officially allocated to the depot in May the same year, the engine would remain an 11A/24L/10A engine for almost twenty years.

Top. Carnforth MPD, Sunday 4th August 1968. Stanier 'Black 5's No's 45390 and 45134. The latter engine - on standby and not rostered to take part in the day's specials - seems to have been abandoned part way through its cleaning. Perhaps the 'cleaners' had run out of time, or may be it was discovered that its classmates were in good shape and unlikely to need replacing.

Above. This picture brings into view the third of the 4-6-0's prepared for duty, No. 45025, which, together with No.45390, would double-head stage three of the LCGB railtour.

First allocated to the Western Region in November 1953, standard 4MT No. 75020 was very much a latecomer to Carnforth when it arrived in June 1967. Its final journey would take it to G.H. Campbell's of Airdrie where it would be broken up in November, exactly 15 years after its completion. No doubt it was a loyal steam follower that decided to add the chalked dedication on the loco's tender. Carnforth MPD, 4th August 1968.

Finishing off my second last film with one or two pictures of standard 4MT No. 75027, I carefully re-wound it back into its cassette. As I tucked it safely into my rucksack, I looked across at the three 4-6-0's and, even though I'd already taken a few shots of them, I couldn't resist taking one or two more. I quickly found my one remaining unexposed film, loaded it into the camera and reeled off another two pictures. And that was it, the last images I would take of BR steam… or so I thought at the time.

Leaving the 'Black 5's simmering in the yard, we climbed up the steps next to the offices on to the footbridge and started walking back to the station. Just as we had done on the evening of the previous Thursday, we stopped about halfway across and, for a few minutes, without commenting on our thoughts, gazed back at the shed and took stock of the view one last time. Amongst the many things that went through my mind, was wondering what on earth I was going to photograph to use up the film I'd just put into my camera!

As already alluded to, there was a lot of disruption to services because of the upgrading of the main line. Many trains were either cancelled or re-routed on Sundays, but luckily we managed to catch a local service not affected by the engineering works as far as Lancaster Castle. Here we changed from train to bus, and arrived at Preston station at about 12.30pm.

Descending the steps to the old platform 7, we found a trolley to sit on and tucked into sandwiches for lunch. We faced a long wait for our train, and knew that there wouldn't be much in the way of activity to occupy our time. We realised, too, that, even though there was a plethora of steam specials busily making their way to and fro all over Lancashire, not one was scheduled to pass through Preston. If we had been really enthusiastic about industrial steam I suppose we would have walked down to the dock railway again – indeed, I might well have finished off my last film photographing Bagnall 0-6-0ST's there. But, as things turned out, thank goodness we decided to content ourselves with what little was happening at the station.

One or two movements did occur, of course (see appendix 32), and amongst these we noted a dmu, Brush Type '4' No. D1636 and English Electric Type '4' No. D339 before something happened that caused us to look at one another in disbelief. From somewhere north of the station we both thought we heard the sound of a steam engine's whistle. Perhaps we had got it wrong and a special was coming through after all. Unsure of whether our ears were playing tricks on us, we moved swiftly towards the end of Platform 5 and waited. And waited. Nothing. Not the remotest sign of any type of engine. After a few minutes we started making our way to the other end of the platform in case the sound had been an echo and had in fact come from the opposite direction.

Looking fervently beyond the south end of the platform, with cameras at the ready, we were once again disappointed to find that there was nothing to be seen and the approaches to the station were clear. On agreeing that we must have been mistaken, we started walking back to where we had been sitting. All of a sudden our eyes confirmed what we thought we had heard after all. Moving surreptitiously, as though it shouldn't be where it was, a 'Black 5' with a single parcel van was leisurely entering the station under Fishergate Bridge almost without making a sound, and heading, we guessed, for No. 1 platform. We thought that she might stop at some point, so we raced up the steps along the footbridge and down to where we could get a closer view. The engine had indeed come to a halt and as we got nearer we realised that it was No. 45212; Preston station may not have been on the route of any of the six specials but, despite this, it would still be graced with the presence of a working steam engine on the last day of BR steam operation after all.

At the time we had no idea what duty the loco was fulfilling or that it had seen continuous employment for about 18 hours, including the penultimate passenger turn the previous evening, the 8.50pm to Blackpool South already mentioned. Preston station was a fitting place for it to find itself on its last booked duty. From 1948 to 1963 the 'Black 5' had been allocated to Fleetwood and then, for a period of about five years, it had found itself allotted to several different sheds. On the closure of Carlisle Kingmoor, No. 45212, together with sister engines No's 44672 and 44878, had experienced its final transfer and found itself at Lostock Hall. My first brush with this engine had come six years earlier on 12th June 1962, while trainspotting on Manchester Victoria station.

Following overnight steam heating duties, she should have gone back to Lostock Hall shed, but this doesn't appear to have happened. I think it extremely unlikely she would have returned to the depot only to be sent back to the station, but then again how would the change of crew been effected? Most fortunately for us, somebody had decided that she should remain at the station on pilot duty for the rest of the day, which in turn meant that I would have no problem in finishing off the black and white film still in my camera! The Stanier 4-6-0 certainly wasn't idle, and moved repeatedly in and out of the station collecting, moving and depositing a variety of parcel vans and wagons. Each time she re-appeared I made a beeline for where she stopped and during a period of about two and a half hours continued to record the 'Black 5's presence on film.

At about 2.20pm the driver positioned his engine in the middle of Platform No.5, alighted, and took a stroll along the platform. At this point, Dennis and I decided to approach him and ask if he would autograph our notebooks. He seemed a pleasant, friendly gentleman and, after hurriedly rewriting 45212 in a space allowing for his signature, he duly wrote 'J Smith' next to the engine's number. I then asked if I could take a photograph of him standing by his engine, which he happily agreed to. Each time the loco moved out of the station I wondered if that would be the last time I would see her. Not knowing how long the 4-6-0 would remain in the station, I decided to use up my last film more quickly than perhaps in hindsight I should have done; by 3.15pm I'd taken my final picture of a BR steam engine working an everyday duty.

Above and following two photographs. 'Black 5' No. 45212 acting as Preston station pilot on the very last day of ordinary standard gauge steam working on BR, 4th August 1968. Further reports that the engine was still carrying out this duty well after 4.00 pm strengthen my conviction that she was the last standard gauge steam engine working a normal roster on BR.

1968 (The Final Farewell to British Steam)

Standing alongside platform 5, this final view of 45212 on 4th August appeared in Steam Railway magazine in May 2007 as a backdrop to W H Auden's poem Night Mail. No one questioned the accompanying details, even though it had been generally accepted that this engine had returned to Lostock Hall shed immediately after completing its overnight train heating duties. However, it must be said that nearly forty years had passed by since steam had finished on British Railways!

We departed Preston for Crewe behind EE Type '4' No. D431 later the same afternoon (possibly the 3.50pm ex-Blackpool South, which left Preston at 4.39pm) and last recall seeing the 4-6-0 about half an hour or so before we headed south. Thoughts about 45212 came to mind while travelling on the first stage of our journey home and how long the 'Black 5' might carry on working for. What, I pondered, would happen if there was a diesel failure? Would steam be called upon to carry out one final rescue? Fanciful, yet understandable thoughts as the final few hours for steam were drawing to a close.

On reaching Crewe we changed trains and Dennis caught the stopping service via Stoke on Trent to Derby; I travelled on to Birmingham New Street via Bescot (to avoid engineering works near Wolverhampton) hauled by Brush Type '4' No. D1961. I had mixed emotions during the time I was on my own. I was looking forward to seeing my girlfriend, but the poignancy of the day wouldn't go away and I was sure Dennis would be experiencing the same sentiments, although he had one further mission - to see the 'Fifteen Guinea Special' the following week. If any consolation could be had from the last rather sad few days, it was that we had been fortunate enough to experience the end of an era, and have memories that would last a lifetime.

Filling the void

Although lacking in authenticity, the flavour and image afforded by the rapidly growing preservation movement would go some way towards providing a reasonable level of enjoyment and satisfaction for those wanting to continue to see steam in action. However, the desire to witness such motive power working under normal conditions, on a day-to-day basis, especially for me, was ever present. I suppose I could stretch the imagination and say that I came close to achieving this when I occasionally observed the ex-GWR pannier tanks operating out of Neasden and Lilley Bridge (Kensington) on the London Transport permanent way trains. But it wasn't quite the same as witnessing and savouring steam engines regularly working everyday passenger and freight turns on the national network.

Swindon-built 0-6-0PT No. 5786 entered traffic in January 1930 and spent its working life on the GWR and Western Region. The pannier tank was purchased from BR in 1958 and, following an overhaul, was renumbered L92. Soon after this picture was taken of the engine passing through Neasden in early October 1969, the Worcester Locomotive Society purchased the loco for £1,100. It was transported by road to the SVR to begin a new life in preservation, eventually becoming a member of the South Devon Railway steam fleet.

An unidentified ex-GWR pannier tank under repair inside Neasden MPD. 510, its last duty number, has been left in place in the frame fixed to the smokebox door; at neither end, or indeed the side of the engine, could its London Transport number be found. By July 1971 the last of the pannier tanks, otherwise known as 'matchboxes', had been withdrawn. October 1969.

The end of steam on our railways had come all too quickly. The images I had wanted to capture were incongruous with the picture of a modern railway system BR was so committed to projecting to the public. The belligerent and shortsighted approach that was taken towards steam power, I believe, led to an enormous amount of money being wasted. Rather than looking a little further ahead and realising the opportunity to invest in further electrification, dieselisation seems to have often been the only option seriously considered. Coupled with the fact that many of the new diesel locomotives were just not up to the job, significant sums of money had been wasted both on the new technology and the scrapping of many steam engines that had barely had time to find their feet. And, as history has proved, especially for a number of heavily used commuter routes, dieselisation certainly turned out to be no more than an interim measure albeit a protracted one. Main lines like those from Paddington to Swansea and Manchester to Liverpool are only now involved in such transformation, well over fifty-five years after the modernisation plan was first revealed.

In stark contrast, West Germany, for instance, would not squander money in such a manner. Instead, the railway system was studied and, while electrification of a number of routes was considered, so too was the continued use of steam locos, especially on those routes still worked predominantly by such motive power. Where possible, rather than dieselisation in the short term, the changeover would be direct. Once the decision had been made to adopt this approach, the necessary preparations were made for several routes to change from steam directly to electric traction with diesel power only used as a temporary measure, if at all. This in turn, of course, meant that some members of the Deutsche Bundesbahn steam fleet would see an extension to their life expectancy and, unlike in the UK, be kept working in tip-top condition for a good while longer. West Germany, and indeed a number of other Western European countries, would soon entice me to travel more miles than ever before to watch, photograph and be close to steam working normal duties on a daily basis.... But that, as they say, is another story.

Postscript

Throughout the years following the fateful day of 4th August 1968, I always believed that Dennis and I had seen, during that Sunday afternoon, the last standard gauge steam engine working a regular, everyday roster on British Railways. Except for coverage of the steam specials organised for this day and on 11th of the month, very little news about steams final movements could be found in either the September or October 1968 issues of Railway Magazine, Railway World or Modern Railways, or indeed any subsequent publications. Certainly nothing was reported about No. 45212 being on duty on the afternoon mentioned. My photograph of the loco standing at the south end of platform 5 was featured in the May 2007 issue of Steam Railway, and accompanying the picture were details of the date, time and the driver's name as signed in my notebook. Remarkably, none of the magazine staff, or indeed any of its many readers, questioned the date and time or (more understandably) the name of the driver standing next to the engine. But, to be fair, time does dim the memory and nearly forty years had passed by!

In view of what I thought to be the historical significance of the 'Black 5's activities that day, I decided to try and seek additional information about the man in charge of the 4-6-0, Mr J Smith. In doing so, I was totally unaware of the difficulties that lay ahead, and that another 'chapter' in the form of this postscript would need to be written so many years later in order to complete this journey back in time.

I made a start in November 2007 with the LMS staff records held in the National Archives at Kew. My own delving met with little success, so I spoke to an advisor there, Paul Sturm, and, as helpful as he was, he concluded that I would have to try an alternative route or routes to find out more about this particular former railway employee. Subsequently, other avenues were explored, including contacting Network Rail and the National Railway Museum, all without success.

By the summer of 2008 I really hadn't made any progress at all. But then I read an article titled 'Lonely silence at Lostock Hall', in the August/September issue of Steam Railway. Describing briefly the shed's history, there was in addition a very small picture of a group of enginemen attending a reunion that had taken place in late July. This gave me a glimmer of hope and I contacted Howard Johnston who had written the article to seek his help. Unfortunately, by December, I still hadn't got any closer to securing a positive identification of Mr Smith, and was beginning to wonder if the person I had photographed was indeed in charge of the 'Black 5' or an engine driver at all! So, I decided to try another line of research and started looking through some earlier publications of a magazine I'd never read before.

I didn't have to go back through many previous issues before coming across an item entitled: 'Preston 3 have 141 years of service' in the August 2008 issue of the ASLEF journal. I decided to get in touch with Graham Fazackerley, Preston Branch secretary, who had submitted the piece to see if he could help. He readily agreed but, unfortunately, after showing a number of his colleagues and ex-railwaymen the picture of Mr Smith early in the New Year, he too couldn't discover anymore about him. Even local railway author, Dennis Sweeney, who I wrote to at the beginning of December, admitted he was struggling to find anyone amongst all of his connections who could help. Mr Smith's photograph had now been seen by a fair number of ex-footplate men from the Preston area and I began to wonder if he actually existed!! Perhaps he was from further afield, hence the problem of recognition? After all this time the omens were not looking good but, in the New Year, my investigations would enter a more productive phase and, unquestionably for me personally, a more interesting and rewarding one, too.

When the labours of Alan Castle, a member of the renown 'MNA', came to fruition, there was at long last a chronological and in-depth account available of the numerous reported movements and workings of steam still in service during the last few months and weeks of their operation. In his book, 'Steam - The Grand Finale', published in July 2008 to mark the 40th anniversary of the end of steam, Alan had managed, together with the help of enthusiasts, photographers, drivers firemen, inspectors, fitters and other railway workers, to paint a picture of steams final contribution to the everyday running of the railway in Lancashire and Yorkshire. When I bought the book, a week before Christmas 2008, I was particularly looking forward to what comments had been made about the 'Black 5's duties and its whereabouts on 4th August 1968.

My first discovery, however, was that while I knew first hand that No. 45212 was still working on that last Sunday, two other engines (in addition to those occupied with the various steam specials), both allocated to Rose Grove, had not quite completed their employment either. They, too, were out and about and engaged in further menial duties. Acting as standby engine for sister loco No. 48773, which had been assigned to the Blackburn to Carnforth leg of the LCGB Rail Tour, Stanier '8F' No. 48519 was used instead of a diesel shunter on a permanent way working. Having passed its final boiler inspection on 28th June, the very much alive, but rather dirty and unkempt engine, proceeded to Rose Grove yard to shunt ballast wagons and use up the energy being generated by what was later described as a rather well-filled firebox.

The other engine, No. 48493, which, it must be said, matched fellow classmate No. 48519 for appearance, had found itself at Lostock Hall shed on Saturday evening and had remained there, in steam, overnight. All the other '8F's had had their fires dropped and were cold. No. 48493 therefore found itself with one final duty and, according to reports, had left the shed quite early in the morning. It, too, had been given a similar task to No. 48519, and was observed in Farington Junction yard shunting ballast wagons. Ironically, the last of seven reasons listed on the Shopping Proposal form, recommending it to be put through works, for what would prove to be the final time in June/July 1965, while allocated to Bletchley, was that it had had to be confined to local work!

Other articles such as 'Nine Down ... Three To Go!' a special supplement in the September 1998 issue of Steam World had suggested that 'Black 5' No.45212 had finished its turn of duty at 8.00am on the morning of 4th August, and had made its way light engine back to Lostock Hall shed to face prompt withdrawal. Indeed, Alan confirmed that 45212's work had ended at this time, but did not mention when it returned to shed. However, as a result of a barrage of additional information coming in following the publication of his book, he produced for Heritage Railway magazine the follow-up article entitled '1968 - the last word'. Under the sub-heading 'The last BR steam station pilot duty', No. 45212 was recorded as leaving Preston station at approximately 8.00am and running light to 10D to be immediately withdrawn.

I decided to write to him to explain that what had appeared in print (through no fault of his may I say) was not accurate, and that the history books might need revising. In my letter to Alan, I also enclosed a copy of the much-viewed picture of No. 45212 and Mr J Smith, with a plea for him to show it to as many of his contacts as possible. As soon as he had received my letter in early January 2009, he called me and at once announced that I'd 'stirred up a hornet's nest!' He could not account for the presence of the engine at any of the three steam sheds at the time in question, and its whereabouts seemed to have been overlooked - it had, he said, been assumed that 45212 had returned to Lostock Hall after its overnight steam heating duties. Furthermore, he was having problems finding anyone who was able to identify the driver, and kindly offered to see if any members attending the next 'Black 5' Club meeting might recognise Mr Smith.

At the end of February 2009 Alan sent me a copy of his circular 'The Very Final Word??' The good news was that someone else had confirmed the presence of No. 45212 in Preston station and that she was still there when they left the building at about 4.00pm. And the bad news? When he checked the name of the driver against the August 1968 staff lists both for Preston signing-on point and Lostock Hall, neither contained the name J Smith! And, to make matters even more bizarre, not one of all the ex-footplate men who had seen my picture recognised the person standing next to the engine. There was one possible lead, however. Peter Whalen, a former 10D fitter, suggested the fireman on the day in question was Stuart Morley. I spoke to Stuart and he explained his shift had finished at 8.00am but, unfortunately, couldn't recall whom the crew were who took charge of the 'Black 5'.

More determined than ever to try and solve the riddle of what I was beginning to think was a ghost driver, I emailed Chris Proctor at ASLEF headquarters on 30th March, and asked if he would be kind enough to put the photograph in the Journal. He was most helpful and promised that an appeal, together with 'The Picture', would be included in the news section of the May issue. Meanwhile, Alan Castle had been in touch with me after he had received one or two suggestions that he said, at the end of the day, amounted to nothing more than speculation as to who the person might be. Despite all my efforts there was still no helpful or encouraging news coming back about Mr Smith and his railway career.

A step forward of sorts came after the May copy of the ASLEF Journal had been circulated. On the afternoon of the 1st May, I had a telephone call from Jimmy Boyle an ex-Preston driver whose career on the railway had begun in April 1955. Just as Peter Whalen had previously suggested, Jimmy first indicated that the crew on the afternoon in question was Stuart Morley and second man Andy Reddington, previously a Wyre Dock fireman and sadly now deceased. Just as Alan Castle had been, Jimmy was intrigued by the uniform Mr Smith was wearing which, as can be seen, was more in keeping with the type worn by drivers of diesel and electric locos. This he suggested was most likely due to a shortage of overalls by this time. He, too, didn't recognise the driver outright, yet something was telling him that he looked like Bob Cooper, who permanently worked 'the Preston shunt.' However, he'd never seen Bob without his trademark flat cap, so it was understandable that he was a little uncertain as to whether it was definitely him.

I had several further conversations with Jimmy over the next few days and he seemed more and more convinced that it was Bob Cooper standing next to 45212. During the last of our chats he kindly asked me if I would like to join the annual reunion of ex-Preston and Lostock Hall men during their visit to the North Yorkshire Moors Railway on 9th May 2009. I think I'd said 'yes please' before he'd finished the invitation! The day for me would prove to be an unforgettable one. Being in the company of so many ex-railwaymen, many of who had been on the regulator (including a number who had been top-link men) is something I would never have dreamt of happening. The icing on the cake came when I heard from Jimmy that we would travel the line in an ex-GWR inspection saloon… hauled by Tornado, the new 'A1.'

During the day of the trip I spoke to several of the group, including Brian Fare, Dennis Halliwell Peter Norris, Mel Parker, Tom Rudd and Peter Whalen. However, the jury was still out as to whether 'Mr Smith' really was Bob Cooper. I wrote to all of the men I had had the pleasure to talk to, and sent them copies of a selection of the pictures I'd taken while at NYMR. This must have provoked further discussion about the yet to be identified driver, and I was given the names of several 'absent friends' who it was thought might be able to shed a little more light on the saga of J Smith/Bob Cooper.

Interestingly, at the end of July, I received a telephone message from Norman Callaghan in Australia who at the time was working for the Western Australia Railway. After reading the May issue of the ASLEF Journal, he had decided to contact me to pass on his thoughts about the mystery driver in the photograph. Once a Preston engineman, he categorically stated that he had not known of a J. Smith from the time he started his railway career at Preston in August 1963, and that it was just possible that the person in the picture may have been a driver from outside the area.

Nevertheless, as time moved on - eight months had passed since I first contacted Alan Castle - I was pretty sure that, despite all of the speculation and debate, the 'Black 5' had been under the control of Bob Cooper. He had been described as a bit of a joker by one or two of his former colleagues, which would help explain his signature in my notebook… that is until I received a call from Jim Thompson, another former steam man, and he said he was pretty sure the gentleman in question was a Harry Dixon!

Completely by accident, I had a break through at long last. By chance, when checking with Jimmy Boyle who I might have missed sending photographs to following the reunion trip to the NYMR, he highlighted Ronnie Clough. In fact Ronnie hadn't taken part in the day's events, and I was obviously unaware of that when I first spoke to him. Consequently he hadn't seen 'The Picture', so I sent him a copy directly after talking to him. He kindly offered to speak to a few of his former colleagues and friends to see what he could find out and, after writing to me at the end of September, he further convinced me that the identity of the driver of 45212 was Bob Cooper. In his letter he told me that one of the people he had spoken to, Bob Tye, a former Preston Parcels Inspector now in his nineties, remembered Bob well as a colleague, but thought family confirmation of his identity might prove difficult as he believed Mrs Cooper had died shortly after her husband and that as far as he was aware they didn't have any children. Once again, like others who had worked with Bob, he recalled what a comedian he was, and that it would have been typical of him to sign our notebooks using a common name like Smith as a pseudonym. On checking a copy of the 1968 staff list for Lostock Hall, Ronnie informed me that his full name was John Robert Cooper, and he had started at the shed in January 1937.

Further information from ex-Lostock Hall driver John Burnett confirmed what others had said about Bob being a bit of a jester. He also mentioned that Bob's route knowledge and, therefore, availability were limited and he would ask for a pilot if he were required to travel more than 25-30 miles from Preston! At this point, it was clear that the majority of those people with a firm opinion believed that it was Bob Cooper. Nonetheless, I still felt it was necessary, not least for my own contentment, I suppose, for him to be identified without doubt or reservation. It was essential that I speak to someone who could state unequivocally it was J R Cooper; I really needed to try and establish contact with members of his wider family, if of course any were still alive.

On 4th November 2009, with the kind help of Peter Richardson, Features Editor of the Lancashire Evening Post, the now infamous picture and an accompanying plea for help regarding my research, was included in the letters section of the newspaper. By the end of the evening I had had several responses. The first, a telephone call, was as disappointing as it was abrupt. I had stated in the newspaper that the 'Black 5' was preserved at the North Yorkshire Moors Railway and immediately the gentleman at the other end of the phone very swiftly corrected me and wished to point out that it was only on loan, and in fact the engine belonged to the Keighley and Worth Valley Railway! And no, he couldn't help with any information regarding the driver!

The next communication received was from David Cooper, who I thought straight away was a family member. When I opened his email, I was disappointed to discover that he wasn't related to Bob at all, although he knew an ex-railwayman, Stuart Morley, (who I'd previously spoken to) and thought he might be able to help.

Dave Hornby, whose father Ken was an ex-Preston man, emailed me only minutes later and explained that Wally Thompson, now in his nineties, but still 'as sharp as a knife' was someone he thought might be able to help, too. Dave also relayed to me a story about his dad, Ken, which as an aside I found both interesting and amusing. On 27th October 1968, after his name had been drawn out of the hat, Ken had the honour of driving the Flying Scotsman. However, another Preston driver frustrated in not being so lucky, had in fact offered Ken £25.00 to change shifts, which he refused to do. Dave was one of six children to feed and clothe and when his mother found out about the offer his dad had turned down, an almighty row ensued! Whilst I was fascinated by such stories and appreciative of the suggestions of other people who might have known Bob Cooper, I was beginning to wonder if he had any surviving family, closely related or otherwise, still living in the locality.

Later the same evening, after several more fruitless emails and telephone conversations, I had the call I had been waiting for: I spoke to someone who instantly dispelled my misgivings and uncertainty. Contrary to previous suggestions that he didn't have a family, Bob Cooper's son, Andrew, telephoned me after seeing the newspaper article and was delighted to be able to confirm, without a shadow of doubt, that it was his father in the picture. He was also pleased to inform me that his mother Therese' was still alive and well and would be able to tell me more about his dad's railway career. It had taken nearly two years but, in the end, the conundrum surrounding 'Mr J Smith' had finally and definitely been unravelled.

John Robert Cooper was born on 22nd July 1918 in Bamber Bridge. He was an only child and after leaving school worked in one of the cotton mills there. His father was licensee of The Lancashire and Yorkshire public house situated next to the level crossing. By the time Bob was eighteen, he decided to look for a job elsewhere. Without saying anything to his parents, he took an afternoon off work and went to Lostock Hall shed to see if anyone could give him advice about securing a job with what was then the LMS. When he arrived home, he told his mum and dad that he was leaving the mill and would be starting work as a cleaner at Lostock Hall shed the following week, on Thursday 21st January 1937.

It wasn't long of course before Bob would face some very difficult times and, unfortunately for him, long lasting effects of the 2nd World War. He served with the Royal Engineers and Andrew recalls the stories his dad told him about working on the coal trains supplying Battersea power station. His army career also took him abroad, and he worked as a driver both in France and Belgium. However, he was recalled at some point, and returned to Lostock Hall for about 10 months to help ease the severe shortage of drivers there. He was badly affected by his experiences at Dunkirk during the evacuation at the end of May beginning of June 1940, and a number of his colleagues suggested to me that this had resulted in Bob both losing confidence and not taking life seriously. By the time the war had ended his dark brown hair had turned completely white.

Harold Griffin helped to fill in more details about Bob Cooper. He said what a great sense of humour he had, and how, many a time, he would be found in his 'local', The Anchor public house, and was always the life and soul of any social gathering there. But he also added that Bob was often self-doubting when it came to work, and this was reflected in his driving duties after the war. Very rarely did he venture further than Blackpool where he occasionally had to travel to when his duties dictated driving some of the extra parcel trains leading up to Christmas. He was quite happy and content to work the 'Preston shunt' and forego the more prestigious freight and passenger turns.

Former Lostock Hall fireman, John Fletcher, recalls one occasion when on the footplate with Bob and how impressed he was with his driver's skill to get them out of a very difficult situation. Hauling a mixed freight, the 'Britannia' they were in charge of had been brought to a standstill by Bob on the incline between Whalley and Wilpshire when it was discovered that two of the wagons had caught fire. At about 4.30am, after separating the burning wagons from the rest of the train and positioning them next to a road bridge, Bob remained with his engine while John set off to find a phone box to call the fire brigade. Fortunately, a lorry driver stopped and gave him a lift and they came across a public telephone after a mile or so. John managed to raise the alarm and a fire engine was soon on its way to the scene. Indeed, the response was so quick that the fire engine crew picked him up not too long after he'd started walking back to the train.

On arrival at the scene, a policeman was already in attendance and appeared to be rather confused and uncertain about whom he had been talking to. He was unsure as to whether the person he had found sitting on the embankment was who he said he was. Wearing a sports jacket and a flat cap, Bob Cooper obviously didn't fit the bill as an engine driver, at least not as far as the officer was concerned. He immediately asked John to confirm that Bob was indeed who he said he was and that he wasn't some crackpot trespassing on the railway! The blaze, having been extinguished by the efforts of several firemen, meant that the footplate fireman could turn his attention to the one in the firebox in preparation to get the loco ready for what was going to shortly be asked of it. Bob Cooper, of course, had the unenviable task of getting his train underway again in rather difficult circumstances.

Starting off on a gradient unassisted obviously presents a far greater challenge than doing so on the level. Bob Cooper would need to use all of his expertise and experience to coax the Pacific to get its load moving again. John explained that after re-coupling the wagons, he was called upon to react to instructions instantly - timing was going to be crucial if Bob's attempt to get the train moving was going to work. He was required to secure the brakes on the tender while Bob moved the loco back a matter of a few inches to use what play existed between the two at the drawbar. At the same time as the regulator was opened, John would have to release the brake on Bob's signal in the hope that the little bit of momentum gained would be sufficient before the train resisted the engines efforts to move it. At the first attempt, the 'Britannia' responded faultlessly to the driver and fireman's timing and, without the slip of a wheel, the engine slowly moved its load forwards.

On Saturday 24th January 1976, almost thirty-nine years to the day after starting out on his railway career, Bob was working with Harold Griffin on shunting duties at Preston station. Feeling the need for a breath of fresh air and to stretch his legs, at around 1.00pm Bob volunteered to fetch the pies that they often looked forward to having for lunch. Tragically, when he was a little over halfway back down the steps to No.1 platform, he suffered a massive heart attack and died on the platform near to where his diesel shunter was waiting. Ironically, Andrew had mentioned to me how his father had often said, because of the nature of the shift patterns that, 'nobody retires from the railway they just drop dead!' Sadly for Andrew, his father's words have remained alongside his memory ever since.

At the time footplate colleagues from Lostock Hall, including Ronnie Clough and Joseph Booth, Cliff Nelson and John Fletcher, John Commons and Ray Haythornthwaite and Vinny Commons and Paul Tuson were in the public and enthusiasts eyes while working steam specials during the final day, I doubt that 'Mr J. Smith' gave them a second thought, and was perfectly happy to keep his 'Black 5' occupied within the confines of, and approaches to, Preston station.

I have often wondered if Bob Cooper ever thought about his shift on what was the final day of normal steam operations on our railway. After all, it was unusual at this time to have a steam loco rather than a diesel shunter to carry out this particular duty. Did he later, as time moved on, even consider that he might have been in charge of the last steam engine working a regular roster for BR? One thing is for sure - if he hadn't have been content with regular employment on what many of his colleagues would probably have regarded as a boring and mundane turn of duty, he would never have been on the regulator of No. 45212 on Sunday 4th August 1968.

I last spoke to Alan Castle in September 2014 while at the Severn Valley Railway. He explained that he had had further information suggesting that 45212 had been seen in Preston station shortly before 4.30pm - the previous 'last' sighting had been advised of was a little after 4.00pm. Sadly, I didn't speak to Alan to establish whether any more sightings of the 'Black 5' had been forthcoming before his untimely death on 18th May 2015.

One question does remain of course: who was Bob's fireman on that historic day? Well, I've tried hard to find out… perhaps the question will remain unanswered.

Glossary of Terms / Abbreviations.

1. ASLEF Associated Society of Locomotive Engineers and Firemen.
2. ATC Automatic Control
3. BSA Birmingham Small Arms
4. Bunk or Bunking. Entering a railway shed, works or such buildings without permission.
5. Cabbed. Climbing up on to the footplate of engine.
6. Cop. Recording an engine for the first time.
7. CLC Cheshire Lines Committee.
8. CW Crewe Works
9. dmu Diesel Multiple Unit.
10. E.E. English Electric.
11. ER, WR, SR and LMR. Post Nationalisation abbreviations for Eastern, Western, Southern, and London Midland Regions.
12. emu Electric Multiple Unit.
13. GSWR Glasgow and South Western Railway
14. GWR Great Western Railway.
15. LCGB Locomotive Club of Great Britain.
16. LMSR London Midland & Scottish Railway.
17. LNWR London and North Western Railway
18. LNER London & North Eastern Railway.
19. LSWR London and South Western Railway
20. L&Y Lancashire and Yorkshire Railway
21. 'MNA' 'Master Neverers Association'
22. MR Midland Railway
23. MPD Motive Power Depot (also referred to as shed or depot)
24. NBL North British Locomotive Company
25. NCB National Coal Board
26. NRM National Railway Museum, York
27. NYMR North Yorkshire Moors Railway
28. On shed. The locos actually noted while visiting a particular shed.
29. RCTS Railway Correspondence and Travel Society.
30. RTC Railway Touring Company
31. SLS Stephenson Locomotive Society.
32. SRPS Scottish Railway Preservation Society.
33. S.R. Southern Railway.
34. S & D Somerset and Dorset or SDJR Somerset and Dorset Joint Railway
35. WD War Department
36. WTL Wheel Turning Lathe

Relevant Shed Codes (as at October 1963)

1A Willesden	10A Carnforth	55A Leeds (Holbeck)
1B Camden	10C Fleetwood	55B Stourton
	10D Lostock Hall	55C Farnley
2A Tyseley	10F Rose Grove	55D Royston
2B Oxley (Wolverhampton)	10H Lower Darwen	55E Normanton
2C Stourbridge	10J Lancaster	55F Bradford (Manningham)
2D Banbury		55G Huddersfield
2E Saltley	12A Carlisle (Kingmoor)	55H Leeds (Neville Hill)
2F Bescot	12B Carlisle (Upperby)	
2H Monument Lane	12C Barrow	56A Wakefield
2J Aston	12D Workington	56B Ardsley
2K Bushbury	12E Tebay	56C Copley Hill
2L Leamington Spa		56D Mirfield
	14A Cricklewood East	56F Low Moor
5A Crewe North	14B Cricklewood West	
5B Crewe South		61B Aberdeen (Ferryhill)
5C Stafford	16C Derby	
5D Stoke and Cockshute	16E Kirkby-in-Ashfield	62A Thornton
5E Nuneaton	16F Burton	62B Dundee
	16J Rowsley	62C Dunfermline
		63A Perth
6A Chester (Midland)		
6B Mold Junction	30A Stratford	
6C Croes Newydd		64A St. Margarets (Edinburgh)
6D Shrewsbury	31B March	64B Haymarket
6E Oswestry		64C Dalry Road
	34B Hornsey	64F Bathgate
8A Edge Hill	34G Finsbury Park	64G Hawick
8B Warrington (Dallam)		
8C Speke Junction	36A Doncaster	65A Eastfield (Glasgow)
8D Widnes		65B St Rollox
8E Northwich	41D Canklow	
8F Springs Branch (Wigan)	41E Staveley (Barrow Hill)	66A Polmadie (Glasgow)
8G Sutton Oak	41J Langwith	66B Motherwell
8H Birkenhead		66D Greenock (Ladyburn)
8J Allerton	50A York	66E Carstairs
8K Bank Hall	50B Hull (Dairycoates)	66F Beattock
8L Aintree	50C Hull (Botanical Gardens)	
8M Southport	50D Goole	67A Corkerhill (Glasgow)
		67B Hurlford
9A Longsight	51A Darlington	67C Ayr
9B Stockport (Edgeley)	51C West Hartlepool	67E Dumfries
9D Newton Heath	51L Thornaby	
9E Trafford Park		70A Nine Elms
9F Heaton Mersey	52A Gateshead	70C Guildford
9G Gorton	52F North and South Blyth	70D Eastleigh
9H Patricroft	52G Sunderland	70E Salisbury
9J Agecroft	52H Tyne Dock	70F Bournemouth

Relevant Shed Codes (as at October 1963 contd.)

9K Bolton
9L Buxton

52K Consett

70G Weymouth
70H Ryde
75D Stewarts Lane

81A Old Oak Common
81E Didcot
81F Oxford

85A Worcester
85B Gloucester (Horton Road)
85C Gloucester (Barnwood)
85D Bromsgrove

82A Bristol (Bath Road)
82B St Phillips Marsh
82C Swindon
82E Bristol (Barrow Road)
82F Bath (Green Park) Highbridge

86A Canton (Cardiff)
86B Newport (Ebbw Jnct.)
86C Hereford
86E Severn Tunnel Junction
86G Pontypool Road

88B Radyr (Cardiff)
88C Barry

83A Newton Abbot
83D Exmouth Junction
83G Templecombe

84A Laira (Plymouth)

Appendices, including those for Part One.

Appendix 1

Small Heath (Golden Hillock Road Bridge) / Tyseley MPD 8th August 1959

```
3673  3792  3840  4111  4140  4153  4155  4172  5101  4903  4907  4912
4914  4930  4932  4942  4974  4978  4979  4983  4990  5005  5008  5012
5058  5089  5096  5308  5331  5350  5911  5926  5930  5957  5964  5988
5993  6006  6008  6009  6024  6026  6029  6129  6314  6325  6348  6375
6819  6820  6822  6834  6836  6851  6853  6904  6938  6961  6967  6968
6971  6984  7015  7031  7424  7903  7910  7912  7927  8108  8468  8700
8713  44450 45199 48415 73013 92053 92240 92244
```

Appendix 2

'The Button Factory' 30th August 1959

```
1000   3664   4104   4155   4648   4902   4946   4990   5018   5063   5070   5332
5658   5909   5977   6003   6017   6022   6311   6374   6821   6851   6971   7024
8415   8700   8713   8737   9735   9753   42267  42794  42896  42925  43122  43738
44774  44818  44845  44856  44897  44931  45013  45015  45189  45401  45325  45591
45620  45651  45674  45681  45682  45690  45704  45742  46123  46409  49126  70050
73010  73013  73022  73025  73155  75021  92152
```

Appendix 3

Tamworth April 1960

```
40108  40164  42061  42761  42799  42810  42824  42870  43043  43047  43092  43248
43482  43510  43583  43668  43680  43799  43938  43963  43991  44077  44112  44130
44296  44002  44439  44839  44841  44851  44875  44890  44920  44968  45058  45111
45124  45149  45184  45186  45189  45240  45253  45305  45351  45416  45504  45512
45519  45550  45559  45580  45626  45656  45662  45663  45668  45676  45679  45726
46106  46108  46116  46138  46146  46156  46170  46204  46221  46232  46233  46242
46244  46245  46248  46250  46258  46422  48002  48005  48053  48124  48131  48193
48287  48312  48319  48392  48398  48435  48510  48563  48601  48662  48667  70049
72002  73138  75009  90391  92014  92093  92118  92135  92151  92155  92167  92218
  D6   D213   D214   D215   D217   D223   D226   D227   D228   D229   D231   D234
 D255   D268  D8004  D8008
```

Appendix 4

Derby Works Open Day 27th August 1960

En-route to Derby from Birmingham New Street

```
42421 42759 42890 43012 43046 43673 43709 43762 44534 44537 44591 44810 44950
44963 45058 45059 45092 45416 45690 47643 48169 48182 48267 48272 48364 48405
48683 48706 48748 48756 61010 61248
```

Derby Works and Motive Power Depot

80 118 158A 1000 40003 41123 41152 41528 42054 42066 42067 42146 42161 42181 42229 42288 42316 42332 42346 42384 42390 42395 42486 42514 42541 42582 42587 43013 43174 43200 43323 43359 43360 43373 43394 43435 43459 43548 43658 43679 43778 43844 43985 44037 44049 44051 44214 44225 44235 44289 44334 44344 44456 44465 44466 44591 44597 44666 44667 44756 44806 44817 44825 44851 44854 44888 45268 45348 45416 45506 45552 45598 45610 45618 45619 45626 45627 45649 45654 45660 45685 45693 46443 46489 46497 46499 46502 47000 47006 47203 47236 47284 47331 47441 47458 47516 47533 47583 47630 47638 47660 47661 48104 48124 48152 48156 48157 48220 48225 48293 48342 48356 48381 48390 48454 48694 58144 61348 61388 70042 71000 73050 73063 73065 73066 73135 73156 73167 75055 76030 90683 92114 92139

En-route from Derby to Birmingham New Street

43122 43242 43521 43563 43668 44663 44941 44945 45625 48194 48687 90719

Appendix 5

Aston MPD 30th August 1961

42552 42945 42957 42966 42974 44110 44448 44876 45058 45237 45322 45344 45448 45647 46134 46427 48718 48719 48752 70017 70024 70027 70031 70043

Saltley MPD 30th August 1961

3821 42419 42823 42903 43012 43017 43041 43435 43599 43668 43680 44137 44179 44185 44517 44571 44659 44759 44780 44791 44810 44839 44859 44919 44944 44945 44962 44981 45268 45269 45272 45532 45569 45643 45649 46122 46132 46137 46157 48183 48220 48339 92004 92055 92131 92139 92151 92155 92165 92231 D79 D80 D90 D119 D123 12066

Appendix 6

Crewe Trip 21st April 1962 (Steam recorded)

4916 5965 6827 40165 40543 41212 41229 42079 42105 42438 42678 42776 42934 42937 42962 42964 43047 43681 43955 44110 44450 44593 44679 44681 44684 44687 44762 44834 44872 45000 45002 45035 45048 45058 45089 45110 45143 45149 45189 45231 45243 45250 45257 45276 45278 45297 45317 45325 45344 45380 45413 45421 45426 45429 45445 45446 45494 45531 45534 45560 45567 45572 45584 45587 45603 45634 45644 45643 45648 45672 45673 45689 45736 45740 45742 46127 46132 46136 46137 46165 46170 46207 46228 46231 46235 46240 46241 46250 46254 46256 47213 47384 47400 47445 47450 47469 47542 47549 47588 47590 47596 47606 48054 48205 48252 48305 48348 48365 48400 48468 48478 48505 48514 48697 48728 48735 48738 48752 49414 49452 70004 70033 70043 70047 71000 73025 73070 73073 78030 84004 90655 92096

Appendix 7 Doncaster Trip (From Manchester) 11th June 1962

32545 42088 44695 44985 45594 48136 60005 60008 60009 60012 60014 60016
60021 60024 60025 60026 60028 60031 60032 60034 60036 60042 60054 60065
60082 60083 60100 60110 60113 60114 60116 60117 60118 60119 60121 60122
60134 60139 60140 60148 60152 60156 60158 60512 60515 60528 60532 60533
60537 60800 60817 60852 60871 60880 60903 60909 60921 60936 60943 61001
61003 61004 61050 61053 61055 61057 61097 61109 61115 61118 61119 61124
61127 61137 61139 61157 61170 61193 61209 61214 61234 61247 61250 61274
61279 61365 61387 61392 61446 61942 61974 62004 62026 62034 62053 62055
62069 63593 63613 63618 63663 63698 63711 63746 63786 63848 63858 63863
68961 68971 68972 68976 68989 70002 70011 70036 70053 73016 73095 73168
76033 78022 90011 90042 90063 90144 90185 90296 90340 90425 90476 90480
90500 90501 90559 90578 90636 92173 92201

Appendix 8 Bristol Trip 17th April 1963 (Steam recorded)

1661 2217 2232 2251 2277 2291 2891 3606 3623 3632 3677 3696
3702 3725 3758 3832 3844 4102 4131 4613 4619 4664 4680 4970
4991 5085 5930 5934 5975 6146 6147 6148 6312 6769 6903 6963
6965 6981 7002 7034 7338 7900 8102 8401 8402 8403 8404 8405
8409 8415 8431 8795 9404 9410 9601 9729 41207 41208 41245 41248
41249 42421 42622 43949 44102 44209 44218 44223 44264 44269 44523 44534
44569 44583 44659 44963 45006 45076 45268 45280 45561 45617 45624 45656
45675 45676 45682 45685 45690 47557 48110 48431 53807 73015 73019 73028
73031 73042 73068 73093 75001 75072 78009 82003 82007 82009 82035 82037
82038 82039 82040 90433 90506 92007 92008 92070 92077 92137 92222 92243
92248

Appendix 9 London Trip 28th September 1963

Willesden MPD

41239 42080 42222 42234 42431 42478 42562 42573 42577 42581 42606 42611
44678 44772 45000 45093 45142 45272 45410 45434 45495 45529 45620 45623
45664 45735 45736 46101 46114 46156 46222 46225 46230 46235 46239 46254
47307 47501 48018 48036 48171 48279 48416 48518 48531 48600 48624 48628
48632 48649 70001 70004 70010 70012 70018 70024 70031 70032 70034 70043
73013 73014 75014 76047 78019 78038 78039 78043 78060

Old Oak Common MPD

1010 1504 1507 2836 2879 3646 3750 4089 4098 4609 4638 4701
4703 4704 4920 5001 5041 5057 5060 5065 5070 5076 5093 5098
5919 5958 6005 6010 6124 6135 6141 6142 6930 6952 6978 6986
6998 7003 7009 7013 7014 7015 7017 7019 7020 7021 7029 7032
7035 7036 7037 7904 7921 7928 8420 8436 8756 8757 8759 8763
8768 9419 9420 9423 9455 9463 9659 9700 9704 9707 9755 9784
92241

Cricklewood West MPD

42070 42086 42092 42954 44690 44984 45197 45234 45334 45342 45346 45417
47202 47432 47434 48107 48163 48306 48332 76035 76036 76037 76039 76041
76042 76089 92127

Stewarts Lane MPD

30534 30537 30540 30928 31305 31542 31822 31893 31894 31896 32337 32340
32343 32347 34090 82023

Nine Elms MPD

120 4672 30035 30249 30320 30585 30902 31613 31617 31621 31624 31634
31796 33001 33004 33040 34001 34007 34009 34019 34028 34031 34037 34048
34056 34060 34077 34078 34082 34085 34089 34095 35012 35020 35024 35026
35030 73041 73065 73081 73082 73086 73087 73110 73119 75077 80148 82010
82014 82016 82017 82018 82022

Appendix 10

Shrewsbury MPD 8th February 1964

3709 3782 3843 4647 5932 5942 5991 6810 6819 6907 6916 6922
6931 6934 6942 6945 6987 7012 7800 9657 41202 41207 42488 44814
45143 45145 45283 45363 45422 45429 45577 46525 48269 48305 48354 48369
48404 48463 48470 48524 48730 48739 48768 73025 73034 73036 73090 73095
80069 80100

Oswestry MPD 8th February 1964

1438 1638 3208 3749 5421 6907 7033 7426 7434 7820 7822 45190
46510 46512 46513 46514 46515 46516 46518 48436 73036 80097 80104 80131
82031 84004

Appendix 11

South West Holiday August 1964

Plymouth 3rd August

1363 34023 41230 41308

Exeter St Davids station 5th August

4692 4694

Exeter MPD 5th August

2214 3205 31812 31854 34075

Exmouth Jnct. MPD 5th August

3746 4610 4655 31837 31849 31855 31856 31859 31875 34014 34015 34017 34033 34054 34057 34058 34059 34062 34066 34070 34076 34078 34080 34082 34083 34084 34086 41295 41317 41322 41323 73161 76008 80036 80038 80064 82030 82035 82039

Exeter Central Station 5th August

3759 4610 4692 4694 31802 34013 34030 34059 35019 35028 41206 41284 82040

Exeter St Davids station 5th August

34107

Appendix 12

Scotland Trip 10th – 23rd July 1965

Burton MPD 10th July

44688 44825 44932 44941 44989 45180 45224 45253 45464 48052 48117 48194 48266 48367 48528 48621 48651 48672 48690 47250 47313 47464 47643 61313 70022 90024 90032 90129 90220 90295 90384 90474 90572 92088 92211

Derby MPD 10th July

44839 44861 45267 48064 48141 48153 48191 48282 48317 48731 45574 90078

Wakefield MPD 11th July

42108 42150 42161 42181 42406 42650 45739 48257 48323 48363 61022 61024 61161 61309 61320 61353 61040 90047 90061 90068 90074 90076 90089 90112 90113 90116 90123 90124 90135 90155 90160 90183 90200 90210 90233 90281 90300 90321 90333 90336 90339 90341 90348 90360 90361 90370 90373 90382 90385 90396 90407 90429 90470 90415 90482 90563 90587 90610 90611 90631 90639 90651 90654 90678 90679 90684 90698 90707 90723

Neville Hill MPD 11th July

42184 42196 42689 43075 60118 60134 60154 60876 63417 63420 63426

York MPD 12th July

42204 43097 43126 44945 48381 48758 60121 60124 60138 60145 60146 60152 60155 60810 60828 60831 60847 60876 60886 60895 60929 60963 61021 61049 61055 61176 61275 61276 61299 62005 62010 62049 62065 65823 65846 65894 70010 90045 90217 90223 90280 92005 92006 92035 92231 92239

Darlington MPD 13th July

42085 42213 42477 43030 43099 43102 43128 43129 45286 48100 48272 48294
48312 48387 48430 48649 60010 60124 60806 60884 60885 61216 62003 62041
62043 62045 63368 63391 65859 68010 68011 68023 68029 68037 68043 68044
68047 68053 68055 68062 90014 90059 90412 90434 90452 90493

Hawick MPD 15th July

76049 78049

St. Margarets MPD 15th July

42128 42691 46462 60027 60041 60052 60813 60816 60824 60844 60846 60931
60970 61039 61134 61191 61324 61396 61397 61404 65234 80006 80007 80022
80026 80055 80114 80122

Dalry Road MPD 15th July

42273 44702 44878 45053 45168 45469 45477 45483 61245 61308 61347

St Margarets MPD 16th July

42128 42691 44878 46115 46462 60027 60041 60052 60813 60824 60844 60931
60970 61029 61099 61134 61263 61324 61397 61404 65234 80007 80022 80055
80114

Dunfermline MPD 17th July

61072 61101 64569 64571 64626 65903 65917 65918 65288 90039 90071 90229
90515 90547

Thornton MPD 17th July

61076 61102 61132 61133 61148 61180 61261 61343 61407 64588 64595 64606
64618 64625 64632 65327 65345 65901 65905 65907 65909 65911 65915 65916
65922 65931 65932 76110 90117 90350 90444 90596 90727

Dundee MPD 17th July

46463 46464 60528 60530 60818 60973 61147 61278 61292 61293 61340 61344
61403 64558 64576 64597 64608 64624 65319 73008 80124 90628

Perth MPD 17th July

44698 44703 44722 44792 44799 44924 44925 44931 44959 44960 44973 44979
44980 45047 45138 45213 45461 45472 45473 60031 60512 61244 70002 70012
70033 73153 73145 75032 80028 80093 80126

Stirling MPD 17th July

44727 45016 45168 45357 45359 45389 45423 70008 70033

St. Margarets MPD 17th July

42128 42691 44704 46462 60041 60824 60931 60970 61029 61099 61134 61180 61191 61345 61350 61354 61397 76050 80006 80022 80026 80055 80114

Bathgate MPD 18th July

65243 65267 65282 65297 76104 76105 76106 76107 76111 78045 78046 78050 78052 78054

Motherwell MPD 18th July

44820 44850 44880 44881 44900 44908 44991 45176 45433 73055 73059 76000 76002 76003 77005 77008 92233

Eastfield MPD 18th July

42176 42209 42478 42649 44903 45160 45202 45364 45387 45442 46460 61008 61103 61116 61140 61357 64592 65910 73078 73108 75012 80020 80024 80057 80113 80118 90168 90727

Polmadie MPD 18th July

42195 42199 44802 44965 45309 45471 45481 45675 60535 73057 73062 73063 73064 73075 73098 73099 73107 73122 76004 80058 80060 80061 80086 80109 80116 80120 80121 80130

Corkerhill MPD 18th July

44699 44705 44724 44758 44798 44977 44999 45463 45697 73009 73102 73103 73106 73120 73121 73124 76114 78026 80000 80004 80046 80047 80051 80063 80112

St. Rollox MPD 19th July

44677 44718 60024 60034 61307 73101 73147 73150 73152 73154

Beattock MPD 20th July

42125 42129 42169 42274 42693 45245 80005 80045

Carlisle Kingmoor MPD 21st July

43000 43004 43028 43045 43049 43121 44668 44672 44677 44692 44724 44790 44792 44802 44870 44873 44877 44898 44900 44901 44902 44989 45012 45028 45075 45082 45129 45135 45138 45195 45235 45259 45294 45295 45340 45490

Carlisle Kingmoor MPD cont.

45491 45530 45531 45573 45588 45629 45742 46128 46160 47471 47641 47667
48158 48500 48536 60027 60052 60846 70002 70003 70005 70009 70016 70029
70037 70038 70039 72006 72007 72008 73033 73101 92010 92015 92018 92114
92126 92130 92233

Carlisle Upperby MPD 22nd July (visit not completed)

41217 41264 42095 42225 43025 43953 43964 44939 46434 47285 48406 70011
70020 70029 70044

Carnforth MPD 23rd July

42118 42147 42198 42247 42322 42613 43027 43066 43103 43105 44300 44778
44816 44828 44904 44905 45014 45092 45095 45212 45230 45234 45328 45342
45372 45374 45390 47201 47531 48108 48400 48519 48707 70017 70048 70052
75015 75017 75057 92016

Lancaster MPD 23rd July

41221 43036 44667 44902 44947 45054 45193 45258 45373 46431 46433 46441
46514 48077 48148 48297 48454 48679

Steam Locomotives noted elsewhere during trip.

42128 42169 42199 42241 42277 43133 43138 44670 44672 44705 44718 44758
44772 44790 44802 44878 44947 45011 45067 45091 45117 45124 45133 45357
45402 45475 45480 45697 46115 48133 48166 48214 48247 48614 48632 48660
60007 60019 60024 60118 60532 60816 60836 60843 60876 60877 60970 61094
61101 61103 61180 61262 61303 61330 61350 61244 62028 62048 63386 65790
65841 65842 65851 65930 65934 68023 70033 73009 73057 73100 73104 73122
73145 73150 73153 76090 76094 76102 78026 80004 80045 80112 80128 90045
90229 90254 90266 90309 90441 90445 90650 92097 92206

Appendix 13

Worcester MPD 25th September 1965

3616 3682 4113 4161 4680 6147 6155 6169 6813 6848 6856 6872
6937 7909 9626 44666 44691 44945 45493 48246 75000 75008 75022 75025

Gloucester Horton Road MPD 25th September 1965

3643 3675 3759 3775 4689 4698 6113 6160 6819 6855 6931 6944
7808 7814 7816 7829 7927 8745 41291 44264 44269 44683 44710 45353
45454 48266 48370 48395 48460 48643 73013 73017 73019 78001 78004 78006
80037 92230

Appendix 14

Saltley MPD Christmas Day 1965

6656 6679 6692 44057 44840 44912 45051 45182 45267 45270 45288 45391 46443 46448 46454 46526 48016 48084 48109 48117 48133 48212 48219 48220 48351 48375 48449 48514 48554 48603 48637 48671 48725 48736 48762 48767 73155 75035 76038 76040 76043 76048 90357 92029 92125 92129 92136 92138 92151 92155 D25 D36 D88 D140 D221 D228 D267 D318 D341 D379 D384 D1588 D1589 D1593 D1653 D1813 D1908 D5183 D5197 D5202 D5223 D5226 D5233 D5234 D5245 D5246 D5266 D5292 D5695 D7508 D7518 D7519 D7570 D7572 D7592

Tyseley MPD Christmas Day 1965

3625 4176 4635 5606 5658 6625 6853 6855 6857 6858 6861 6864 6879 6937 6951 6952 6953 8767 9774 43052 43098 44658 44663 44666 44859 44937 44948 45134 45292 46428 46470 48546 48755 61121 90471 92002 92004 92073 92118 92132 92134 92139 D1065 D1604 D1914 D7587

Appendix 15 South West Trip 2nd – 11th April 1966 (Depot/Works visits only)

Oxford MPD 2nd April

3677 5971 6126 6134 6136 6849 6872 6923 6932 6937 6953 6956 6959 6967 6991 6993 6999 7904 7907 7914 7919 7922 9773 73003 73166 90258

Salisbury MPD 3rd April

33006 34006 34026 34056 34066 34089 34100 34108 73065 73169 76007 76008 76012 76018 76059 76067 80152

Weymouth MPD 2nd April

34034 34037 34044 34086 35007 35017 35022 35028 35030 41284 41298 73016 73080

Weymouth MPD 4th April

34044 34057 34086 35007 35017 35022 35028 41301 73080 73110 76011

Bournemouth MPD 4th April

34002 34026 34037 34040 34047 35027 41230 41295 41312 41320 73016 76005 76009 76010 76014 76026 76033 76057 76066 80011 80013 80019 80085 80094 80134

Ryde MPD 5th April

14 16 21 26 27 29 33 35

Ryde Works 5th April

18 22 28 30(Cut up)

Eastleigh MPD 7th April

30053 30069 30926 31803 31816 31873 34021 34023 34025 34041 34048 34077 34079 35022 35029 41287 41294 45418 73155 75076 76018 76019 76033 76063 76064 76069 80016 80082 80139 80142 DS233

Guildford MPD 7th April

30072 31405 31408 31411 31639 31791 34088 34097 41319 73037 73043 73065 73081 73087 73089 73093 73118 76031 77014 80154

Nine Elms MPD 8th April

33006 34002 34017 34038 34057 34066 34071 34087 34095 35011 35012 35026 73080 73085 73117 73169 73171 80015 80089 80095 80144 82006 82018 82019 82023 82024 82026 82029

Stratford MPD 10th April

120 6000 1008 30245 30587 30777 30850 30925 33001 42500 49395 61194 63460 63601 NCB67

Nine Elms MPD 10th April

33006 34002 34019 34071 34102 35011 35012 35022 35028 73085 73110 73117 80012 80015 80089 80095 80133 80143 80145 82006 82019 82024 82026 82028 82029

Appendix 16

Scotland Trip 16th – 30th July 1966

Shrewsbury MPD 16th July

8718 44731 44775 44821 44865 44913 44931 44935 45000 45058 45231 45348 46446 46508 47677 48122 48404 48418 48436 75002 75006 75012 75053 75063 78018 78038 78039 78058 78063

Croes Newydd MPD 16th July

1638 1660 3709 5605 6697 8767 9610 9630 9641 9669 45045 45130 45198 45344 47507 48147 48252 48440 48665 75021 75033 75046 75048 75060 75071 92074

Chester MPD 16th July

1628 42616 44717 44766 44800 44831 44917 44993 45001 45044 45048 45051 45064 45111 45250 45285 45322 45325 45403 45419 45493 47389 47598 47659 48055 48349 48705 48754 70021 76035 76047 76052 92150 92112 92118

Birkenhead MPD 16th July

42121 42606 42613 42765 42782 42812 42859 42942 44933 45249 45369 47272 47324 47447 47533 47674 48115 48421 48501 48502 48626 48741 92011 92021 92024 92026 92032 92046 92047 92048 92049 92085 92086 92092 92096 92100 92104 92105 92107 92108 92113 92120 92121 92123 92131 92133 92159 92160 92163 92165 92166

Aintree MPD 17th July

44659 46419 46489 46500 46502 46523 47279 47289 47327 47367 47444 48168 48176 48340 48605 48650 48676 75064 90054

Bank Hall MPD 17th July

41211 41244 41304 42078 42132 44675 44737 44806 44877 44950 45055 45386 45388 45407 45627 48294 48476 48493 75026 75027 75049

Speke Junction MPD 17th July

42574 44771 44809 45059 45071 45114 45137 45188 45201 45223 45282 45329 45338 45370 45412 45417 45441 45466 46516 48161 48203 48296 48305 48374 48509 48520 48544 48632 48709 48723 90639 92008 92012 92022 92025 92027 92050 92070 92091 92117 92122 92158 92227

Trafford Park MPD 17th July

42066 42069 42071 42076 42080 42081 42267 42287 42583 44708 44735 44804 44815 44851 44895 44918 45073 45150 45220 45233 45239 45333 45352 45404 48178 48344 48371 48535 78007 78012 78023 78062

Patricroft MPD 17th July

44712 44766 44834 44853 44962 45080 45221 45234 45275 45310 48139 48154 48208 48213 48292 48390 48491 48553 48636 48663 48770 73006 73010 73011 73033 73035 73053 73094 73125 73126 73127 73129 73131 73133 73134 73137 73138 73140 73143 73144 73158 73159 73160 82000 82003 82009 82031 82034

Agecroft MPD 17th July

44677 44781 44782 44816 44817 44928 44929 45062 45096 45197 45258 47201
47202 48011 48111 48118 48164 48224 48257 48264 48289 48397 48411 48521
48666 48671 48708 48714 48743 48745 48775 73000 73025 73034 73050 73067

Southport MPD 18th July

42968

Springs Branch (Wigan) MPD 18th July

42102 42233 42235 42462 42577 42587 42647 42963 44678 44679 44848 45019
45024 45128 45281 45395 45408 45431 45481 46447 46517 47314 47603 47671
48050 48114 48121 48125 48165 48261 48275 48338 48410 48468 48494 48675
48727 48742 48751 61306 75043 76076 76080 92134 92161

Lostock Hall MPD 18th July

42096 42187 42297 42431 42436 42472 42625 43041 43046 43118 43119 45054
45055 45107 45328 45346 45368 45402 45421 45450 47293 47336 48062 48077
48160 48257 48263 48438 48445 48470 48618 48622 48679 48707 48739 70002
70010 73135 78002 78037 78041 78057 90351

Carnforth MPD 18th July

42095 43004 43023 43027 43066 43095 43103 43105 44709 44733 44778 44832
44874 44889 44892 44894 44915 44948 45017 45092 45095 45221 45227 45373
45374 45390 45399 45424 45495 45675 46400 46422 46431 46441 46486 46499
48089 48093 48247 48254 48426 48473 48519 70052 73100 90633 90707

Barrow MPD 19th July

42134 42252 44311 44394 44500 44882 45141 45383 47373 47667 47675 48177

Workington MPD 20th July

42236 43008 43017 43036 43047 43073 43122 46424 46452 46491 47612 92015

Carlisle Upperby MPD 20th July

41207 41217 41264 45226 45238 45296 45393 46455 46458 46513 48177 48381
70022 70024 70032

Carlisle Kingmoor MPD 20th July

43000 43040 43049 43121 44669 44671 44674 44677 44692 44726 44727 44762
44767 44792 44795 44802 44878 44887 44898 44902 45012 45013 45019 45082
45097 45106 45138 45147 45185 45195 45212 45217 45253 45274 45363 45364
45437 45481 46115 47471 47531 47641 48275 48280 48670 70001 70002 70009

Carlisle Kingmoor MPD contd.

70010 70017 70036 70037 70038 70039 70040 70042 70050 72006 73059 73100 73102 92009 92043 92093 92113 92130 92208

Dumfries MPD 23rd July

45480

Stranraer MPD 23rd July

44718 44792 44982 45126 45164 45483 78016

Ayr MPD 23rd July

42702 42737 42789 42795 42801 42803 42861 42863 42908 42913 42919 44724 44788 44974 44977 44999 45016 45161 45177 45423 45432 45467 45474 73145 76001 76073 76092 76096 76101 76103 78051

Hurlford MPD 23rd July

42736 45115 46451 73102 76021 76024 76091 77007 77017 77018 77019 80004

Motherwell MPD 23rd July

44786 44820 44850 44880 44881 44908 44991 45029 45176 45359 45437 60528 73107 73154 76000 76002 77005 77008 77009 92249

Crewe South MPD 24th July

43020 43024 43026 43034 43052 43113 43151 44680 44761 44762 44765 44814 44829 44834 44839 44844 44863 44864 44873 44876 44878 44897 44898 44917 44942 44963 45031 45033 45050 45051 45056 45070 45132 45224 45231 45243 45281 45297 45326 45393 46495 46512 47397 47494 47530 47590 47592 48092 48255 48287 48446 48505 48544 48551 48554 48738 48765 70014 70016 70023 70027 70028 70029 78010 78019 78031 78036 92032 92067 92078 92090 92128 92150 92203 92223 92234

St Rollox MPD 24th July

60034 70034 73150 73151 80057

Polmadie MPD 24th July

42176 42197 42216 42264 42277 44879 44972 45025 70002 70006 70010 70011 73055 73059 73060 73063 73064 73072 73079 73099 76004 76070 76098 76104 80001 80002 80027 80045 80058 80061 80086 80116 80118 80120 80121 80122 80123 80130 92233

Corkerhill MPD 24th July

44675 44723 44798 44993 45214 45236 45488 45675 46460 73005 73009 73101 73105 73120 76046 76093 76094 76114 77015 78026 80000 80004 80024 80025 80046 80047 80051 80063 80112 80128

Eastfield MPD 24th July

42690 42739 42917 44699 45273 60024 61008 61132 61342 65912 65914 73146 80005 80007 80054

Perth MPD 25th July

44698 44703 44704 44705 44720 44796 44797 44997 44998 45461 45472 45475 60026 70008 80028 80092 80093 80126

Dundee MPD 25th July

45127 45473 46464 60530 60813 60818 61102 61180 61262 61263 61293 61403 64576 64577 64597 64608 64620

Thornton Junction MPD 25th July

61103 61133 61148 61261 61308 61330 61347 61349 64569 64570 64588 64606 64618 64623 65327 65345 65901 65905 65907 65909 65910 65911 65915 65921 65922 65925 65929 65931 90117 90168 90199 90350 90441 90444 90468 90596 90600 90628 90640

St Margarets MPD 25th July

42128 42691 44925 45047 45162 45469 60824 60868 60955 60976 61345 65234 78049 80006 80055 80113 80114 80124

Aberdeen Ferryhill MPD 26th July

44703 60004 60009 60019 60532 61262

Dunfermline MPD 26th July

61072 61350 61407 64611 65288 65918 65930 65934 76110 90039 90041 90071 90386 90489 90534 90547 90560

St Margarets MPD 27th July

42128 44691 44925 45047 45127 45483 60824 60868 60919 60955 60976 61345 65234 78049 80006 80026 80113 80114 80124

Dunfermline MPD 27th July

61072 61350 61407 64611 65288 65918 65930 65934 76110 90039 90071 90386 90534 90547 90560

Dundee Tay Bridge MPD 27th July

44879 45473 46464 60818 61102 61180 61262 61263 61293 61403 64547 64577 64597 64602 64608 64620

Cowlairs Works 28th July

44722 44992 45357 57566 60041 60836 61029 61140 61278 62059 73096 90020

Eastfield MPD 28th July

42690 42739 42917 44699 45273 60034 61008 61342 65912 73146 80005 80007 80054 90117 90468

St Rollox MPD 28th July

44998 60024 73149 73150 73151 73153

Polmadie MPD 28th July

42197 42216 42277 44883 45025 45455 73055 73060 73063 73064 73099 76004 76104 80001 80002 80027 80045 80061 80086 80116 80118 80122 80123

Bathgate MPD 28th July

46462 61307 65243 65267 65319 78046 78047

Aberdeen Ferryhill MPD 29th July

44703 44794 44879 60004 60009 60019 60532 90628

Carstairs MPD

42274 44700 44953 44954 44956 45112 45309 45492 61116 70040 73060 73078 76090 76113

Appendix 17

Saltley MPD Christmas Day 1966

42436 44944 45410 46421 46454 48061 48107 48133 48153 48321 48351 48364 48456 48477 48516 48529 48556 48603 48645 48725 48755 92013 92028 92136 D23 D88 D105 D117 D121 D142 D153 D1593 D1635 D1662 D1720 D1748 D1749 D1802 D1836 D1869 D1873 D3020 D3107 D3115 D3576 D3577 D3582 D3775 D3838 D3973 D3974 D5186 D5187 D5190 D5199 D5200 D5204 D5207 D5212 D5224

Saltley MPD contd.

D5228 D5230 D5232 D5257 D5263 D5266 D5282 D5290 D5298 D7508 D7520 D7524 D7528 D7553 D7557 D7563 D7570 D7584 D7629 D7647 D7655 D7657 12035 12041 12042 12043 12061

Tyseley MPD Christmas Day 1966

1638 4696 7029 9610 9630 9774 44663 44833 44840 45089 45241 46442 46501 73127 73130 D211 D302 D321 D1682 D1686 D1689 D1692 D1718 D1936 D3026 D3085 D3167 D3950 D3952 D3956 D3957 D3969 D3983 D3985 D5008 D5010 D5012 D5020 D5032 D8134 12066

Appendix 18

Oxley MPD 3rd March 1967

44808 44856 44865 44876 44919 44945 45040 45186 45264 45283 45344 46428 48035 48105 48180 48450 48460 48464 48475 48531 48724 76039 76087 92123 92152 92159

Appendix 19

Salisbury MPD 30th May 1967

34006 34018 34023 34052 34056 34098 34104 34108 75074 76007 76031

Bournemouth MPD 30th May 1967

34004 34025 34034 41224 41230 41295 75075 76008 76009 76011 80011 80146

Weymouth MPD 30th May 1967

35003 35013 35014 35026 73118 76006 76053 76069

Eastleigh MPD 30th May 1967

30067 34044 34060 34071 34077 34095 34102 73115 73117 75076 75077 76033 76063 76066 80016 80019 80133 80139

Appendix 20

Crewe South MPD 10th August 1967

43001 43003 43007 43021 43088 44681 44684 44765 44766 44777 44778 44800 44812 44814 44819 44831 44832 44833 44843 44859 44865 44898 44899 44911 44944 45006 45021 45027 45040 45042 45052 45089 45145 45186 45241 45243 45253 45264 45280 45298 45308 45321 45349 45493 48010 48018 48133 48194 48220 48252 48293 48334 48336 48351 48364 48374 48436 48449 48450 48460 48474 48505 48517 48522 48531 48603 48725 48728 48729 48767 48768 71000

Crewe South MPD contd.

70029 75029 92022 92032 92137 92160 92223 92249

Appendix 21 North of England trip 16/17th September 1967

Royston MPD 16th September 1967

48055 48070 48084 48093 48113 48160 48162 48169 48202 48222 48276 48281
48337 48352 48394 48439 48454 48473 48537 48622 48664 48703 48710 48721
92082

Wakefield MPD 16th September 1967

42149 42196 42235 42236 42269 42287 42650 42699 43130 44853 44946 45675
48104 48157 48265 48452 48466 61123 61189 77002 77012 90047 90160 90233
90236 90300 90306 90362 90363 90396 90404 90409 90617 90620 90625 90650
90654 90678 92155 92205 92211 92215

Normanton MPD 16th September 1967

42093 42138 42189 42252 42574 43043 43044 43125 43129 44824 44854 44857
45075 90243 90281 90345 90430 90644 90682 90699 90722

Low Moor MPD 16th September 1967

42055 42066 42072 42116 42145 42251 42587 42616 42665 42689 44693 45208
45363 61030 61306 61337 61388 90318 90605 90633 90642 90721

Leeds Holbeck MPD 16th September 1967

42152 44803 44826 44828 44836 44852 44884 44889 44896 44943 44983 45080
45219 45254 45562 45593 48158 48283 48332 48399 62005 70004 70023 70025
70029 92016 92020 92118 92212 92249

York MPD 16th September 1967

60019 62048 63455 90200

West Hartlepool MPD 16th September 1967

63344 63387 63431 90061 90074 90076 90116 90210 90230 90309 90339 90360
90431 90459 90478 90627 90677 90695

Sunderland MPD 16th September 1967

63395 65795 65811 65855 65882 65892 90009 90135 90321 90348 90378 90382
90417 90698

Carlisle Kingmoor MPD 17th September 1967.

42134 43049 43120 43139 44672 44674 44677 44682 44691 44759 44775 44790
44795 44817 44840 44844 44858 44862 44872 44882 44883 44887 44898 44899
44900 44902 44928 44936 44937 45013 45028 45041 45048 45120 45176 45236
45267 45268 45273 45274 45279 45292 45295 45296 45330 45340 45349 45368
45437 45455 45481 45493 47293 47612 48045 48053 48163 48200 48287 48322
48433 48503 48544 48730 70003 70005 70006 70010 70012 70013 70015 70016
70022 70023 70029 70033 70037 70038 70039 70040 70042 70045 70046 70047
70049 70052 75035 75041 92009 92018 92019 92052 92071 92074 92110 92114
92122 92125 92137 92139 92233

Carlisle Upperby MPD 17th September 1967

41264 44770 44910 44932 45262 45447 46455 46457 46470 46486 48400 48451
75019 75027

Tebay MPD 17th September 1967

75024 75030 75037 75039

Carnforth 17th September 1967

42210 43105 44667 44675 44733 44758 44778 44780 44792 44822 44874 44892
44894 44905 44948 44963 45001 45014 45017 45025 45072 45092 45135 45193
45209 45227 45374 45342 45390 45394 45421 45424 45435 45445 46400 46431
46433 46499 48012 48308 48338 48384 48393 48467 48519 70025 70027 70051
73128 75009 75010 75015 75020 75021 75033 75034 75040 75043 75048 75058
75059 75062 92028 92077 92118 92126 92212

Lostock Hall MPD 17th September 1967

42187 42611 43004 43019 43033 43046 43088 43119 44713 44802 44809 44915
44917 44942 44971 45107 45149 45226 45339 45345 45347 45373 45391 45402
45436 45444 48062 48077 48164 48266 48307 48320 48438 48445 48470 48517
48618 48637 48707 48758 73011 78020 78021 78037 78041 92012

Springs Branch (Wigan) 17th September 1967

44658 44679 44683 44732 44819 44831 44842 44920 45055 45116 45281 45282
45312 45321 45395 45449 46432 46515 48082 48117 48125 48132 48167 48261
48272 48275 48319 48325 48410 48614 48675 48678 48715 48722 48724 48764
73140 76077 76081 92162

Appendix 22

Crewe South MPD 1st November 1967

4498 42647 43001 43003 43007 43021 44680 44681 44684 44805 44808 44811
44812 44821 44832 44833 44843 44865 44944 45006 45021 45042 45052 45089

Crewe South MPD contd.

45136 45270 45278 45297 45298 45308 45349 45405 45494 46520 48018 48220
48364 48402 48460 48474 48522 48531 48543 48548 48603 48725 75029 76051
92100 92120 92218

Appendix 23

Buxton MPD 20th January 1968

48190 48336 48424 48471 48495

Sockport Edgeley MPD 20th January 1968

44781 44836 44842 44855 44868 44916 44940 44988 45027 45046 45073 45200
45225 45261 45279 45312 48170 48267 48278 48319 48369 48464 48626 48673
48731 48768

Newton Heath MPD 20th January 1968

44697 44734 44780 44803 44809 44818 44846 44855 44867 44884 44888 44893
44910 44949 44962 45038 45083 45190 45202 45203 45221 45246 45254 45255
45268 45330 45382 45411 45420 45424 48010 48074 48090 48115 48132 48197
48321 48368 48373 48519 48553 48612 48678 48729 48758 70023 73128 92109

Patricroft MPD 20th January 1968

44858 45282 45285 48033 48214 48282 48325 48382 48390 48407 48453 48491
48609 48700 48714 70012 73000 73010 73011 73025 73033 73034 73035 73053
73067 73073 73096 73125 73126 73127 73129 73131 73132 73133 73134 73135
73136 73138 73140 73142 73143 73158 73159 73160

Appendix 24

Speke Junction MPD 17th February 1968

44663 44708 44725 44730 44772 44806 44834 44844 44859 44877 44907 44950
45034 45057 45071 45130 45131 45201 45231 45232 45242 45280 45292 45299
45349 45386 45388 45407 45412 45417 48017 48119 48206 48268 48305 48371
48450 48551 70024 92002 92008 92014 92020 92022 92023 92024 92025 92026
92046 92049 92054 92055 92069 92079 92084 92086 92102 92112 92113 92151
92152 92153 92160 92162 92163 92166 92204 92249

Lostock Hall MPD 17th February 1968

43006 43019 43027 43033 43088 43106 44672 44683 44761 44800 44878 44942
45041 45149 45212 45227 45295 45345 45353 45391 45421 45436 48077 48438
48492 48510 48646

Bolton MPD 18th February 1968

44664 44715 44728 44802 44947 45104 45110 45260 45290 45294 45318 45377
45381 45435 48026 48046 48090 48200 48380 48425 48436 48469 48504 48559
48652 48702 48740 48764 48773 73004 73040 73069

Trafford Park MPD 18th February 1968

44665 44735 44804 44807 44815 44851 44895 44929 44965 45096 45258 45269
45316 48308 48317 48319 48344 48345 48351 48356 48763

Appendix 25

Carnforth MPD 2nd March 1968

6441 44709 44758 44874 44889 44894 44897 44942 44963 45001 45017 45054
45076 45095 45096 45134 45209 45212 45259 45342 45390 45394 45424 45435
48167 48323 48410 48445 70013 70021 75009 75015 75020 75021 75024 75034
75039 75041 75043 75048 75058 75062 92004 92077 92088 92110 92118 92212
92218 92223

Appendix 26

Heaton Mersey MPD 30th March 1968

44663 44903 45114 45253 45279 48063 48107 48117 48168 48192 48193 48201
48224 48317 48319 48322 48344 48503 48507 48546 48551 48677 48683 48723

Appendix 27

Rose Grove MPD 21st April 1968

44690 44848 44899 45350 45397 48062 48081 48167 48247 48257 48310 48323
48348 48375*48384 48393 48400 48410 48441 48448 48468 48476 48519 48544
48666 48727 48730 75032 75048   * Cabside of loco only.

Appendix 28

Stockport Edgeley MPD 4th May 1968

44836 44855 44868 44871 44888 44940 45013 45027 45034 45200 45312 48182
48437 48546 48745 92069

Heaton Mersey MPD 4th May 1968

44663 44903 45065 45190 45253 45392 48063 48107 48117 48191 48192 48197
48201 48224 48252 48292 48317 48322 48329 48344 48365 48471 48503 48507
48551 48683 48684 48723

Speke Junction MPD 4th May 1968

44708 44838 44906 44933 45005 45131 45201 45386 45388 45395 45426 48060
48153 48206 48450 48493 48617 92008 92024 92091 92094 92160 92162 92165
92249

Edge Hill MPD 4th May 1968

44711 44777 44864 44877 44926 45076 45156 45231 45284 48012 48045 48056
48168 48293 48294 48308 48374 48433 48467 48529 48614 48665 48692 48715
48722 48746 48752

Newton Heath MPD 4th May 1968

44780 44781 44809 44818 44845 44851 44890 44891 44910 44949 45046 45076
45101 45203 45206 45254 45255 45268 45310 45342 45397 45411 48132 48321
48368 48369 48373 48612 48620 48678 70013 92054

Appendix 29

Newton Heath MPD 20th May 1968

44803 44809 44818 44851 44884 44890 44891 44949 45101 45202 45206 45254
45255 45268 45310 45330 45411 45420 48356 48529 48533 48612 48665 48687
48746 92054

Patricroft MPD 20th May 1968

44777 45055 45156 45187 48033 48170 48212 48267 48282 48325 48338 48374
48390 48453 48467 48549 48553 48749 48775 73000 73034 73040 73050 73053
73067 73125 73126 73128 73132 73133 73134 73135 73136 73138 73142 73143
73157 92218

Bolton MPD 20th May 1968

44664 44781 44829 44871 44888 44947 44965 45073 45110 45269 45312 45318
45381 48026 48090 48111 48168 48380 48465 48532 48652 48702 48744

Carnforth MPD 20th May 1968

 6441 42073 42085 44874 44877 44891 45001 45017 45134 45149 45209 45231
45342 45382 45390 45394 45424 45435 45444 48124 61306 70013 75009 75020
75027 75034 75048 92004 92009 92088 92091 92118 92160 92167 92223

Appendix 30

Newton Heath MPD 22nd June 1968

44735 44780 44781 44803 44809 44818 44884 44890 44891 44949 45076 45101
45202 45206 45254 45268 45310 45330 45394 45411 45420 48132 48321 48356

Newton Heath MPD contd.

48368 48369 48373 48529 48533 48612 48620 48665 48678 48687 48746 92054

Patricroft MPD 22nd June 1968

44777 45156 45187 45287 48033 48170 48175 48212 48267 48282 48327 48338
48374 48390 48453 48467 48491 48549 48553 73010 73040 73050 73069 73125
73126 73128 73133 73135 73138 73142 73143 73157 92218

Bolton MPD 22nd June 1968

44664 44802 44829 44871 44877 44888 44929 44947 45046 45073 45104 45110
45260 45269 45290 45312 45318 45381 48026 48111 48168 48319 48340 48380
48392 48465 48504 48532 48652 48692 48702 48720 48744 48773

Rose Grove MPD 22nd June 1968

44690 44899 45350 45382 45397 45447 48081 48115 48247 48257 48267 48278
48291 48323 48348 48384 48400 48410 48423 48448 48451 48493 48519 48666
48715 48723 48727 48730 75027

Carnforth MPD 22nd June 1968

6441 42073 42085 44709 44713 44758 44874 44894 44897 44963 45017 45025
45095 45134 45209 45231 45342 45390 45424 45435 45445 48062 48124 48393
61306 70013 75009 75019 75020 75048 92077 92088 92091 92118 92160 92167
92223

Lostock Hall MPD 23rd June 1968

43019 43027 43106 44683 44761 44806 44816 44878 44942 44950 44971 45149
45212 45305 45345 45353 45386 45407 45436 45444 48253 48293 48294 48445
48476 48546 48646 48763

Appendix 31

Crewe South MPD 20th July 1968

4498 70013

Carnforth MPD 20th July 1968

6441 42073 42085 44709 44735 44758 44809 44871 44874 44877 44894 44897
44915 44963 45017 45095 45134 45200 45206 45209 45268 45330 45390 45394
45424 45435 45445 48124 61306 73069 75009 75019 75020 75027 75048 92077
92088 92091 92118 92160 92167 92223

Lostock Hall MPD 20th July 1968

43019 43106 44683 44713 44806 44816 44878 44888 44942 44950 44971 45055
45110 45149 45212 45231 45260 45269 45305 45310 45318 45353 45386 45388
45407 45436 45444 48253 48293 48445 48476 48546 48646 48723 48763

Rose Grove MPD 20th July 1968

44690 44899 45096 45156 45287 45350 45382 45397 45447 48062 48115 48167
48191 48247 48257 48278 48294 48323 48340 48348 48384 48393 48400 48410
48423 48448 48451 48493 48519 48665 48666 48715 48727 48730 48765 48773
48775

Appendix 32

Lostock Hall MPD 2nd August 1968

43019 43027 44683 44713 44816 44871 44878 44888 44942 44950 44971 45017
45055 45073 45110 45149 45260 45269 45305 45345 45353 45386 45388 45436
45444 48253 48293 48294 48445 48476 48546 48646 48723 48763 48765 48775

Rose Grove MPD 2nd August 1968

44690 44899 45096 45156 45350 45382 45397 45407 45447 48062 48115 48167
48191 48247 48257 48323 48340 48348 48384 48393 48410 48448 48451 48666
48715 48730 48773

Lostock Hall MPD 3rd August 1968

43019 43027 44683 44713 44781 44816 44871 44874 44878 44888 44894 44942
44950 44971 45017 45055 45073 45110 45149 45212 45260 45269 45287 45305
45318 45345 45353 45386 45388 45407 45436 45444 48253 48293 48294 48340
48445 48476 48493 48546 48646 48723 48763 48765 48775 70013 73069

Rose Grove MPD 3rd August 1968

44690 44899 45096 45156 45350 45382 45397 45447 48062 48115 48167 48191
48247 48257 48278 48323 48348 48384 48393 48400 48410 48423 48448 48451
48519 48665 48666 48715 48727 48730 48773

Carnforth MPD 4th August 1968

 6441 42073 42085 44709 44735 44758 44877 44897 44963 45025 45134 45200
45206 45209 45231 45310 45330 45342 45390 45394 45424 45435 45445 48124
61306 75009 75019 75020 75027 75048 92077 92088 92091 92118 92160 92167
92223

Preston Station 4th August 1968

D1636 D339 45212* D3374 D3580 D1956 D1624 D1964 D431   * Station Pilot

Acknowledgements (including those for Part One)

I would like to express my sincere thanks to the following, a number of whom I have pestered on numerous occasions for help not only with regard to Bob Cooper but other railway matters too: Stewart Blair (Carlisle Evening News & Star), Jimmy Boyle, John Burnett, Norman Callaghan, Alan Castle, Ronnie Clough, Noel Coates, Andrew Cooper, Therese' Cooper, Bernard Crick, Heather Crook, Brian Fare, Peter Fitton, John Fletcher, Albert Ford, Ron Gardner, Bob Gregson, Harold Griffin, Peter Groom, Dennis Halliwell, John Hill, Dave Hornby, Mick Kelly, Ian Matthews, Stuart Morley, Barry Morton, Peter Norris, Mel Parker, Richard Pearson (NRM Shildon), Chris Proctor (ASLEF), Jack Procter, Peter Richardson (Lancs. Eve. Post), Herbert Ridge, Tom Rudd, Derek Sharpe, Dennis Sweeney, Mike Taylor, Richard K Taylor (RCTS), Bob Tye and Peter Whalen. Thanks, too, to Steve Waddington and David Crossland at Amadeus Press.

Sadly, some of the aforementioned are no longer with us.

Last and by no means least my thanks to my old school chum, Dennis Perfect, who has read through and made many corrections to the text and helped fill in the blanks that my memory served up on numerous occasions. Any mistakes or oversights are entirely my responsibility.

Bibliography

BR Motive Power Allocations 1959 – 1968 Vol. 1, by Paul Teal (Ian Allan 1985)
British Railways Locomotives 1955 and 1962 both by Chris Banks (OPC 2001 & 2005)
British Railways Steam Locomotive Allocations 1948 - 1968, by H. Longworth (OPC 2014)
British Standard Steam Locomotives Vols. 1-5 (RCTS 1994 – 2012)
British Steam Motive Power Depots, by Paul Bolger (Ian Allan 1981 – 84)
Firing Days at Saltley Vols. 1 & 2 by Terry Essery (D Bradford Barton)
LMS Engine Sheds Vols. 1-5, by Hawkins & Reeve (Wild Swan Publications Ltd. 1981- 87)
LMS Engine Sheds Vols. 6&7, by Hawkins, Reeve and Stevenson (WSP Ltd. 1989 – 90)
Locomotive Stock Book 1960,1963,1966 & 1969 (RCTS)
Peto's Register of Great western Railway Locomotives. Various Volumes (Erwell Press)
Steam Locomotives of British Railways, by H C Casserley (Hamlyn 1973)
Steam The Grand Finale, by Alan Castle (Mortons Media Group Ltd. 2008)
The Book of The Royal Scots, by Richard Derry (Irwell Press 1999)
The Book of The Merchant Navy Pacifics, by Richard Derry (Irwell Press 2001)
The Book of The WC & B of B Pacifics, by Richard Derry (Irwell Press 2002)
The Stanier 4-6-0's of the LMS, Rowledge & Reed (David & Charles 1981)
The Stanier Class Five 4-6-0s, John Jennison, (RCTS 2013)
The Complete BR Diesel & Electric Locomotive Directory, by Marsden (OPC 1991)
Various issues of Steam Railway, Railway Magazine, Railway World, Trains Illustrated, Modern Railways and Heritage Railways.

Footnote

The accuracy of the details concerning the disposal and scrapping of BR steam locos has long been a subject of discussion, even more so since it was discovered that deliberately false and misleading information had been accepted by many as fact. It must be born in mind, therefore, that where such particulars are included here, their reliability cannot be guaranteed.